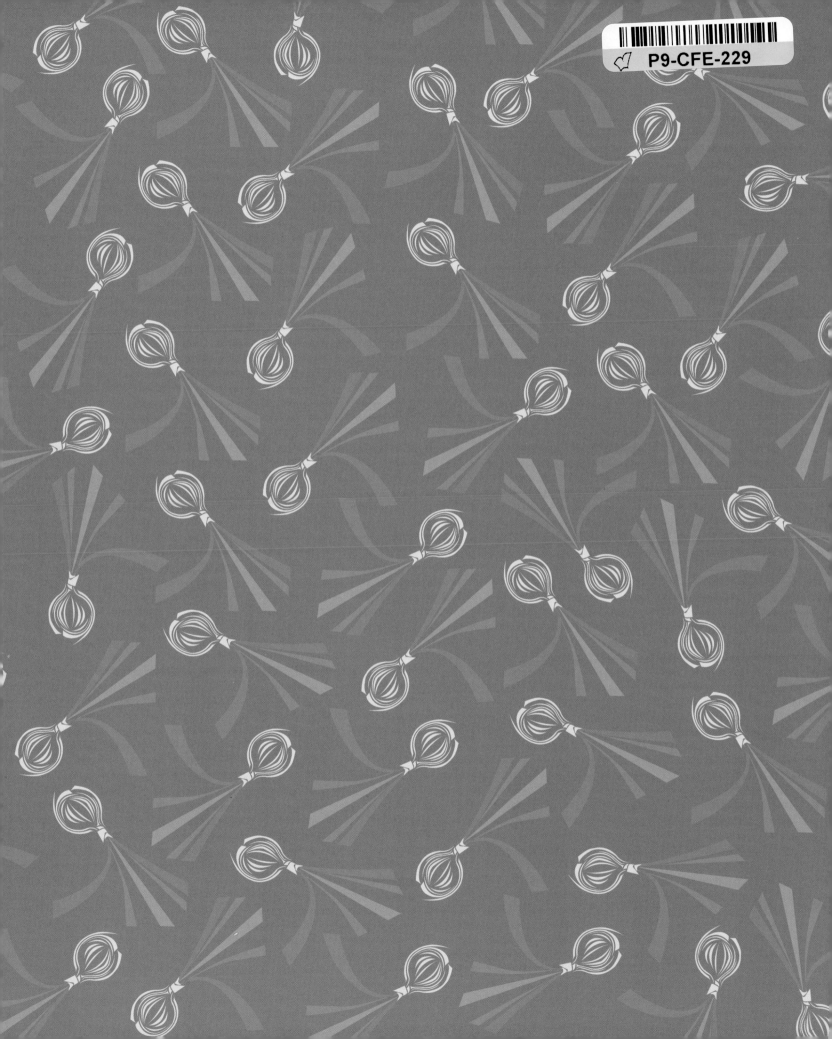

THE CULINARY INSTITUTE OF AMERICA®

IDENTIFICATION · FABRICATION · UTILIZATION

PRODUCE

**By Brad Matthews,
Paul Wigsten**

The Culinary Institute of America

KITCHEN PRO SERIES

THE CULINARY INSTITUTE OF AMERICA®

PRODUCE

By Brad Matthews, Paul Wigsten

IDENTIFICATION · FABRICATION · UTILIZATION

DELMAR
CENGAGE Learning™

Australia • Brazil • Japan • Korea • Mexico • Singapore • Spain • United Kingdom • United States

KITCHEN PRO SERIES

KitchenPro Series: Guide to Produce Identification, Fabrication and Utilization
Brad Matthews, Paul Wigsten

President: Dr. Tim Ryan '77

Vice-President, Dean of Culinary Education:
Mark Erickson '77

Senior Director, Continuing Education:
Susan Cussen

Director of Intellectual Property: Nathalie Fischer

Editorial Project Manager: Margaret Wheeler '00

Editorial Assistant: Shelly Malgee '08

Editorial Assistant: Erin Jeanne McDowell '08

Photography: Keith Ferris, Photographer,
Ben Fink, Photographer

Vice President, Career and Professional
Editorial: Dave Garza

Director of Learning Solutions: Sandy Clark

Acquisitions Editor: Jim Gish

Managing Editor: Larry Main

Product Manager: Nicole Calisi

Editorial Assistant: Sarah Timm

Vice President Marketing, Career and
Professional: Jennifer McAvey

Executive Marketing Manager: Wendy Mapstone

Marketing Manager: Kristin McNary

Marketing Coordinator: Scott Chrysler

Production Director: Wendy Troeger

Content Project Manager: Glenn Castle

Senior Art Director: Bethany Casey

Technology Project Manager: Chris Catalina

Production Technology Analyst: Tom Stover

© 2011 Delmar, Cengage Learning

For product information and technology assistance, contact us at
Cengage Learning Customer & Sales Support, 1-800-354-9706

For permission to use material from this text or product,
submit all requests online at **www.cengage.com/permissions.**
Further permissions questions can be e-mailed to
permissionrequest@cengage.com

Library of Congress Control Number: 2009942320

ISBN-13: 978-1-4354-0121-1

ISBN-10: 1-4354-0121-2

Delmar
5 Maxwell Drive
Clifton Park, NY 12065-2919
USA

Cengage Learning is a leading provider of customized learning solutions with office locations around the globe, including Singapore, the United Kingdom, Australia, Mexico, Brazil, and Japan. Locate your local office at:
international.cengage.com/region

Cengage Learning products are represented in Canada by Nelson Education, Ltd.

To learn more about Delmar, visit **www.cengage.com/delmar**

Purchase any of our products at your local college store or at our preferred online store **www.CengageBrain.com**

Notice to the Reader

Printed in China
4 5 6 7 17 16 15 14

Contents

Recipe Contents

ABOUT THE CIA

THE WORLD'S PREMIER CULINARY COLLEGE

The Culinary Institute of America (CIA) is the recognized leader in culinary education for undergraduate students, foodservice and hospitality professionals, and food enthusiasts. The college awards bachelor's and associate degrees, as well as certificates and continuing education units, and is accredited by the prestigious Middle States Commission on Higher Education.

Founded in 1946 in downtown New Haven, CT to provide culinary training for World War II veterans, the college moved to its present location in Hyde Park, NY in 1972. In 1995, the CIA added a branch campus in the heart of California's Napa Valley—The Culinary Institute of America at Greystone. The CIA continued to grow, and in 2008, established a second branch campus, this time in San Antonio, TX.

From its humble beginnings more than 60 years ago with just 50 students, the CIA today enrolls more than 2,700 students in its degree programs, approximately 3,000 in its programs for foodservice and hospitality industry professionals, and more than 4,500 in its courses for food enthusiasts.

LEADING THE WAY

Throughout its history, The Culinary Institute of America has played a pivotal role in shaping the future of foodservice and hospitality. This is due in large part to the caliber of people who make up the CIA community—its faculty, staff, students, and alumni—as well as their passion for the culinary arts and dedication to the advancement of the profession.

Headed by the visionary leadership of President Tim Ryan '77, the CIA education team has at its core the largest concentration of American Culinary Federation-Certified Master Chefs (including Dr. Ryan) of any college. The Culinary Institute of America faculty, more than 140 members strong, brings a vast breadth and depth of foodservice industry experience and insight to the CIA kitchens, classrooms, and research facilities. They've worked in some of the world's finest establishments, earned industry awards and professional certifications, and emerged victorious from countless international culinary competitions. And they continue to make their mark on the industry, through the students they teach, books they author, and leadership initiatives they champion.

The influence of the CIA in the food world can also be attributed to the efforts and achievements of our more than 40,000 successful alumni. Our graduates are leaders in virtually every segment of the industry and bring the professionalism and commitment to excellence they learned at the CIA to bear in everything they do.

UNPARALLELED EDUCATION

DEGREE PROGRAMS

The CIA's bachelor's and associate degree programs in culinary arts and baking and pastry arts feature more than 1,300 hours of hands-on learning in the college's kitchens, bakeshops, and student-staffed restaurants, along with an 18-week externship at one of more than 1,200 top restaurant, hotel, and resort locations around the world. The bachelor's degree programs also include a broad range of liberal arts and business management courses to prepare students for future leadership positions, as well as a Wine and Food Seminar travel experience in one of the world's top culinary regions.

CERTIFICATE PROGRAMS

The college's certificate program in culinary arts is designed for students interested in an entry-level position in the food world and those already working in the foodservice industry who want to advance their careers. The CIA also offers an accelerated culinary arts certificate program (ACAP), which provides graduates of baccalaureate programs in hospitality management, food science, nutrition, and closely related fields with a solid foundation in the culinary arts and the career advancement opportunities that go along with that skill base.

PROFESSIONAL DEVELOPMENT PROGRAMS AND CONSULTING

The CIA offers food and wine professionals a variety of programs to help them keep their skills sharp and stay abreast of industry trends. Courses in cooking, baking, pastry, wine, and management are complemented by stimulating conferences and seminars, online culinary R&D courses, and multimedia training materials. Industry professionals can also deepen their knowledge and earn valuable ProChef® Certification and Certified Wine Professional™ credentials at several levels of proficiency.

In addition, the college offers expert culinary consulting to the industry through its CIA Consulting group. Headed by a seasoned team of Certified Master Chefs and supported by the college's acclaimed international faculty, CIA Consulting offers foodservice businesses a rich menu of custom consulting services in areas such as product innovation, menu R&D, restaurant strategy and design, and culinary training.

FOOD ENTHUSIAST PROGRAMS

Food enthusiasts can get a taste of the CIA educational experience during the college's popular Boot Camp intensives and Weekends at the CIA courses offered at all three campuses. In addition, the college's CIA Sophisticated Palate programs at Greystone offer the very best of Napa Valley's food and wine scene, including exclusive visits to area growers, vintners, and purveyors.

CIA LOCATIONS

MAIN CAMPUS—HYDE PARK, NY

Bachelor's and associate degree programs, professional development programs, food enthusiast programs

The CIA's main campus in New York's scenic Hudson River Valley offers everything an aspiring or professional culinarian could want. Students benefit from truly exceptional facilities that include 41 professionally equipped kitchens and bakeshops; five award-winning, student-staffed restaurants; culinary demonstration theaters; a dedicated wine lecture hall; a center for the study of Italian food and wine; a 82,000-volume library; and a storeroom filled to brimming with the finest ingredients, including many sourced from the bounty of the Hudson Valley.

THE CIA AT GREYSTONE—ST. HELENA, CA

Associate degree programs, professional development programs, certificate programs, food enthusiast programs

Rich with legendary vineyards and renowned restaurants, California's Napa Valley offers students a truly inspiring culinary learning environment. At the center of it all is the CIA at Greystone—a campus like no other, with dedicated centers for flavor development, professional wine studies, and menu research and development; a 15,000-square-foot teaching kitchen space; demonstration theaters; and the Ivy Award-winning Wine Spectator Greystone Restaurant.

THE CIA, SAN ANTONIO—SAN ANTONIO, TX

Certificate program, professional development programs, food enthusiast programs

Created to promote Latino diversity in the U.S. foodservice industry, the CIA campus in San Antonio, TX provides a variety of educational opportunities. In addition to a 30-week certificate program in culinary arts, the CIA's southwest campus also hosts Latin American cuisine courses for foodservice professionals as well as programs for food enthusiasts. The campus is currently undergoing an expansion that will grow its facilities from 5,500 to 25,000 square feet. Opening in fall 2010, it will include three new kitchens, one bakeshop, a 125-seat demonstration theater, and an outdoor cooking facility.

AUTHOR BIOGRAPHY

Brad K. Matthews

Director of Purchasing and Storeroom Operations

The Culinary Institute of America

Brad Matthews is director of purchasing and storeroom operations at The Culinary Institute of America (CIA). Directing a storeroom staff of more than two dozen, Mr. Matthews is responsible for all purchases on the college's Hyde Park, NY campus, including more than $6.5 million of food products for the college each year. Mr. Matthews and his staff must assure the value of those purchases through proper receipt, evaluation, storage, and timeliness of deliveries. He also oversees the distribution to the 41 kitchens and bakeshops of all food coming into the CIA campus.

Mr. Matthews is a 1974 CIA graduate. Before joining the staff of his alma mater in 1989 as manager of food purchasing and storeroom operations, he cooked at various restaurants in the Hudson Valley, managed an independent catering business, and ran the foodservice operation at Mount St. Alphonsus Seminary in Esopus, NY.

In addition to his CIA degree, Mr. Matthews holds a Bachelor's degree in organizational communications, which he earned from the State University of New York, Empire State College in 1991.

In 1990, Brad began a program of working with local farmers to ensure a steady supply of quality fresh local products for the CIA and to foster stronger ties with the college's neighbors. The program continued to expand to the point where Brad hired area farmer Paul Wigsten in 2004 as the college's produce buyer and farm liaison.

The CIA now spends more than $500,000 a year for fruits, vegetables, eggs, and dairy products from about 20 Hudson Valley farms. Matthews and Wigsten shared the Glynwood Harvest Good Neighbor Award in 2006 for their efforts in supporting local agriculture.

Paul Wigsten

Farm Liaison/Produce Buyer

The Culinary Institute of America

The Culinary Institute of America's produce buyer Paul Wigsten owns and operates Wigsten Farm in Pleasant Valley, NY with his family. Throughout his youth, Paul worked on the family farm, but in 1982 he moved to New York City to pursue a career in commercial real estate.

After spending 12 years in New York City, Paul returned to Pleasant Valley in 1994. Recognizing a strong demand for locally grown fruits and vegetables, Paul converted the Wigsten family farm from dairy to produce, and he also placed new emphasis on sustainable farming practices and heirloom varieties.

Paul began selling produce to The Culinary Institute of America (CIA) in 1996, and quickly developed a reputation as a source for high-quality produce. This relationship flourished for eight years, and eventually the CIA offered him a full-time position as its produce buyer.

During Paul's tenure at the CIA, he has worked with local growers throughout New York's Hudson Valley to expand the CIA's long-standing practice of buying locally.

Now the third and fourth generations operate the Wigsten Family Farm, including Paul and his wife Robin, and their son William. In 2002, Wigsten Farm was awarded the Agri-Business Award by the Dutchess County Economic Development Corporation.

Under the guidance of Paul and the CIA's storeroom staff, the college spends more than $500,000 purchasing locally grown foods—from produce to eggs and dairy and cheese—each year. His efforts in supporting Hudson Valley farms earned Paul the 2006 Glynwood Harvest Good Neighbor Award.

ACKNOWLEDGEMENTS

I grew up in a family that valued good food. Family gatherings were always centered around the table and the kitchen and I saw the joy in placing wonderful things to eat in front of people you love. I began to try my hand in the kitchen under my mother's nervous eye when I was ten years old and subjected my family to my first creative exploits at the stove.

When I was eleven, to my great joy, my Uncle Rim came back home from Chicago with my Aunt Wilma. They both worked in restaurants and from them I learned much more about food and treating people with hospitality. I learned the magic of garlic's sweet pungent punch and the zest that lemon brought to your palate; and to respect the food you were going to prepare. What I learned under my uncle's tutelage formed the basis for everything I have done professionally since; whatever I have accomplished was because of his faith in me. I cannot properly express my appreciation for what my aunt and uncle have taught me.

After high school I was working in the kitchen of their restaurant when the chef Artie Rhome, gave me a newspaper clipping saying that The Culinary Institute of America was moving to Hyde Park, just across the river. The suggestion was strongly made by this chef that a person with my interests should attend this renowned institution and grow from a cook into a chef. With a fairly healthy shove from my uncle I decided to take that advice. That education prepared me to go out into the world to cook and learn about foods of every description especially the incredible range of colors, textures, and flavor that fresh produce brings to the palate. Over time it also taught me that much of the excellent food I enjoyed and used seasonally was now available more often but it didn't taste quite the same. I also learned that finding these foods locally was becoming a bigger challenge as farms gave way to housing developments and strip malls.

In 1989 I was honored with the opportunity to come back to the CIA as an employee and charged with the purchase of all the food required by its demanding faculty. Shortly thereafter, with the encouragement of now President Tim Ryan and Senior Vice President Charlie O'Mara, I was given the opportunity to reach out to the Hudson Valley's excellent farmers and build a strong partnership tying their efforts and products with the Institute's needs. This has been the most rewarding aspect of my tenure here. One of the farmers I forged a lasting relationship with is my co-author Paul Wigsten. He sold me his beautiful produce until he agreed to join me as my produce buyer and the Institute's liaison to local agriculture and all the local growers he knew so well. This partnership has greatly improved the Institute's role in supporting our farming neighbors and lead to this book. It has been a great deal of fun accomplishing this together.

My most heartfelt appreciation must be expressed to my wife, Lissa. She has shared in my love for this subject and accompanied me through an amazing number of farm stands and markets, and our membership in the Taliaferro Farm CSA. Her support in that and her understanding of the time this project took made the trip all the more enjoyable. Our exploration of the Hudson Valley farm markets and products also included our son Ryan. He hopes to one day follow me at The Culinary Institute of America and my dream is that he will still have all this local bounty to utilize and enjoy. This book is dedicated to Ryan and his hopes for the future.

—Brad Matthews

For as long as I can remember, agriculture has been a part of my life. One of my earliest memories is of walking across the road with my grandfather to get a can of milk from our dairy cows for breakfast. Growing up on a working farm was a wonderful experience for a young lad. Calves to feed before breakfast, hay to bale all summer. and of course cows to milk twice a day, every day, even Christmas. It was traditional for my father and I to milk on Christmas to give the hired men that day off.

There was always a large vegetable garden and my mother and grandmother did a lot of preserving of fruit and vegetables for the long cold Hudson Valley winters. Many years ago I decided to grow vegetables on the family farm. Dairy farming as a lifestyle was just not for me and on top of that, as a dairyman, you have little to no control over the prices you receive for your product. My folks Warren and Betty were very helpful. Dad helped with the tractor work and Mom, a retired Home Economics teacher, developed recipes to hand out at the farmers' markets we attended. Later when I married my wife, Robin, she left her teaching job and joined me full time on the farm. Now our 15-year-old son, William, is an active participant in every aspect of our farm operation. Robin's folks Ernie and Elaine, her sister Vicki and her husband Chris have also been very helpful around the farm. We have a true family farm and I feel very blessed. I would like to dedicate this book to the two most important men in my life, my father Warren and my son William. Perhaps William will one day carry the farming torch or maybe not; only time will tell.

I would like to thank The Culinary Institute of America and President Tim Ryan for giving me the opportunity to spread the word about buying locally while providing me with an inspirational work environment. Brad Matthews and I had a lot of fun writing this book together. We would both like to thank the people who made this possible. Maggie Wheeler, our editor, and Keith Ferris and Shelly Malgee for the photography and Jared Walton, CIA class of 06, of Baldor Specialty Foods, Bronx NY for answering many questions.

—Paul Wigsten

INTRODUCTION

The range of produce raised or gathered and sold into the foodservice industry and home kitchen covers a myriad array of fruits and vegetables. These many produce items encompass a wide range of seasonal concerns, handling and storage considerations, and quality standards. The issues of organic, sustainability, seasonality, and defining what is local are now very relevant to the subject of produce and how it is perceived by the chef, the buyer, the grower, and the consumer.

In this we look to present these produce items from the perspective of both the field and the kitchen. The experiences of farmer, salesperson, purchaser, and chef have been utilized to show what, when, and how to buy as well as how to store and prepare these items that make up such a major role in a healthy and delicious diet.

In defense of our industry, the small farmers, the land, and simply the quality of what we eat, this book will be a clear proponent of supporting local agriculture and the benefit of chefs buying directly from their neighbors the farmers and the benefit of the farmers working with their neighbor the chefs to grow the type of crops that will please their customers. Slow Food and Farm to Fork initiatives are strengthening and getting wider acceptance as are Community Sponsored Agriculture (CSA) farms. The intent of these programs and organizations is to not only keep local farms solvent, but to keep the variety and quality of food that should be desired available for our tables.

Supporting local agriculture lends itself to the belief that is best to buy produce when it is in season. Produce is not only at its best when it is in season; it is much more plentiful, costs less money, and is therefore a much better value. This is more than good food, its good business.

It is the rare restaurant, however, that can buy strictly local in season. Cranberries don't grow in Texas nor pineapples in New York; still it is good to know when any given item will be at its peak and how best to receive and store it once it arrives in your kitchen. This book is designed to enhance your ability to make these decisions and take full enjoyment of the incredible range of color, texture, flavor, and nutrition that produce provides.

SELECTING PRODUCE

Fresh produce is an integral component of quality foodservice operations. The choices made when purchasing and receiving exceptional produce help determine whether your customers will just get fed or be delighted with their experience. The following types of decisions will impact the type of product you buy; whether it is in season, its country of origin, whether it is organic, sustainable, or traditionally grown, the range of textures and colors desired on the plate(s), and the nutrition content of the dish.

Given the range of items in the market today, the options and combinations of items you can serve are almost endless, limited only by one's imagination and financial constraints. These plentiful options are also adaptable to the type of foodservice operation being managed, from fine white tablecloth dining to institutional operations.

Carefully purchased produce will provide much of the visual appeal, texture, aroma, nutrition, and a whole gamut of taste sensations on the plate. Best of all, when produce is purchased in season, it is most likely at its very best and most plentiful, which will drive down the price. What other food items will you find at their best when the price is down? This defines the concept of value, and shows the importance of well-chosen produce in your operation.

Yield is also a consideration when determining an item's true value. Produce purchased locally and in season should have little to no trim loss and a better shelf life than a similar item purchased from across the country or globe. For example, a case of lettuce grown on a large commercial factory farm may be of good quality when it's picked, but it will be packed, chilled, shipped for days by truck, and then potentially held for an unknown number of days in a purveyor's walk-in before arriving at its destination. This product may cost 15 percent less than a similar case of lettuce grown locally, but the trim loss and shortened shelf life may well require 20 percent or more of the case weight to go into your recycling barrel. Plus, the fresher product should have better texture and flavor. Which is the better value?

The idea of buying locally in season is a very good one, at least the majority of the time. This practice builds goodwill and more financial security with your neighborhood farmers, it helps keep tracts of land green instead of paved, the food you use will be fresher, and you will know how safely it was grown. Additionally, it won't need to travel thousands of miles, which consumes fuel.

However, being designated as local does not in itself automatically make something better. The farmer must know his trade and needs to grow quality products that meet your needs. The weather plays a huge role in growing quality and the product needs to arrive at your door before it is too late to utilize and at a price that allows you to turn a profit. The ability for growers to sell directly to foodservice is a challenge, but one that can yield great benefit to both parties. The key is in the planning and communication.

FARM TO FORK INITIATIVE

It is valuable for chefs and/or buyers to sit down with the farmers they deal with at least three times each year. February, when the new seed catalogs are out, is the appropriate time to talk about the upcoming season and what new items may be needed. Chefs and buyers should plan their approximate usage of each product and try to evenly distribute quantities among the farmers who grow that particular crop. This practice gives the farmers a strong sense of security going into the season as they know there will be a market for what they are growing. Additionally, the chefs should try to make at least one on-farm visit early in each season. The chefs have the opportunity to see for themselves how the crops are growing and what they can expect and when. Farmers work very hard and are justifiably proud of their accomplishments; they welcome a scheduled visit for a look at what is going on. Sadly, farmers cannot control the weather, so growers and chefs should work together to be prepared with a plan B should disaster strike. In November or December, it is a good idea to sit down again and review the past season. Chefs can invite the farmer into the restaurant to see where and how the product is featured and thank the farmer for his or her good work. This is a time for both parties to talk about the successes and failures of the prior season.

Developing a good working relationship with farmers takes some time and effort. Chefs need to be clear about prices to determine what is fair to the grower and still

allows for a profit to the chef, and to review prices as markets change. Chefs should set realistic order and delivery times and stick to them. It must be remembered that when placing an order, the product has yet to be harvested, washed, packed, and delivered. The farmer cannot service his accounts properly if he doesn't have enough notice to plan, harvest, and deliver. Also, it is advantageous to be flexible with menu planning. On a rainy day, green beans cannot be harvested because they will rust, so perhaps another green vegetable such as zucchini will do, which can be harvested in the rain.

Management must understand that prompt payment is very important. Many small farmers operate on a very slim margin and cannot usually wait more than a week or two for payment. The intent here is to create a viable long-term business relationship that profits all parties.

On the other side of the equation, farmers need to understand that chefs and buyers are running a business. Being accessible by cell phone is important if the chef or buyer needs to add to an order or reschedule a delivery time. A professional packing job is a key element to the farmer's reputation; this ensures the chef will know what each case will weigh and that the product is safely protected and properly boxed for storage in the coolers. Industry standards have been established for each type of fruit or vegetable on the market and these standards need to be adhered to by the farmers.

Farmers need to be prompt with deliveries and able to act on short notice when an emergency develops. It is imperative to notify their clients when an expected product is not going to be available so that alternate plans can be made. Buying local produce does present some challenges but the rewards for both parties should exceed any small inconveniences that may arise. Most importantly, the dining customers will appreciate the difference and the effort.

FINANCIAL CONSIDERATIONS

The choices made when selecting, buying, and receiving produce have a direct impact on an operation's bottom line. This impact is felt in several ways both before and after the produce arrives in the receiving area or kitchen. As discussed earlier, seasonality is a key factor. Purchasing product well out of season can drive up the food cost to over 100 percent higher than optimal seasonal pricing. Purchasing an item just as it comes into season will almost guarantee that it will be much higher in price than waiting just a few days or weeks until the markets have ample inventory. Some items, like berries, when purchased out of season, may need to be cooked or augmented in some way to improve their palatability and will still command a premium price. Freezing delicious and affordably priced berries in season and then using the frozen berries in the winter months will yield a better tasting product for a lesser cost. Otherwise, consider leaving berries off the menu in the winter and utilize those items when they are in season and a better value.

Proper turnover of inventory is also a factor affecting the bottom line. Produce held too long in storage will not maintain its value. Even if the product appears in reasonable condition upon receipt, it will not retain its vibrant appearance or its bright flavor over time. Also, many produce items will dehydrate as they sit on the shelf under refrigeration. This is detrimental to both their flavor and texture. Water loss is the equivalent of pounds of produce purchased and never served or sold. Inventory levels need to be determined by factoring the rate at which the product is sold and the frequency of available deliveries. Purchase only what is needed to meet demand from one delivery to the next. Being overly cautious to ensure that product is always in inventory, or stocking to fill all available kitchen space, will cost you both in dollars and customer satisfaction over the long run. Diligence in monitoring inventory levels and adjusting par stocks is also important. Running short and either looking for produce from a less than optimal source, or running out of product and letting down your customers, is also harmful to the bottom line.

Proper utilization is also a key factor in maximizing yield and improving the value of your produce purchases. Utilizing all usable vegetable trim in soups or stocks, finding a use for all edible, but often wasted, parts such as papaya seeds and fennel fronds, and utilizing the same item in several menu applications to ensure rapid turnover are all ways to further a product's value. Puréeing and freezing excess product for soups or freezing, pickling, or canning product bought in season when plentiful and low priced for use later in the year are also ways you can improve the bottom line.

SOCIAL RESPONSIBILITY

Your personal ethics and beliefs will play a role in how you identify and choose the produce you purchase and these factors may drive your decision-making process, even if they are not always geared to improve the bottom line. These choices may include the product's country of origin and their practices in regard to chemical usage, sanitation, or labor practices. Actions such as purchasing organic and sustainable produce instead of conventionally grown produce, opting not to buy out-of-season product despite customer requests, or buying domestically or only locally, all make statements about the business you wish to operate. Your choice of produce will have an impact on that. Influencing these choices are other factors such as product availability in your area, financial pressures, customer demands, and your employer's priorities. There are no right or wrong choices but these are questions you want to consider when planning what produce to buy and how to obtain it.

Such options and choices need not be black or white, but geared to what is realistic for your operation and location. Organic produce may be a viable option to strive for, if available for a reasonable cost in season. However, the same items may become prohibitively expensive when not in season; this means you will need to change menu items or ease your standards at these times.

SPECIFICATIONS AND STANDARDS

Whatever your choices and standards, it will be imperative to develop detailed specifications. These are determined by the management, chefs, and buyers to make certain everyone is in agreement on the organization's standards. These specifications should then be given to the operation's vendor(s) to guarantee that the vendors are clear as to what is expected and so they can advise you if anything requested will be difficult for them to procure. These exact specifications should be detailed on each purchase order or, if you maintain a steady relationship with one, or several, produce vendors, your specifications can be placed on file with them and updated as necessary. These can be as detailed as you deem necessary and will provide your vendor with the means to fully comprehend and meet your expectations.

Proper specification sheets will list each item by the exact name of the product, such as Ruby Red Grapefruit. Other quality standards and receiving conditions such as case weight or count, proper skin coloration, state of ripeness, and USDA (United States Department of Agriculture) grade if applicable, should also be clearly stated.

Acceptable product substitutions should be included if deemed necessary and available. Failure of your vendor to provide produce that meets all required specifications should result in the product in question being refused and returned for credit. The reason the product failed to meet your specifications should be noted on the credit memo to ensure there is no disagreement about the credit with the vendor later on.

INDUSTRY TERMS

When determining your specifications and standards in regard to purchasing produce, it is worth discussing the meaning of some terms used when talking about where and how product is grown. There is much debate on the exact meaning of some of these

terms but this should provide a general overview of the terms and how they apply to fresh produce.

SEASONALITY

Seasonality is simply a term meaning to buy what is growing best at that time of year. Seasonal produce charts are helpful when researching this but weather is the wild card in determining what is in season. If the weather remains cold and wet well into spring, the season will start late; likewise if there is a hard frost early in the fall, the season will end early. The amount of precipitation will also affect the season; being too wet or too dry will adversely affect the availability of a product. Similarly, if it is too hot or too cold, the season and yield of the product will be affected. The calendar will give you a guide to when something might be expected but it cannot make that product grow. Interaction between the chef and grower or vendor is important as seasons change. Purchasing according to season will give you the best product at the best price; it's a great way to buy. However, adhering to this philosophy may also limit your choices and require more flexibility in planning your menu.

Supporting your local grower and lessening your carbon footprint are reasons to limit purchases to local and regional product and indicates you also employ seasonal purchasing practices. The limit on how "local" or "regional" are defined is a question that can only be determined by you, but is worth some discussion. How rigid are you as a chef or buyer willing to be when making these choices? Can chefs in the northern parts of America opt to not purchase citrus, bananas, and coffee? Possibly, but more than likely customer demand will dictate purchasing to some extent. That said, there still will be many produce options available that are only limited by what you determine those boundaries to be. Domestic product only, produce from the "tri-state region,"

a 200-mile-radius menu, or raising as many of your own animals and produce as your location allows are all indicative of the different definitions people use to determine what regional or local can mean. Other chefs may believe that to please their customers they will purchase whatever is available at a reasonable cost from anywhere it is grown in the world and not operate at all with a local or regional agenda. These are decisions that can only be made based on the operation's needs.

SUSTAINABILITY

Sustainability is one of the main terms that seems to most defy an agreed upon definition. Growing product in a way that does not deplete the environment or that is not harmful to people and animals in addition to ensuring that the land will continue to support both the growth of product and the farmer in the future is seen as being sustainable. Simply put, this means to satisfy the needs of people now without any risk to the people and environment later on.

These practices include making sure that the soil is neither depleted by erosion nor depleted of nutrients with excessive use of chemical additives such as phosphates.

Another issue of sustainability includes the management of water to guarantee that the produce grown can survive on the amount of water that is renewably available and that the water is not contaminated by animal waste or chemical runoff.

The wages and living conditions of the farm workers, the distance the produce is shipped to market, and other factors are also argued to be part of the sustainability equation. Defining whether, what, and how much artificial or chemical means of fertilization to use is also part of the sustainable debate.

The Slow Food Movement is a grassroots effort to promote the sustainability of our food system. They are advocating that the food we eat be good both for our bodies and the ecosystem in which the produce is grown and economically fair to those who grow it. The idea is simply that the food we raise and eat should be good for the planet and those eating it. The process should be economically fair to both grower and consumer and this will supply food that simply tastes better.

ORGANIC

Organic produce refers to plants that are cultivated without the use of any artificial or chemical herbicides, pesticides, or fertilizers. Instead, organic farmers rely on renewable and natural means to grow their product without damage to the soil or water. This is the fastest-growing segment in agriculture and its popularity is attracting the interest and involvement of the large players in both agri-business and retail vending. Large corporate influence in this segment of the industry may serve to diminish the standards that have been used for produce to be certified organic.

Alternatively, many small farms that are growing their produce properly in a sustainable and organic fashion opt not to be certified organic due to the time and expense of the certification process. This drives home the point that the best way to be absolutely sure that your produce is grown in a manner that meets your standards is to learn about your source and, if possible, know and visit the grower. Labels and certifications

are an indication that the produce meets the standards that you are expecting, but nothing beats knowing your source whenever this is possible.

HEIRLOOM

Heirloom produce is grown from original native seeds, not hybridized variations that are developed to grow faster, extend the shelf life, or have the ability to grow in a broader season. Some growers insist that heirloom seeds must have been introduced from up to a century ago to be truly heirloom; others feel anything that is unique in look and flavor when it is introduced can be considered an heirloom. This produce is not as pretty or uniform in appearance and is much more fragile and difficult to package and ship. Therefore heirlooms represent just a small portion of the produce market; heirloom tomatoes comprise the largest segment of that. What these fruits and vegetables do offer is a much richer and more fully developed flavor. Heirloom varieties are most commonly found in farm stands and from specialty vendors. They command a higher price due to their quality, high perishability, and lower yield. The flavor and unique colors can make them well worth it however. In addition to tomatoes, other heirloom produce items include: potatoes such as Purple Peruvians, apples such as the Golden Russet, and some varieties of melons, eggplant, cherries, peaches, and asparagus. Many of these, however, are rarely found in the commercial market.

WILD AND FORAGED

There is another category of produce on the market that could certainly be characterized as heirloom because no one has introduced these items as a seed into the market. These are fresh produce items that are found or dug up in nature and are not cultivated. The items classified as wild or foraged only grow in their own season when the weather and growing conditions are correct. These circumstances bring uniqueness in appearance and flavor to the produce that is only available when nature permits. These traits and the need for specially trained foragers to go out into the wild and find them cause this product to drive a steep price, but those who crave their woodsy, grassy, or funky goodness find them well worth the price they bear. Wild foraged mushrooms include morels and chanterelles and the exquisitely expensive truffles. Nettles, ramps, cress, amaranth, lamb's quarters, and fiddlehead ferns are all green, foraged produce items found in fields and along the edges of forests. Certain wild berries can also be found on occasion. Sea beans are a crisp and salty vegetable that grows along the ocean shore and is foraged in certain places in North America, Europe, Asia, and Australia; they are prized in salads and with seafood.

When purchasing wild produce items, *especially mushrooms,* it is critical that they be purchased from someone very knowledgeable and experienced as some wild items can be confused with other similar-looking plants that are poisonous. Also, many foraged items may cause allergic reactions unless cooked thoroughly. Items foraged alongside highways or near industrial sites can be contaminated from the environment and therefore can be dangerous for consumption. Having a trustworthy source is critical when buying wild foraged items.

STORAGE

Once your menu is set and you have determined your needs, specifications, and other standards for your produce, it is time to purchase and receive your product. This must be done carefully so that everything is in keeping with your exact specifications. After the produce has been received, it needs to be properly stored. Determining how much storage space is required is not easy and it is difficult to cite an exact means of doing so. You must determine what will work for your operation to protect the quality and integrity of what you buy. Factors to consider include, most simply, the square footage your operation can make available for cold and dry storage and what will fit in this space without overloading your ability to store properly. Seasonal fluctuation is also a consideration; you will likely have access to a greater number of higher quality fresh products during the growing seasons than during the winter, when your needs change. Next to consider is how often you can receive deliveries; this is key because you need to both quickly turn over your produce and occupy only as much space as is required to meet your needs during the interval. Fresh product delivered daily is an ideal situation; holding produce no more than a few days is important.

Refrigeration will be the major concern both because of the space it takes up and the cost of the unit. The exact temperature requirements for each type of produce is addressed with that item in this book but, with the exception of tomatoes, unripe avocados, potatoes, bananas, and dry onions, all of your produce items will likely require

refrigeration. There is an ideal temperature range for each type of produce, generally starting at about 33°F/1.5°C and then going upwards to 45°F/7°C. However, many smaller food service operations may not have enough refrigerator space to meet both the high and low end of this range. If one walk-in cooler is all that is available, careful arrangement of your produce from the warmer area near the door to the coldest area, which may be near the blower, may have to suffice. Additionally, if space is limited you will probably need to turn over your inventory rapidly which will help maintain the quality. The relative humidity should also be high, around 80 to 90 percent to reduce dehydration. Ideally you will have separate fruit and vegetable walk-ins, but such is not always the case.

Produce that is stored under refrigeration should be kept as dry as possible to lessen the spoilage rate. Avoid washing produce prior to storage or placing produce with an ice pack over other product. Produce often has its own outer wrapping to preserve freshness. Do not peel vegetables or remove the outer leaves from lettuce or cabbage until ready to use. However, the leafy tops of items such as carrots, radishes, and beets should be removed as they continue to absorb the moisture and nutrition from the vegetable.

Some fruits such as stone fruits and pears should be held at room temperature until fully ripened. They can be refrigerated at that point but should be quickly utilized to maintain quality. Fruits and vegetables that emit a great amount of ethylene gas such as melons, bananas, and apples can actually promote the ripening of under-ripe produce, but just as quickly promote the spoilage of already ripe produce. Obviously these items should never be stored near anything that is fully ripe. Vegetables with powerful odors such as onions can also taint the flavor of other refrigerated items (e.g., dairy products and absorbent fruits). Using caution when storing these items is also prudent.

Daily inventory counts of produce items will show the volume of each item moved on both a daily basis and also how that volume may fluctuate according to the day of the week. These trends become apparent quickly and can be used to develop a par stock level which will give you a high and low range to maintain your product needs from one delivery date to the next. Once determined, it is important to constantly monitor these pars to ensure they remain relevant to the current volume of business. Changes in seasonal availability and menu selection are other factors that will require your inventory par levels to remain fluid and quickly adjustable. Spikes in usage due to holiday rushes or lulls and extra banquet needs should be realized and compensated for without a rash judgment to raise or lower pars on a daily basis. Consistently over-ordering or under-ordering your produce is tough on both product quality and customer satisfaction.

Purchasing and properly storing fresh produce is an ongoing process that must be correctly adjusted to the season, customer demand, and availability. Doing this well and adopting practices such as buying locally, in a sustainable manner, in season, and opting to use the wide palette of flavors, textures, and colors available to you takes effort but yields gratifying results. These efforts also can add to the economic benefit of agriculture in your area and to your bottom line. They may not all be required to provide good quality produce for your menu but they can improve the seasonal quality and customer satisfaction when applied.

SALAD AND COOKING GREENS

Greens are wonderfully flavorful, varied, and nutritious ingredients. They are also relatively easy to prepare and adaptable to many dishes and cuisines. In general, these vegetables are fairly inexpensive, making them a good nutritional value for your dollar.

Thorough cleaning is essential due to the large amounts of sand and grit that collect, in the leaves. Always place the greens in a large amount of cold water and agitate the dirt away. Pull the greens from the water so as to leave the grit behind. This procedure may have to be repeated, often several times, until there is no evidence of grit when the greens are removed from the water.

Some greens can be large and tough and lend themselves well to low, slow cooking, whereas others are very tender and can be cooked quickly or simply dressed and served raw. Because of the range in sizes and textures and the culinary applications that suit them, they will be classified as either salad or cooking greens.

SALAD GREENS

Salad greens are an excellent nutrition source, low in calories, and come in a myriad of colors, textures, and flavors to challenge the chef and delight the diner. The key, which holds true for all fresh produce, is to utilize what is fresh and best in that season and, when possible, what is grown locally. Salad greens can be mild and silky in texture and flavor, such as the butterhead lettuces or crunchy with a spicy bite like arugula or baby mustard greens and everything in between. Salad greens can also be utilized in various combinations to afford the diner a contrast of flavors and textures.

The different varieties of salad greens can be dressed with an almost equal array of flavors, but the dressing should only complement the green, not drown or overshadow it. Rich, creamy, and cheesy dressings do well with larger, crisp leaf lettuces but will overwhelm a mix of baby lettuce greens. Assertive bitter greens fare better with a dressing and flavors that will balance their bitterness. Other salad greens are well served when wilted with a hot dressing or even when they have been lightly grilled before dressing. The possibilities are as varied as the chef's imagination.

The range of flavors and textures of salad greens mean that almost every choice will have two or three others that may work well as a substitute. The key then is to shop and construct the salad according to what is best and freshest in the marketplace that day. This is more freeing and will yield better results than developing your menu and trying to source what is required. Often this will yield better financial benefits as well because the best product in the market is the most seasonal and plentiful, which results in much better value. Using local sources, and especially working directly with local growers, is critical to finding the best and freshest ingredients. Interacting with local growers in the off season can yield chefs exactly the type and size product desired once the season begins. This aids the chef and the farmer in planning ahead and guarantees one a source and the other a market. Urban area chefs can seek out local greenmarkets to source fresh product and to cultivate relationships with the growers that come there. Once again, a willingness to adapt and create according to the market will provide the best results and a living menu that reflects the season, the location, and the personality and skill of the chef.

LEAF LETTUCES

Leaf lettuces are generally grown to be eaten cold in sandwiches, salads, tacos, and the like. They are cooked in some cultures but are rarely utilized in that manner in the United States. The texture varies with type but they are typically composed of large leaves around a short, dense stalk. If the lettuce is not harvested in time, the stalk will continue to grow through the head and may flower. This is termed *bolting* and is not a desirable condition for purchase. Additionally, when purchasing, the lettuce should be moist and fully colored with no wilting, browning, or holes, and it should have a good weight for its size. Types of leaf lettuces commonly found in U.S. markets are butterhead (Boston or Bibb), romaine or Cos, crisphead or iceberg, and looseleaf lettuces like lolla rossa and oak leaf. Also available in season, mostly at farm stands, is a lettuce similar to iceberg, but with a crisper, denser head known as Summer Crisp.

Lettuces grown locally can command a premium price in comparison to product from large industrial farms; however, the latter were likely shipped for many miles and/or held for days in cold storage. This higher cost is generally offset by improved flavor, longer shelf life, and considerably less trim. The improved flavor and yield can make this product a better value, even with a higher per case price.

BUTTERHEAD

Butterhead lettuces consist of two main types, Boston and Bibb, and are characterized by soft, tender, silky leaves and small stalks. Boston is round and similar to iceberg in shape but is much less dense. It comes twenty-four heads to the case if field-grown or twelve heads per case if grown hydroponically, each in a plastic "clam shell." Hydroponic lettuce is more expensive, and some feel less flavorful, but the heads are more consistently beautiful to behold and have a very high yield percentage. Field-grown Boston lettuce is sometimes available in a red leaf variety, which adds contrast when used.

The Bibb variety, also referred to as limestone lettuce, is similar in consistency, flavor, and feel to the field-grown Boston, but the head is shaped more like Romaine with slender stalks running up the lower outside portion of the leaves. These lettuces may be utilized interchangeably and work well with nuts and fruity salad dressings. The larger outer leaves also make great finger food wrappers for things such as chicken salad. Look for full, thick heads with soft, tender leaves when receiving. Avoid those that are very sparse or have tough discolored leafs. Reject anything shriveled or showing any signs of slime.

Pack Size: 24 or 12 heads per flat
Shelf Life: Several days to one week under refrigeration
Storage Conditions: 34° to 36°F/1° to 2°C
Season: Available year-round but best when purchased at your local farm stand

Nutritional Information

Serving Size:	3-1/2 oz/100 g
Water:	95.63 g
Calories:	13
Protein:	1.35 g
Fat:	0.22 g
Saturated Fat:	0.029 g
Fiber:	1.1 g
Sodium:	5 mg
Iron:	1.24 mg
Potassium:	238 mg
Vitamin C:	3.7 mg

FIGURE **2.1** Butterhead Lettuce

GREEN LEAF LETTUCE

This is a very common lettuce with several varieties (such as Tango), all of which are similar in appearance and application. Leaves are large, tender, loosely packed, and generally have frilly ends. The heads are typically somewhat triangular in shape. Some varieties will have slightly chewier leaves in the warmer months, probably due to a lower water content during those months. Leaf lettuces are excellent in salads, on sandwiches, or as a plate liner for other salads and cold presentations. Leaves may also be used as wrappers for finger foods. This lettuce typically packs twenty-four heads to the case.

Red leaf lettuce has different colorations towards the ends of the leaves. They also often have a more tender leaf, but are used in virtually identical applications and are found in the same pack size as green leaf. With either red or green leaf lettuce, look for heads that have fully colored, tender leaves with no brown or yellow coloration and no slime or dehydration.

FIGURE **2.2** Green Leaf Lettuce

FIGURE **2.3** Red Leaf Lettuce

Pack Size: 24 heads per flat
Shelf Life: Several days to one week under refrigeration
Storage Conditions: 34° to 36°F/1° to 2°C
Season: Available year-round but best when purchased at your local farm stand

Nutritional Information

Serving Size:	3-1/2 oz/100 g
Water:	95.07 g
Calories:	15
Protein:	1.36 g
Fat:	0.15 g
Saturated fat:	0.02 g
Fiber:	1.3 g
Sodium:	28 mg
Iron:	0.86 mg
Potassium:	194 mg
Vitamin C:	18 mg

OAK LEAF LETTUCE

Available in green and red leaf varieties, this lettuce is similar in softness to the butterhead varieties with very tender, frilly leaves and a crisp stem. This lettuce is highly perishable and generally has a shelf life of no more than two or three days. Oak leaf is beautiful when used in salads or as a plate liner under broiled fish. It has a wonderful delicate mineral flavor and should not be only utilized for garnish. If using in a salad, dressings should be delicate and light to balance the fragile nature of the leaf; citrus flavors complement the flavor of the lettuce well. Oak leaf lettuce is very fragile and tender, so look for well-formed heads with no shriveling or slime in the soft leaves. There should be no discoloration or rusting.

Pack Size: 24 heads per flat
Shelf Life: 2 to 3 days under refrigeration
Storage Conditions: 34° to 36°F/1° to 2°C
Season: Available year-round but best when purchased at your local farm stand

LOLLA ROSSA

Lolla rossa is a variety of red leaf lettuce with brightly colored red and green leaves that are deeply frilly and bent. This lettuce is available as full-sized heads packed twenty-four to a case or in baby-sized heads packed twelve to a 2-1/2-pound flat. This lettuce is extremely eye-catching and adds texture, depth, and color to the plate. Lolla rossa is more assertive in flavor than red leaf lettuce, with a fuller taste and slightly bitter finish. The excellent visual appeal, neutral flavor, and crisp, frilly leaves allow this lettuce a great many creative applications by adding volume and height to the dish. Lolla rossa is prized for its color and texture, so look for full, crisp heads with a vibrant color. Avoid anything that has begun to wilt or slime at the edges; the texture should be crinkly and crisp.

Pack Size: 12 baby heads or 24 mature heads per flat
Shelf Life: Several days to one week under refrigeration
Storage Conditions: 34° to 36°F/1° to 2°C
Season: Available year-round but best when purchased at your local farm stand

ROMAINE

Romaine is a Cos type of lettuce with elongated leaves and a long, white stalk running much of the way through the center. Romaine has a fairly rigid, slightly bitter leaf, which will stand up to more assertive and richer dressings. Its texture is showcased in the Caesar salad for which romaine is most famous. The density and firm texture of the leaf matches up well with the anchovies, citrus, and eggy cheese dressing. Romaine's assertive flavor and strong texture make it one of the few salad lettuces that has excellent cooking applications. Try sautéing it in olive oil and garlic or braising it with stock and white beans.

In warmer months, be aware of the potential for bolting which reduces the yield and the quality of the head. Romaine is also available in a red leaf variety, but this is more commonly seen in the baby form. Avoid heads with excess rusting, dehydration, or decay at the leaf tips.

FIGURE **2.4** Romaine Lettuce Hearts

Pack Size: 24 to a case; baby romaine packs 12 heads to a 2-1/2–pound flat
Shelf Life: One week under refrigeration
Storage Conditions: 34° to 36°F/1° to 2°C
Season: Available year-round but best when purchased at your local farm stand

Nutritional Information

Serving Size:	3-1/2 oz/100 g
Water:	94.61 g
Calories:	17
Protein:	1.23 g
Fat:	0.30 g
Saturated Fat:	0.039 g
Fiber:	2.1 g
Sodium:	8 mg
Iron:	0.97 mg
Potassium:	247 mg
Vitamin C:	24 mg

ICEBERG

Sometimes referred to as crisphead due to its very crunchy leaves, iceberg was at one time the staple lettuce in American kitchens. After falling from popularity in many homes and upscale eateries, it has regained some of its former appeal in recent years. Its cool, refreshing, and crunchy nature make it a natural on sandwiches, tacos, and in salads with rich, creamy dressings, such as the Wedge Salad. Beware of rusting spots through the center of the head and on the leaf stems that can severely limit its yield and eye appeal. Look for a hefty, round head with limited leaf trim. As with all lettuce, avoid limp and discolored outer leaves and decay at the stem end. The stem can easily be removed by a sharp whack on the stem and simply pulling it away. Also, as with romaine, steer clear of stems that are bolting through the head.

FIGURE **2.5** Iceberg Lettuce

Pack Size: 24 heads per flat
Shelf Life: Several days to one week under refrigeration
Storage Conditions: 34° to 36°F/1° to 2°C
Season: Available year-round but best when purchased at your local farm stand

Nutritional Information

Serving Size:	3-1/2 oz/100 g
Water:	95.64 g
Calories:	14
Protein:	0.90 g
Fat:	0.14 g
Saturated Fat:	0.018 g
Fiber:	1.2 g
Sodium:	10 mg
Iron:	0.41 mg
Potassium:	141 mg
Vitamin C:	2.8 mg

MESCLUN

Mesclun is essentially a mixture of small salad greens, lettuces, and herbs that gets its name and derivation from the Provençal region in southern France. Mesclun began appearing on menus and farm stands in the early to mid-1980s and has grown in popularity, if not quality, since that time. Mesclun should contain a wide variety of greens and lettuces, and often herbs, developed to present a large range of shapes, colors, textures, spiciness, and flavors. Mixtures should present a minimum of a dozen varieties and some specialty farms, depending on time of season, can utilize three times that many. Each leaf should be small and tender with a vibrant appearance and taste. Typically mixtures include red and green oak leaf and romaine, lolla rossa, frisée, tat soi, pak choy, arugula, baby spinach, orach, mizuna, dandelion, baby mustard, and cress. When in season, the best place to source quality mesclun is from your local farmer, their stands, or greenmarkets.

Large commercial farms sell vast quantities of a spring mix marketed as mesclun in a 3 lb pillow pack. Such packs may have their place in certain operations but are generally inferior mixes with much less variety and a more homogenous bland flavor. They are targeted to the mass market with a much lower price point. Local mesclun, which is usually cut by hand using scissors or a sharp knife, will be more expensive but a much higher-quality product. Consider using a better mixture and stretching it with leaf or Boston lettuce, if need be. In either case look for a product with fresh good color, small leaves (not torn larger ones), and with no wilting or slime.

Mesclun should be dressed with delicate light vinaigrettes so as to not mask their appearance and flavor. Mesclun salads should be presented in ways that showcase their color and variety to the dining customer.

> **Pack Size:** 2-1/2 to 4 lb/1.13 to 1.81 kg flats
> **Shelf Life:** Several days is optimal, but farm-fresh mesclun may last over a week
> **Storage Conditions:** 34° to 36°F/1° to 2°C
> **Season:** Available year-round but best when purchased at a local farm stand

FRISÉE

Frisée is a member of the endive family with a small head and thin, spiky or frilly leaves and is also referred to as Italian or French curly chicory. Frisée is relatively biting and bitter in nature and should be dressed assertively to complement its forceful flavor. Many chefs prefer the heads to be blanched before harvest to provide a very pale color and mellower flavor. This is accomplished by covering the heads to block out sunlight and neutralize the chlorophyll. Frisée that is allowed to grow into full, large heads is also referred to as curly endive or chicory. Chicory will have the same bitter, curly, slender leaves and a desired bleached heart only in a

FIGURE **2.6** Frisée

full-sized head, similar to escarole. Avoid curly endive that is discolored, wilted, showing signs of slime, or is very large and tough in texture. Be alert for rust and molding spots, which can occur if the heads were covered while wet. Smaller heads will be more tender with a lesser bite.

Pack Size: 12 to 24 heads per flat
Shelf Life: Several days to one week
Storage Conditions: 34° to 36°F/1° to 2°C
Season: Available year-round

MÂCHE

Like the butterhead lettuces, mâche (or corn salad) has very tender and mildly flavored leaves. The head is much smaller with narrow elongated leaves that lay in a rosette pattern. Mâche is widely available on the wholesale market. This product is beautiful on a plate and is most frequently grown hydroponically in small trays. It is more expensive, by the pound, than most lettuces or greens. In salads, this can be used in similar applications to Boston lettuce. Mâche is also referred to as field lettuce. As with all greens, a vibrant leaf and color with no wilting or slime is desired.

Pack Size: 24 plugs or small heads per flat
Shelf Life: 2 weeks under refrigeration
Storage Conditions: 34° to 36°F/1° to 2°C
Season: Available year-round as a hydroponically grown product

FIGURE **2.7** Mâche

BELGIAN ENDIVE

Belgian endive is the torpedo-shaped sprout that grows out of the top of the chicory root or, primarily in the United States, is grown hydroponically from a root cutting. Belgian endive is generally pale yellow to white and should have tightly sealed heads with no browning. Red or California endive is a beautiful white to burgundy red color but should likewise have closed heads and no browning. These are beautiful but less common and red endive is often twice as expensive as white.

Endive is highly flavored and slightly bitter; it can be eaten raw in salads, shredded into slaw, used as a garnish on cold meat and cheese plates, used as an edible spoon for hors d'oeuvres, or served as cooked greens (a good use for open or large heads). Cooked Belgian endive can be braised, grilled, or sautéed.

FIGURE **2.8** White Belgian Endive

Pack Size: 6 to 10 lb/2.72 to 4.54 kg case
Shelf Life: Several days to one week
Storage Conditions: 32°F/0°C
Season: Available year-round

Nutritional Information

Serving Size:	3-1/2 oz/100 g
Water:	93.79 g
Calories:	17
Protein:	1.25 g
Fat:	0.20 g
Saturated Fat:	0.048 g
Fiber:	3.1 g
Sodium:	22 mg
Iron:	0.83 mg
Potassium:	314 mg
Vitamin C:	6.5 mg

ESCAROLE

Escarole is another green that is delicious when served raw or cooked. The heads are large and lettuce-like in shape with broad, flat leaves. The escarole head should still hold its shape and not be completely flattened and open. The coarser and assertive outer dark green leaves are excellent braised, especially with garlic and white beans. The tender, pale yellow, inner leaves are delightful in salad or, if tender enough, both outer and inner leaves can be combined and served together. Avoid heavily browned heads or those appearing limp and/or slimy.

FIGURE **2.9** Escarole

> **Pack Size:** 18 lb/8.16 kg cases
> **Shelf Life:** Several days to one week under refrigeration
> **Storage Conditions:** 32°F/0°C
> **Season:** Available year-round but best when purchased at your local farm stand

RADICCHIO

Radicchio is available in several types and colors, but the claret-colored, firm, round head known as Chiogga (also the name of a variety of beet) is what is generally available and known in the United States as radicchio. The Verona type is very similar but brighter in color and with less firmly compacted heads. Radicchio is immensely popular, especially in Italian cuisine, and is enjoyed raw in salad as well as braised and grilled. Intense, spicy,

FIGURE **2.10** Left to right: Chiogga Radicchio and Trevisano Radicchio

and bitter in flavor, radicchio is generally preferred when blended with other ingredients or with assertive or heavier, creamy dressings to minimize the strong bitterness. It is excellent braised with other greens, in soups, or grilled and the outer leaves can be used to wrap fish or cheese before grilling them. Look for large, firm radicchio that hasn't been trimmed down as it aged. Heads should be solid and firm without sponginess and browning outer leaves.

Radicchio Treviso or Trevisano has rapidly gained popularity in the last several years. Trevisano can be nearly twice as expensive as standard radicchio. Shaped like romaine with less dense and more brightly colored heads, this is delicious in its own right or as a substitute for the more typical radicchio. Dressed in garlic and oil and grilled with a sheep's milk cheese, it makes a great first course.

Pack Size: Radicchio packs in 6 lb/2.72 kg flats. Trevisano sells in 5 lb/2.27 kg flats; the head count may vary according to size.
Shelf Life: Several days to one week
Storage Conditions: 34° to 36°F/1° to 2°C
Season: Available year-round

Nutritional Information

Serving Size:	3-1/2 oz/100 g
Water:	93.14 g
Calories:	23
Protein:	1.43 g
Fat:	0.25 g
Saturated Fat:	0.060 g
Fiber:	0.9 g
Sodium:	22 mg
Iron:	0.57 mg
Potassium:	302 mg
Vitamin C:	8 mg

FIGURE **2.11** Watercress

WATERCRESS

There are several delicious types of cress available in the market, but the most widely known and popular cress in the United States is watercress. This item is almost always available in its cultivated form, but can also be found grown hydroponically, like mâche. Even rarer still, wild cress is sometimes available in season; it is very similar to the cultivated cress but has a sharper, richer flavor. Recently cress has been available in a micro green form that is beautiful, highly flavored, and expensive. Generally consumed raw in the United States, many cultures use cress as a cooking green and as a medicinal herb. Upland cress, not surprisingly, is grown on land rather than along waterways and is milder in flavor. Pepper cress has small, curled, round leaves and gets its name for its sweet/hot peppery bite. Use watercress as a garnish, in salads, or as a bed for grilled meats. When combining with other salad items, balance its heat and spice with bland or mild-tasting vegetables. When cooking cress, it should be handled quickly in stir-fries or simply wilted.

Look for cress that is not wilted, slimy, or badly bruised by ice. Remove any tie or stem band as soon as possible to avoid further damage. Avoid cress with a sour scent.

Pack Size: 24 bunches to the case
Shelf Life: Several days
Storage Conditions: 32°F/0°C
Season: Available year-round

Nutritional Information

Serving size:	3-1/2 oz/100 g
Water:	95.11 g
Calories:	11
Protein:	2.3 g
Fat:	0.1 g
Saturated fat:	0.027 g
Fiber:	0.5 g
Sodium:	41 mg
Iron:	0.20 mg
Potassium:	330 mg
Vitamin C:	43 mg

ARUGULA/ROCKET/ROQUETTE/RUGULA/RUCOLA

Through its origins that are not exactly known, the delicious green rocket has become known primarily as arugula in this country. While wildly popular in the culinary world in the past several decades, this green has been cultivated for food and medicine for centuries. Arugula is sold in a number of varieties. It is found most commonly in its standard size, which is an irregular dark green leaf about two to three inches in length, often with a small root bundle at the base of the stem. Baby arugula is now very popular and is also found as a micro green. Rarely, it can be found grown using the hydroponics method and attached to its soils and root ball. Arugula has a peppery, radish, or mustard-like flavor and is very assertive and pungent. It marries well with a variety of flavors including sweet, salty, acidic, bland, and rich ingredients, which accounts for its great popularity.

Look for and avoid product that is bruised, wilting, discolored, or that is starting to slime. Slight drooping is generally not a problem but only buy as much as needed because of its brief shelf life. The best indicator of quality is a bright pungent aroma and bright colorful leaves.

Pack Size: Standard arugula is available in 10 lb/4.54 kg cases; baby rocket is available in 2.5 lb/1.31 kg flats
Shelf Life: 4 to 6 days under refrigeration
Storage Conditions: 34°F/1°C
Season: Available year-round but best when purchased at your local farm stand

FIGURE **2.12** Arugula

Nutritional Information

Serving Size:	3-1/2 oz/100 g
Water:	91.71 g
Calories:	25
Protein:	2.58 g
Fat:	0.66 g
Saturated Fat:	0.086 g
Fiber:	1.6 g
Sodium:	27 mg
Iron:	1.46 mg
Potassium:	369 mg
Vitamin C:	15 mg

COOKING GREENS

This category of greens is often associated with southern cooking in the United States but it is integral to the cuisines of many cultures. This grouping consists of greens from the looseleaf cabbage family such as collards and kale to the pungent mustards to the softer and rich-flavored chards. Historically, many of these were trimmed and cooked slowly with a piece of pork but they can be cut finely and cooked relatively quickly to add a more pungent jolt of flavor to many dishes. Although rich in flavor when served relatively plain, these greens lend themselves to a variety of strong seasonings and marry well with beans, potatoes, pastas, soups, and various meats.

Heartier greens such as the kale and collards are best in late fall and early winter, but can be found year-round. The best quality and selection will be found at the local greenmarket and farm stands, but these greens can usually be found in reasonable quality from your produce wholesaler or retail market. Always look for cool and moist greens with a rich green color and no dryness, yellowing, or wilted edges.

FIGURE **2.13** Spinach

SPINACH

As you probably learned during childhood, spinach is really good for you. It may actually be one of the most healthy, nutrient-rich foods that you can eat or serve to others. The fact that it's delicious, extremely versatile, economical, and widely known and available, makes it all the easier to provide such good nutrition. This wonderful green is good for the heart, vision, and bone strength, and has iron for energy as well as many other minerals and vitamins. Be aware that spinach can produce allergic reactions or thyroid issues if consumed in too great a quantity, but such problems are rare in comparison to its health benefits.

Spinach is generally available in three forms. Savoy spinach has dense, dark, thickly curled leaves and is available loose or in cello pack. Flat leaf spinach has smaller, more tender leaves and is available bunched or "triple washed" in large cello pillow packs. Baby spinach is now very popular as well and is excellent when used in salads. Spinach is a pre-washed item, but it makes good sense to wash all greens prior to preparation.

The methods of preparation for spinach are many and some are best suited to the type of spinach available. The heavier Savoy is best when serving creamed spinach, braised with bacon, or in something like a strata. The smaller, more tender flat leaf is great in lighter cooking methods such as simply wilted with garlic, sautéed with eggs or in a quiche, or in soups. It, like baby spinach, is also delicious in salads if the leaves are small and tender enough. All spinach can be eaten raw, but it is actually easier for the body to access all the nutritional value when it has been cooked in some fashion.

Spinach enjoys year-round availability but has the best quality in the early spring and fall. In the summer your local farm stand may sell what is called summer spinach; this is a paler, limper, and heavily stemmed product, but is also delicious when properly and simply cooked.

Pack Size: 20 lb/9.07 kg crate bunched; loose 2-1/2 lb/1.13 kg bag, washed; 3 to 4 lb/1.26 to 1.81 kg pillow pack of baby spinach
Shelf Life: Several days under refrigeration
Storage Conditions: 32°F/0°C
Season: Available year-round but best in spring and fall at your local farm stand

Nutritional Information

Serving Size:	3-1/2 oz/100 g
Water:	91.40 g
Calories:	23
Protein:	2.86 g
Fat:	0.39 g
Saturated Fat:	0.063 g
Fiber:	2.20 g
Sodium:	79 mg
Iron:	2.71 mg
Potassium:	558 mg
Vitamin C:	28.1 mg

CHARD

Chard is a green most commonly, and incorrectly, referred to as Swiss chard. Chard can be purchased as white stemmed (the most common and widely known as Swiss), red stemmed or red chard, and rainbow, which has brightly colored stems of several different colors. Chard has a slightly earthier and more complex flavor than its cousin, spinach.

Unlike spinach, chard stems are edible and delicious, although often neglected. The stems should be trimmed out, cleaned, sliced or diced, and then slowly sautéed or braised until tender. The leaves can be cooked in much the same ways as spinach; sautéed, creamed, or quickly braised. The stems and leaves can be served separately, but

FIGURE **2.14** White Chard

FIGURE **2.15** Red Chard

the flavors meld perfectly when mixed together for service. Chard is wonderful in cheesy strata with a crunchy crust. Generally available year-round, chard is at its peak from late spring until early fall. In addition to the quality of the leaf, look for chard with stems that are not brittle, drying, browning, or dehydrated so that nutritious part of the plant is not wasted. Considering its versatility, excellent nutritional value, and great flavor, chard is a vegetable that deserves more recognition and appreciation.

Pack Size: 20 to 25 lb/9.07 to 11.43 kg crate
Shelf Life: 3 days to 1 week
Storage Conditions: 34° to 36°F/1° to 2°C
Season: Available year-round but best when purchased from June through September at your local farm stand

MUSTARD GREENS

These greens are as varied as the cultures that prize them; mustard greens come in a variety of species which account for the broad range in size, colors, textures, flavors, and levels of heat found in greens classified as mustard. American mustard has a large, frilly, pale green, thin leaf with a radish-like, moderate level of heat. Most widely desired in southern or soul cooking, mustard greens are almost always prepared by simmering in a large amount of liquid with a fatty cut of pork to flavor it. Outside the South, this mustard green is rarely utilized.

The stems are tough and fibrous and should be removed prior to cooking. Aside from the method of boiling with pork, tender mustard greens can be served wilted with a bacon dressing or steamed briefly for a much more pungent flavor. They can also be served in a fiery Indian dish with chiles and other bitter green vegetables. Mustard greens should be a bold, vibrant green color with a firm but wrinkled texture. Avoid those greens that are turning pale to yellow or showing signs of mold or slime.

Wrapped heart mustard is generally only found in Asian markets. The large Romaine-like heads are generally trimmed down and only the stalk sections or even the heart is used. Fiery in flavor, it is usually found in a heavily seasoned stir-fry or made into kimchee. Dark jade in color, when cooked it makes for great presentation on the plate.

FIGURE **2.16** Mustard Greens

Japanese mustards are green and dark maroon to purple-red in color and found in large leaf (giant-leaf) as well as miniature and micro-size leaf version. The larger leaf is usually only found in pickles, but the small and micro leaf varieties are often found in this country utilized in Asian salad mixes and as a pungent accent or garnish on a plate.

In fact, most mustard greens utilized outside the South are the micro leaf variety because its appearance and forceful flavor have found favor in recent years.

Pack Size: 15 to 25 lb/6.8 to 11.34 kg crate
Shelf Life: Several days to 1 week under refrigeration
Storage Conditions: 32°F/0°C
Season: Mustard greens are available year-round but are best in the colder winter months

Nutritional Information

Serving Size:	3-1/2 oz/100 g
Water:	90.8 g
Calories:	26
Protein:	2.7 g
Fat:	0.2 g
Saturated fat:	0.01 g
Fiber:	3.3 g
Sodium:	25 mg
Iron:	1.46 mg
Potassium:	354 mg
Vitamin C:	70 mg

COLLARDS

Collard greens are a member of the cabbage family as is kale. These are types of cabbage that do not form into heads or bolt in the center, and are also known as colewort. The word collards was probably derived from this term.

Collards can be cooked in various ways. However, they are most popular in the South boiled or braised until tender with some type of pork product. The tender leaves can be thinly sliced and quickly sautéed for a cleaner, bright flavor, simmered in broth like cabbage, or used as a wrapper for other ingredients much liked stuffed cabbage. The stems of the collard greens are very tough and should be stripped out of the greens prior to cooking. Collards have a flavor that can be appreciated unadorned but that can also handle cooking with pungent and powerful flavors and aromatics. This versatility is clear in the many cultures that have embraced this green and made it integral to many national dishes such as Caldo Verde, Feijoada, Jamaican Rice-up, and the Southern "mess o' greens," which combines collards with whatever other greens are available with salt pork or ham hocks. With this dish, the broth, or "pot likker," is often drunk.

Pack Size: 15 to 25 lb/6.8 to 11.34 kg crate
Shelf Life: Several days to 1 week under refrigeration
Storage Conditions: 32° to 34°F/0° to 1°C
Season: Collards are available year-round but are best from late fall well into winter

KALE

Like collards, kale is a member of the non-bolting cabbage family. Its origins and much of its popularity come from the colder, northern regions of Europe where it is utilized in a myriad of ways. Kale has an earthy flavor and is extremely nutritious. It is available in several varieties. The most common is curly kale, which is long with dark green to bluish-green leaves. Curly kale is used in soups, traditionally cooked until completely soft, sautéed and served chewy or crunchy to the bite, puréed into a sauce, or braised with beans or potatoes and other vegetables. Its flavor, like many other slow-cooking greens, melds well with a great many assertive flavors. Kale should have vibrant, full, curly blue-green leaves; avoid anything beginning to yellow, wilt, or show signs of slime.

FIGURE **2.17** Collard Greens

FIGURE **2.18** Kale

Tuscan Kale, not surprisingly, came out of the Tuscan region of Italy hundreds of years ago. It is also called Lacinto or black kale and has rich dark green/black plumed leaves that speak of its full flavor. This variety of kale has gained popularity in recent years and is becoming much more readily available, especially at local farm stands. Aesthetically, its beautiful appearance fades into a rich, meaty mass when cooked. However, the complex flavor complements the flavors of its origins, combining well with rich ingredients such as pork, cheese, and olive oil. Tuscan kale must be stripped of its tough fibrous stems to be palatable, and is more costly than many greens. However, it is well worth the effort and expense when used in the appropriate manner. Red Russian kale gets its name from its origins and its red stems and bright color, especially when grown in the cooler months. The leaves are frillier and appear more delicate than other kales, but it is tough to the bite and very assertive in flavor. Accordingly, this kale should be combined with other assertive ingredients and served with big-flavored cuts of meat. Red Russian kale is most prized when picked in its small, delicate, baby form and used as an assertive flavor point in salad mixes such as mesclun.

Pack Size: 10 to 15 lb/4.54 to 6.8 kg crates
Shelf Life: 3 to 10 days under refrigeration
Storage Conditions: 32° to 34°F/0° to 1°C
Season: Available year-round but best when available at your local farm stand

DANDELION GREENS

Dandelion greens are not all that commonly used culinarily. Although they are available commercially in its wild or cultivated form, they are most commonly considered a weed. Its appearance is similar to frisée or chicory with narrow, spiky, green leaves. Dandelion greens can be served raw in salad, steamed with vinegar, or sautéed with aromatics. Highly nutritious, this is a much-maligned green. Dandelion greens should be slender and brightly green colored; avoid anything wilting or beginning to slime. The greens you dig from your lawn as weeds can be consumed, provided you are certain no pesticides or other poisons have been used to treat your or your neighbor's lawn. Now that's eating locally!

Pack Size: 15 to 20 lb/6.8 to 9.07 kg crates
Shelf Life: Several days under refrigeration
Storage Conditions: 34° to 36°F/1° to 2°C
Season: Generally only available in spring and summer months

FIGURE **2.19** Dandelion Greens

Nutritional Information

Serving Size:	3-1/2 oz/100 g
Water:	85.6 g
Calories:	45
Protein:	2.7 g
Fat:	0.7 g
Saturated Fat:	0.17 g
Fiber:	3.5 g
Sodium:	76 mg
Iron:	3.1 mg
Potassium:	397 mg
Vitamin C:	35 mg

BEET GREENS

Beet greens are the sprouting tops of the beet root and are closely related and similar to chard. More frequently than not, and wastefully so, these delicious and nutritious greens are typically lopped off the desired beet and discarded. When buying fresh beets, the quality of the tops should also be evaluated and utilized to maximize the financial and nutritional value of the beet. Young and tender tops with bright red stems will obviously be preferred, but larger greens in good condition with certainly suffice. Avoid greens with yellow or brown spots or those that are wilting and slimy. Beet greens will keep longer if left attached to the beet but then the quality of the beet will suffer as the greens continue to drain moisture from the beet itself. Cook in the same manner as you would spinach or chard; the flavor will complement many other ingredients. Turnip greens may be utilized in much the same manner.

Pack Size: 12 to 18 lb/5.44 to 8.16 kg crates
Shelf Life: Several days
Storage Conditions: 34° to 36°F/1° to 2°C
Season: Best quality will be found in late spring and summer when farm fresh beets are in the market

FIGURE **2.20** Beet Greens

Nutritional Information

Serving Size:	3-1/2 oz/100 g
Water:	91.02 g
Calories:	22
Protein:	2.2 g
Fat:	0.13 g
Saturated Fat:	0.02 g
Fiber:	3.7 g
Sodium:	226 mg
Iron:	2.57 mg
Potassium:	762 mg
Vitamin C:	30 mg

CABBAGE FAMILY

The mustard family (Brassica) is a large and varied group of vegetables, mostly referred to as a type of cabbage, which, despite its presence in many of the world's cuisines and its huge range of applications and flavors, never seems to get a lot of respect. Perhaps it's the "peasant food" connotation of many of its members, or that funky cabbage smell, but the group's reputation seems to be in direct contrast to its prevalence and popularity. The number-one selling side dish in the United States is coleslaw, kimchee is practically synonymous with Korean food and a variety of cabbages proliferate in all Asian cuisines, while much of Germany and Alsace's cuisine features braised and pickled cabbage as a prominent ingredient, and southern cooking in the Unites States frequently features collard greens and kale.

So, ignore the bad press and enjoy and experiment with this group of vegetables. Please note that if that cabbage smell is too pungent, it likely means that the product has been held in storage for too long. Many of these items can look fresh for a long time. However, for that all-important aspect of flavor, fresher is generally better. Beyond aroma, another indication of freshness and flavor quality is color; avoid graying, dull, or off colors when receiving these items.

There are two main categories in this classification: head-forming cabbages and non-head forming or stalk-forming cabbages. Head-forming cabbage grows into a dense, firm, rounded bolting head or a dense, squat, barrel shape. The non-head forming cabbages grow on stalks of varying thickness. Some are edible whereas others are not. Brussels sprouts seem to fit both categories because each sprout looks like a tiny red or green head of cabbage. These "little cabbages" are really the buds of the plant that grow on long stalks.

Kale and collard greens are technically classified as members of the cabbage family and are very green and leafy with tough, thin stalks. Given that they are prized for their leafy greens, and how these greens are prepared, they are often thought of as a cooking green. To that end, they are addressed in Chapter 2 of this book (pages 33–35).

There are a great number of different horticultural and culinary items that fall in the cabbage family. They are nutritious, an excellent source of dietary fiber, and most are relatively inexpensive. They have culinary applications to suit most every taste and season and they are present in almost every ethnic cuisine. Many can be served hot or cold, raw or cooked, utilizing many different methods of preparation, and seasoned mildly or in a very assertive manner. Whatever your culinary plans are, it is likely some member of the Brassica family would be a good fit.

HEADING CABBAGES

Clearly the predominant form of cabbage from the Brassica family, heading cabbages are any of four main types that form into compact, usually round, bolting, dense heads. These include green cabbage (sometimes referred to as white), red cabbage, the crinkly and crisper Savoy cabbage, and Napa, which forms more into a tall stalk or barrel than a tight ball. All should have good color without blemishes, a waxy surface, a short stem that has not bolted up through the center of the head, and be heavy for their size (indicating high moisture content). Cabbage with a dull gray or whitish hue has likely been held in storage too long. Originating in Northern Europe, heading cabbages are extremely popular in many cultures. From sauerkraut to braised cabbage, on fish tacos and in kimchee, cabbage enjoys great popularity. Rich in vitamin C and a good source of roughage, it is a nutritious part of any diet.

GREEN CABBAGE

Probably the most popular variety of cabbage, green cabbage is one of the workhorses of the cabbage family. This cabbage forms into round, firm, heavy heads, usually weighing several pounds, and should have very few heavy wrapper (outer) leaves. Pale green to white in color with a sulfuric cabbage aroma and flavor profile, green cabbage is tremendously popular because of its versatility and low cost. In the United States, green cabbage is mostly used raw in coleslaw, the ubiquitous side for every picnic and barbecue, and it comes with most diner sandwiches and burgers. When making coleslaw, shred the cabbage as thinly as possible for a more pleasing bite and flavor. A nice, more nutritious change of pace is utilizing cabbage on tacos, especially fish tacos, instead of iceberg lettuce. Green cabbage is often cooked around St. Patrick's Day and served with corned beef. This cabbage is also good braised with bacon, onions, and beer as an accompaniment to pork or wursts in German and Alsatian dishes. Sauerkraut is pickled cabbage and is excellent when cooked in the same fashion; sauerkraut can be braised, steamed on franks, or added to a Reuben sandwich.

FIGURE 3.1 Green Cabbage

Pack Size: 50 lb/22.7 kg
Shelf Life: 1 week
Storage Conditions: 32°F/0°C
Season: Available year-round but the peak season is in late summer and fall.
Also, when seen at farm stands locally.

Nutritional Information

Serving Size:	3-1/2 oz/100 g
Water:	92.18 g
Calories:	25
Protein:	1.28 g
Fat:	0.10 g
Saturated Fat:	0.034 g
Fiber:	2.5 g
Sodium:	18 mg
Iron:	0.47 mg
Potassium:	170 mg
Vitamin C:	40 mg

RED CABBAGE

Red cabbage has a very similar flavor profile and texture to green cabbage. In fact, the size, texture, and flavor are all comparable, only the color is different. However, this color adds visual appeal and contrast to green cabbage in many dishes in raw form. When cooked, the color will turn more bluish, unless an acid is added, and can bleed into other items in the dish. When braised with onions and caraway, it makes a beautiful and flavorful side for pork or braised beef dishes.

Recent studies have shown that anthocyanins, the color compounds that give this cabbage its purple color, may have strong health benefits that can make it a better dietary choice than its paler cousins. These compounds are believed to supply antioxidants that aid in cardiac and brain function as well as cancer protection. Be sure the heads have good even color with no blackening of the leaves or deterioration.

Pack Size: 50 lb/22.7 kg
Shelf Life: 1 week
Storage Conditions: 32°F/0°C
Season: Available year-round but the peak season is in late summer and fall.
Also, when seen in farm stands locally.

Nutritional Information

Serving Size:	3-1/2 oz/100 g
Water:	90.39 g
Calories:	31
Protein:	1.43 g
Fat:	0.16 g
Saturated Fat:	0.021 g
Fiber:	2.1 g
Sodium:	27 mg
Iron:	0.80 mg
Potassium:	243 mg
Vitamin C:	57 mg

FIGURE **3.2** Red Cabbage

SAVOY CABBAGE

Similar in size and color to green cabbage, Savoy cabbage has a thinner leaf with a crinkly texture that makes for a lighter, brighter flavor and crunchier bite. The crinkly heads generally weigh less than either the green or red varieties. The milder flavor, texture, and gradation of colors from pale to dark green make this an excellent cabbage for cooking and for slaws. Some believe it is best only when cooked. The outer large dark green leaf makes an excellent wrapper for stuffing applications. The crinkled leaves make this cabbage lighter in density than the green or red varieties, but they should still be firm with good heft indicating high water content.

Pack Size: 35 to 40 lb/15.88 to 18.14 kg
Shelf Life: 1 week
Storage Conditions: 32°F/0°C
Season: Available year-round but the peak season is in late summer and fall. Also, when seen in local farm stands and greenmarkets.

Nutritional Information

Serving Size:	3-1/2 oz/100 g
Water:	91 g
Calories:	27 g
Protein:	2 g
Fat:	0.1 g
Saturated Fat:	0.013 g
Fiber:	3.1 g
Sodium:	28 mg
Iron:	0.40 mg
Potassium:	230 mg
Vitamin C:	31 mg

NAPA CABBAGE

Napa cabbage is often referred to as Chinese cabbage because it actually originated in China. This variety of cabbage has a head shaped more like a barrel than a ball. There is a similarly shaped but thinner and elongated Chinese cabbage that is often sold as Napa. However, that variety is actually Michihli. The two are similar and can be used interchangeably but the latter variety is stronger in texture and has a higher moisture content.

FIGURE **3.3** Savoy Cabbage

FIGURE **3.4** Napa Cabbage

Napa cabbage has a reasonable shelf life, but the quality and moisture content diminish quickly. The flavor can range greatly, from very mild and sweet to a mild horseradish flavor, and is not a recommended substitute for other head cabbages, even though it is frequently substituted. There are a number of ways this cabbage can be cooked and served. It can be shredded in soups, stir-fried, or braised. The stalk can be served separately from the soft leaves for added crunch, the cabbage can be used raw in slaws, as a wrapper, or pickled in kimchee. This is a versatile, nutritious, and inexpensive vegetable. Look for heads that appear full, crisp, and vibrant with no wilted or shriveled leaves. Napa can be prone to rust-colored flecks, which greatly affect the visual appeal of the finished product and can result in excess trim loss.

Pack Size: 40 to 45 lb/18.14 to 20.41 kg
Shelf Life: 1 week
Storage Conditions: 32°F/0°C
Season: Available year-round but the peak season is in late summer and fall. Also, when seen at farm stands locally.

Nutritional Information

Serving Size:	3-1/2 oz/100 g (cooked)
Water:	96.33 g
Calories:	12
Protein:	1.10 g
Fat:	0.17 g
Sodium:	11 mg
Iron:	0.74 mg
Potassium:	87 mg
Vitamin C:	3.2 mg

NON-HEAD FORMING CABBAGES

BROCCOLI

This widely available member of the cabbage family has Italian origins and its name comes from the Italian term for stalk. This is a highly nutritious, delicious, and versatile vegetable, despite its occasional bad press. Look for very tight florets with no budding or flowering and stalks that are not very woody. Almost always bright green in color, broccoli can sometimes have a purplish cast on the florets, but this is not a quality issue. Yellow broccoli, however, should be avoided as it is much too old. Broccoli is usually served boiled or steamed, but can be stir-fried, used in soups, and served raw in crudités. The stems are best utilized by peeling, slicing, and stir-frying. When receiving broccoli, insist on a good ice pack. This will give you a fresher product.

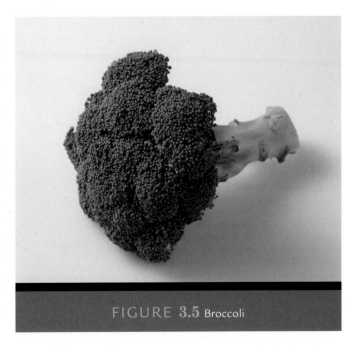

FIGURE **3.5** Broccoli

Pack Size: Loose crowns — 10 lb/4.54 kg; bunched — 14 bunches, 20 lbs/9.07 kg

Shelf Life: 4 days

Storage Conditions: 32°F/0°C

Season: Available year-round but the peak season is generally considered to be October through April

Nutritional Information

Serving Size:	3-1/2 oz/100 g
Water:	89.30 g
Calories:	34
Protein:	2.82 g
Fat:	0.37 g
Saturated Fat:	0.039 g
Fiber:	2.6 g
Sodium:	33 mg
Iron:	0.73 mg
Potassium:	316 mg
Vitamin C:	89.2 mg

BROCCOLI RABE, RAPINI

This bitter and highly nutritious member of the cabbage family also originated in Italy. Broccoli rabe has thin, tough stems, edible dark green spiked leaves, some small florets that look similar to broccoli, and is usually purchased bunched. Despite its name, this vegetable is more closely related to the turnip. The florets often have small yellow flowers that are edible. Although the thicker ends of the stems may be edible, they are not pleasant to eat. Discard the stems just below the leaves; only the more tender stems should be utilized when cooking. Broccoli rabe is often steamed or braised but it is best if cooked by blanching quickly to reduce the bitterness and then sautéing in olive oil with garlic and chili flakes. The seasoning should be very assertive to complement this vegetable's strong, pungent flavor and bitterness. Woody stems, a strong bitter odor, and slime should be avoided when purchasing this item.

FIGURE **3.6** Broccoli Rabe/Rapini

Pack Size: 20 lb/9.07 kg

Shelf Life: 5 days

Storage Conditions: 32°F/0°C

Season: Available year-round but generally the peak season is considered to be September through April

Nutritional Information

Serving Size:	3-1/2 oz/100 g
Water:	92.55 g
Calories:	22
Protein:	3.17 g
Fat:	0.49 g
Saturated Fat:	0.05 g
Fiber:	2.7 g
Sodium:	33 mg
Iron:	2.14 mg
Potassium:	196 mg
Vitamin C:	20.2 mg

BROCCOLINI, ASPIRATION

This tasty green vegetable has the best attributes of broccoli, without the sulfurous or cabbage-like flavor or waste. The stems are smaller, thin, and tender with no trim, and the small florets are tender and delicious. Sweeter than broccoli, broccolini has been likened in flavor to asparagus. The labor-intensive nature of harvesting this vegetable due to its more delicate texture and the need to trim and bunch can drive up the price, but the almost-100% yield greatly improves its value. Proper purchasing and receiving is essential to take advantage of this value, so be sure the product is very fresh with no yellowing florets and tender with no thick or woody stems.

Broccolini is very similar to Chinese broccoli (see following), so it naturally lends itself to various Asian influences in cooking. However, its versatility and likeability make it a good choice for many different cuisines and cooking styles and is excellent served both hot and cold.

FIGURE **3.7** Broccolini/Aspiration

As noted, Chinese broccoli (Gai Lan) is related to, and very similar to the aforementioned broccolini. The stems are not quite as tender, nor the florets as sweet, but this vegetable is very similar in flavor. The appearance is also similar in the size of the stalks, but can be leafier with fewer florets. This vegetable is rarely seen other than in Chinese food preparations, but its versatility makes it a good candidate for many cuisines.

Pack Size: 6 or 10 lb /2.72 to 4.54 kg cases
Shelf Life: 4 days
Storage Conditions: 32°F/0°C
Season: Available year-round but the peak season is generally considered to be September through April

CAULIFLOWER

This crunchy, relatively unappreciated vegetable has a pale floret or curd and is more ball-shaped than its broccoli relative. The outer leaves and thick core or stalk are not edible. The florets, depending on the variety and place of origin, can be pale yellow, orange, green, or purple, but in the United States are almost always purchased as pure white. The white curds come from "blanching" or surrounding each head in its outer leaves to prevent exposure to the sun. This adds to the cost of the product but yields a milder flavor and brighter appearance more acceptable to the American palate. Look for fresh, large, heavy heads without a pronounced sulfur odor.

FIGURE **3.8** Cauliflower

Cauliflower can be cooked in several ways, but overcooking quickly ruins its texture and appeal. Heads can be cored and cooked whole or cut into florets off the stem and handled that way. Consider steaming rather than boiling to avoid a soggy or water-logged product. Cauliflower may also be cooked in the microwave, baked in a sauce, pickled, served raw, or deep-fried. Seasoning can range from very simple and light to accentuate the mild, nutty flavor to fiery chili sauces used in Indian cooking. Watch for bruising, discoloration, or black spots on the heads.

Pack Size: 9 to 20 head flats (approximately 25 lb/11.34 kg per flat)
Shelf Life: 4 days
Storage Conditions: 32°F/0°C
Season: Available year-round but the peak season is generally from December to March

Nutritional Information

Serving Size:	3-1/2 oz/100 g
Water:	91.91 g
Calories:	25
Protein:	1.98 g
Fat:	0.1 g
Saturated Fat:	0.015 g
Fiber:	2.5 g
Sodium:	30 mg
Iron:	0.44 mg
Potassium:	303 mg
Vitamin C:	46.4 mg

BROCCOFLOWER, ROMANESCO BROCCOLI

Broccoflower is a green cauliflower, but gets its name from the fact that it looks like a cross between cauliflower and broccoli. It is usually marketed, however, as brocco-flower rather than simply "green cauliflower." The Romanesco version of this vegeta-ble is identical in color but has unusual and beautiful conical-shaped bulbs instead of a simply rounded head of green curds. This product is not common in the market and is grown almost exclusively in California.

Although similar in flavor and texture to cauliflower, the broccoflower can be milder and a little sweeter. The heads are also smaller and less dense in mass, but like cau-liflower are very dependent on freshness for a good sweet flavor. The scarcer Romanesco has a more refined and delicate flavor to complement its appearance. Smell is your best indicator of freshness and quality with both vegetables; avoid a harsh cabbage-like aroma. The best time to source these items is in late summer to late fall. Cooking methods and applications, not surprisingly, are essen-tially the same as with cauliflower.

FIGURE **3.9** Broccoflower

Pack Size: 12 large or 18 small heads per flat (approximately 25 lb/11.34 kg per flat)
Shelf Life: 4 to 5 days
Storage Conditions: 32°F/0°C
Season: The peak season is late summer to late fall

BRUSSELS SPROUTS

Brussels sprouts look like tiny green cabbages, to which they are related. These "little cabbages," typically 1 to 1-1/2 inches/2.5 to 3.75 centimeters in diameter, are the edible buds that grow on a long, tough, inedible stalk. They are rarely seen on the stalks but are generally sold in pint buckets or in bulk bags. These are best when purchased in the fall and through early spring; they are scarce and not at their best in summer. Purplish red-budded Brussels sprouts exist and are beautiful; however they are very rarely found in the market.

FIGURE **3.10** Brussels Sprouts

Look for fresh, preferably domestic sprouts and the smaller, the better. They can be steamed whole, halved, or quartered, boiled gently in any form, roasted, or shredded, stir-fried, and seasoned liberally. In any case, trim the stems, remove the older outer leaves, and soak in salted water for about ten minutes prior to cooking to make sure no bugs are hiding inside. Proper cooking time is essential in all preparations as either overcooking or undercooking Brussels sprouts will yield a poor-tasting product. Brussels sprouts held in storage too long develop a strong odor and flavor that detracts from their enjoyment; check for odor when received and utilize quickly.

Pack Size: 25 lb/11.34 kg bushel or twelve 1-pint flats
Shelf Life: 6 to 7 days
Storage Conditions: 32°F/0°C
Season: The peak season is fall and winter

Nutritional Information

Serving Size:	3 1/2 oz/100 g
Water:	86 g
Calories:	43
Protein:	3.38 g
Fat:	0.3 g
Saturated Fat:	0.062 g
Fiber:	3.8 g
Sodium:	25 mg
Iron:	1.4 mg
Potassium:	389 mg
Vitamin C:	85 mg

BOK CHOY

Also referred to as Chinese cabbage, there are several forms of this delicious Asian cooking cabbage. The standard bok choy has a long, heavy white stalk with a flat green leaf at the upper half of the stalk. This type has two sizes: the large, mature bok choy or the smaller Dwarf, or baby, bok choy. There is also a Shanghai bok choy that has a smaller, pale green stalk and a smaller, more tender leaf. Both types are similar in flavor and texture. They are very juicy and utilize similar methods of preparation. Both the stalk and leaves are edible and are often simply cut up and cooked together.

Better results are achieved by separating the stalk from the leaf and beginning the cooking process with the thicker and longer cooking stalk. The more tender leaves can then be added in the final stages of cooking for a better tasting and more appealing product. Before purchasing, and cooking, be sure the stalks are firm and satiny with no dehydration and the leaves are unblemished and vibrant. Bok choy is delicious stir-fried and well seasoned; this vegetable is also wonderful braised with shreds of meat or slowly simmered in a soup.

Because Napa cabbage and bok choy are both often referred to as Chinese cabbage, be certain you know what you are purchasing as they are decidedly different in texture, appearance, and flavor. There are several other varieties of bok choy grown but they are less widely known in this country. However, one variety, the small, tender baby Tatsoi, which has a lush, dark green leaf and tiny stem, is growing in popularity, especially as a salad green. It is prized for its subtle mustard flavor.

FIGURE **3.11** Baby Bok Choy

Pack Size: Sold by the bushel (approximately 30 lb/13.6 kg)
Shelf Life: 3 to 4 days
Storage Conditions: 32°F/0°C
Season: Available year-round

KOHLRABI, GERMAN TURNIP

An ancient vegetable with origins in many places of the world, kohlrabi has shown little growth in popularity in the United States despite its crunchy, sweet flesh. As one might expect from its multiple places of origin, this vegetable has diverse uses in both cooking methods and cuisines. Because it is very crisp and juicy, it is excellent and refreshing served cold and raw in crudités or as a salad component. It can also be cooked by first peeling, then blanching the bulbs in water, then sautéing and simply seasoning or saucing. The greens can be stripped of their tough stems and cooked in butter, oil, or pork fat and served separately or in combination with the bulbs. Kohlrabi is excellent stuffed, or puréed and used as a sauce for roasted meats. More elaborate recipes exist, depending on the origin of the dish.

Most readily available in the summer, kohlrabi is hit or miss in the market at other times of the year. Bulbs can be any size but they should not be dried or cracked from age. The leaves, as with other greens, should be

FIGURE **3.12** Kohlrabi/German Turnip

fresh and vibrant with no slime or yellowing. The edible fleshy parts of the bulb will always be golden yellow despite the fact the outer peel can be found in various colors.

Pack Size: Sold by the bushel (approximately 24 heads or 25 lb/11.34 kg)
Shelf Life: 1 week
Storage Conditions: 32°F/0°C
Season: The peak season is spring through fall

Nutritional Information

Serving Size:	3-1/2 oz/100 g
Water:	91 g
Calories:	27
Protein:	1.7 g
Fat:	0.1 g
Saturated Fat:	0.013 g
Fiber:	3.6 g
Sodium:	20 mg
Iron:	0.4 mg
Potassium:	350 mg
Vitamin C:	62 mg

MUSHROOMS

Mushrooms are the fruiting body of a fungus; they draw their nutrients from their host and have very high water content. Edible mushrooms comprise only a few percent of the many types of mushrooms and fungi that exist. Most mushrooms, by volume, used for culinary purposes are now cultivated by man. There are also a wonderful and delicious variety of wild mushrooms prized by chefs in foodservice. Wild mushrooms should never be foraged by or purchased from anyone other than a certified expert. There are far more wild mushrooms that are poisonous than those that are edible and some look strikingly similar. The need to be cautious and knowledgeable in the use of wild mushrooms cannot be stressed enough. Wild mushrooms should always be thoroughly cooked to prevent allergic reactions as well.

The types of mushrooms available in foodservice come in a broad array of appearances, flavors, shapes, sizes, consistencies, and textures. They offer the chef a great selection when choosing which one will best complement the other foods being prepared. However, due to this wide range, one mushroom will not necessarily substitute well for another in a particular dish. This is especially true with the wild varieties, but common sense needs to play a role in the selection of the commercially grown types as well. A good rule of thumb is to know that the bigger and darker a mushroom gets, the more pronounced and assertive the flavor will be. Mushrooms are prized in any culture that has a temperate climate that fosters their growth. European, Asian, and American cuisines all take strong advantage of the culinary possibilities provided by mushrooms, and each prizes certain varieties over others.

Commercially grown mushrooms are available year-round. Wild mushrooms are only available fresh in the appropriate season and then only when the weather is cooperative. Also, many of these wild varieties are usually available in dried form.

COMMERCIALLY GROWN MUSHROOMS

The following mushrooms are all commercially grown and were evolved from numerous wild varieties, some of which are still found wild. These are grown in large commercial farms and smaller boutique operations. Those grown in factory-like settings, most commonly in Pennsylvania and second most commonly in California, will be more homogenous in flavor and appearance. Those grown in smaller operations will have a more pronounced flavor and reflect the growing style and medium used by that grower; these will also come with a higher price point. Your style of foodservice and the availability in your specific area will determine which is the best choice for your operation.

CREMINI MUSHROOMS

The cremini mushroom is of the same family of mushroom as the common white mushroom, *Agaricus bisporus,* but is a different strain. It will have the same conformation but differs in that it is a darker brown color and is firmer with a more pronounced flavor. This was the common strain of mushroom in American markets until the white was so heavily marketed in the early 1900s. The price for this mushroom is often comparable to the common white variety, but may run somewhat higher. This mushroom cooks and is used in virtually the same ways as the white mushroom; just expect a more assertive flavor and more bite in the texture.

Look for dry, firm mushrooms with closed gill veils when receiving. Avoid those that are shriveled, damp, or show signs of mold or a sour smell. Clean with a quick rinse followed by drying on towels or use a brush if less moisture is required in cooking.

Pack Size: 5 or 10 pound/2.27 to 4.54 kg boxes
Shelf Life: 2 to 3 days
Storage Conditions: 34°F/1°C
Season: Available year-round

FIGURE **4.1** Cremini Mushroom

Nutritional Information

Serving Size:	3-1/2 oz/100 g
Water:	92.3 g
Calories:	27
Protein:	2.5 g
Fat:	0.1 g
Saturated Fat:	0.014 g
Fiber:	0.6 g
Sodium:	6 mg
Iron:	0.4 mg
Potassium:	448 mg
Vitamin C:	0.0 g

ENOKI MUSHROOM

Enoki mushrooms are very small, thin, white mushrooms. They are only a couple inches in length with a very small cap and are Japanese in origin. They grow and are packaged in small clusters. These are as delicate in flavor as they are in appearance and so are best enjoyed raw as a salad garnish, or simmered quickly in a light broth. Their flavor is more fruit-like than the woodsy nature of most other mushrooms. Enokis are exceedingly popular in Asian cultures, making this little mushroom one of the most heavily cultivated species in the world. Look for pure white and firm, thin mushrooms that are not wet or beginning to brown. Trim the enokis from the root base just prior to use. Gently rinse or brush away any foreign matter carefully so as not to damage this slender mushroom.

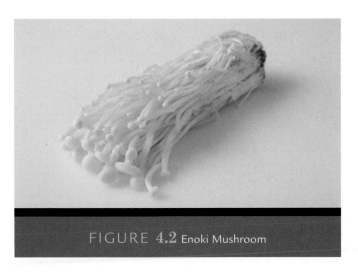

FIGURE 4.2 Enoki Mushroom

Pack Size: 4 or 8 oz/113 or 227 g package
Shelf Life: 2 to 3 days
Storage Conditions: 34°F/1°C
Season: Year-round

Nutritional Information

Serving Size:	3-1/2 oz/100 g
Water:	88.54 g
Calories:	44
Protein:	2.56 g
Fat:	0.32 g
Fiber:	2.7 g
Sodium:	3 mg
Iron:	1.09 mg
Potassium:	368 mg
Vitamin C:	0.0 mg

MAITAKE MUSHROOM, HEN OF THE WOODS

The Maitake (or Hen of the Woods) is another mushroom of Japanese origin that is both cultivated and found in the wild but should not be confused with Chicken of the Woods. This mushroom grows in thick clusters and appears almost solid in nature. The fluffy tops come in a range of gray to brown hues and the underside is characterized by having pores rather than the more typical gills. This mushroom's texture is best appreciated by gentle slow cooking with plenty of moisture or fat although the flavor can also be accentuated by either sautéing or roasting quickly with herbs. Farm-raised maitakes require very little cleaning; lightly brushing them will remove any foreign materials.

Look for clusters with a thick, dense base of stems, light feathery tops, and a clean sweet scent. Anything smelling sour or showing mold or decay at the tips should be avoided. Wild maitakes are best in the fall.

Pack Size: 3 lb/1.36 kg box for commercially grown and by the pound for wild
Shelf Life: 3 to 4 days
Storage Conditions: 34°F/1°C
Season: Year-round

FIGURE **4.3** Maitake Mushroom

Nutritional Information

Serving Size:	3-1/2 oz/100 g
Water:	90.53 g
Calories:	37
Protein:	1.94 g
Fat:	0.19 g
Saturated Fat:	0.03 g
Fiber:	2.7 g
Sodium:	1 mg
Iron:	0.3 mg
Potassium:	204 mg

OYSTER MUSHROOM

The oyster mushroom is a wild and cultivated mushroom that comes in a variety of shapes and hues. The most common oyster mushroom is grayish-white to beige or light brown in color with multiple stems coming from one root ball or cluster. The caps can be small and domed or have a spoon-like shape with gills growing up the bottom side from the stem to the curved rim. The oyster-like flavor of this mushroom becomes milder as it cooks and so it is best paired with a limited number of flavors that are also soft in texture such as cream or veal, poultry, and seafood. Sadly, this mushroom can be, and quite often is, grown quickly in poor environments which only further erodes its delicate flavor. Know your source, when possible, to be assured that this popular mushroom is grown properly in order to yield the desired quality.

FIGURE **4.4** Oyster Mushroom

There are several less-commonly-found varieties of the oyster mushroom. Pink oysters are rare and incredibly perishable. Yellow oysters are also quite perishable but not so much as pink oysters, and have a delightful texture when roasted or simmered in a broth. The blue oyster mushroom is a better culinary bet; these are small with bluish caps and white stems that grow in clusters. They have a pleasingly delicate flavor and firmer texture that provide a better shelf life. These mushrooms are similar to the black oysters, which have a dark gray cap with pale gray gills. These are also fragile but have an excellent pronounced flavor. Having the best flavor, however, comes with a higher cost. White oysters are also known as white trumpets as they have a more cornet-like shape, which differentiates them from common oyster varieties. Cook gently so that they may hold their shape when cooked for the pretty eye appeal they will offer.

Trumpet Royale mushrooms are not marketed as oyster mushrooms, but are in the same family. This mushroom has a denser flesh and solid stem that makes it hold up well under any cooking method, be it braising, grilling, sautéing, or roasting. The cap and the stem of this mushroom cook up and eat exactly the same; there is little trim loss.

Choose only firm and well-textured mushrooms that have a delicate clean aroma. Avoid anything wet, shriveled, or exhibiting signs of mold. Clean these mushrooms by removing the tough stem and quickly rinsing out the gills to prevent any more water absorption than is necessary and immediately dry on paper towels.

Pack Size: 5 or 10 lb/2.27 or 4.54 kg boxes
Shelf Life: 2 to 3 days
Storage Conditions: 34°F/1°C
Season: Year-round

Nutritional Information

Serving Size:	3-1/2 oz/100 g
Water:	88.8 g
Calories:	43
Protein:	3.31 g
Fat:	0.41 g
Saturated Fat:	0.02 g
Fiber:	2.3 g
Sodium:	18 mg
Iron:	1.33 mg
Potassium:	420 mg

PORTOBELLO, PORTABELLA MUSHROOM

This mushroom is a fully grown or overgrown cremini. The caps range from 3-1/2 to 6 inches in diameter and the gills will be fully open. Due to its size and age, this mushroom will have a more firm and meaty texture and a full, assertive, woody flavor. This mushroom can be sliced and sautéed or the entire cap grilled or broiled. The slices can also be breaded and fried. The grilled cap will have a big meaty flavor and texture and is often served whole like a burger or sliced like a steak sandwich. Clean these by brushing any dirt or debris from the gills and wiping the cap tops with a damp towel. Remove the woody stem with a small sharp knife to prevent cracking or breaking up the cap. The stem is woody, but can be used as a flavoring for soups or stocks.

Avoid portobellos with wet or slimy gills and cracked or molding edges on the caps. Look for large, heavy, firm mushrooms with an even color and pleasant smell.

Pack Size: 5 lb/2.27 kg box
Shelf Life: 2 to 3 days
Storage Conditions: 34°F/1°C
Season: Year-round

Nutritional Information

Serving Size:	3-1/2 oz/100 g
Water:	91.2 g
Calories:	26
Protein:	2.5 g
Fat:	0.2 g
Saturated Fat:	0.026 g
Fiber:	1.5 g
Sodium:	6 mg
Iron:	0.6 mg
Potassium:	484 mg

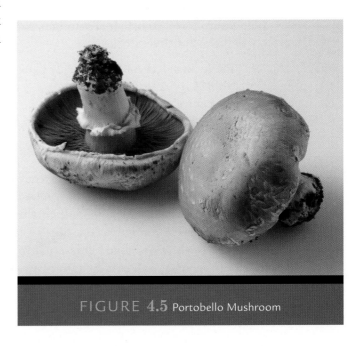

FIGURE 4.5 Portobello Mushroom

SHIITAKE MUSHROOMS

The shiitake mushroom is originally from Asia and its influence on the cuisine and culture in that part of the world is ancient and immense. For many years this mushroom was rarely seen in the West unless it was dried, and then only in Chinese and Japanese markets. That has changed dramatically in the last forty years and this wonderful mushroom is commonly raised commercially in many areas of the world, including North America. Shiitake mushrooms are raised on dead tree trunks, primarily oak trees, and the name comes from the Japanese for tree mushroom.

FIGURE 4.6 Shiitake Mushroom

The rapid expansion of this mushroom's popularity in a short time has created inferior product that is being rushed to market. Properly grown shiitakes will be very firm in texture with an equally assertive flavor. Avoid limp or soggy product as it will be short on taste. The better the shiitake, the more complex the flavor will be and the denser the meat.

Larger caps are often the most popular, but the tender and sweet small or button cap shiitakes will be superior in flavor and texture. Not surprisingly, given its heritage, the shiitake's full rich flavor pairs well with Asian aromatics such as garlic, ginger, green onions, soy, and herbal flavors. It also pairs well with the starches from that region such as rice and noodles. This mushroom may be sliced and stir-fried, braised, or broiled. Care must be taken to add enough fat or moisture to prevent dehydration during cooking.

Choose product with dark brown, thick, domed caps with the edges still curled under, which indicate fresh and moist mushrooms. The gills should have a thin veil or the remnants of the gill veil still attached. The caps should be dry and tender, not tough or open and limp. Fresh shiitakes will have a smoky, woody aroma. Clean shiitakes with a damp towel or brush. The stems should be removed before cooking, but can be used to flavor broth or stock.

> **Pack Size:** 3 or 5 lb/1.36 or 2.27 kg box
> **Shelf Life:** 2 to 3 days
> **Storage Conditions:** 34°F/1°C
> **Season:** Year-round

WHITE MUSHROOMS

Depending on their size and how they are marketed, white mushrooms are also called Fancies, Buttons, Stuffers, or jumbo and field mushrooms. The white mushroom constitutes the vast majority of all mushrooms sold. This mushroom has the typical gilled cap on a stem configuration. Ideally, the gill veils should be closed and the cap should be pure white or beige. This mushroom will be the mildest in flavor, lends itself to many recipes, and can be eaten raw. The flavor will become more pronounced if the gills open with age. However, as this mushroom is generally chosen for its mild flavor, it is preferable to purchase the mushrooms with the gills closed. The texture and flavor is better when these mushrooms are smaller. The large caps are best suited for stuffing, as the flavor of the filling will help offset the more watered-down flavor of the larger cap. This mushroom's mild woodsy flavor allows it to complement many other flavors and cooking methods: broiling, baking, sautéing, stuffing, or simmering in soups. Grinding for duxelles or slicing them raw for salads or as a pizza topping are all common methods of preparation.

FIGURE **4.7** White Mushrooms

Look for white or pale brown mushrooms that are dry with tightly closed caps and a mild aroma. Avoid those that are soft, spotty, shriveled, show signs of mold, have open wet gills, or have a strong or sour scent. Clean these mushrooms by rinsing in cool water and drying on towels or use a brush to whisk away dirt without allowing the mushroom to absorb more liquid. The longer mushrooms are in storage, the more water is lost through evaporation, so they are best used in a day or two.

Pack Size: 3 or 10 lb/1.36 or 4.54 kg boxes
Shelf Life: 1 to 2 days
Storage Conditions: 34°F/1°C
Season: Available year-round

Nutritional Information

Serving Size:	3-1/2 oz/100 g
Water:	92.43 g
Calories:	22
Protein:	3.09 g
Fat:	0.34 g
Saturated Fat:	0.043 g
Fiber:	1.0 g
Sodium:	5 mg
Iron:	0.5 mg
Potassium:	318 mg
Vitamin C:	2.1 mg

WILD MUSHROOMS

Wild mushrooms are a product of nature and its variables. These mushrooms will be more varied in size and flavor, more expensive, and availability will be driven by the season and the weather. Still, these are delicious items and highly prized. Look for them when available, but only from licensed and qualified foragers.

CEPE, PORCINI, KING BOLETE

The cepe or porcini is also known as the king of mushrooms because it is so prized for its thick, rich, meaty texture and full woodsy flavor. These mushrooms have thick, chewy stems and caps with a texture that can be delicate, or creamy, while still substantial, which allows them to complement many dishes and work with a variety of cooking methods. The stem is pale in color and rounded while the cap is dark brown with a thin tube on the underside. This mushroom can grow to be quite large.

The mushroom's texture is suited to hot, quick cooking, but be sure to use a fair amount of cooking fat to ensure they stay moist. Many chefs believe the flavor and texture is maximized by a slower sauté or braise in a liquid that will absorb the essence of this wonderful mushroom. The porcini is one of the very few wild mushrooms that can also be safely served raw. Whatever cooking method is used, this mushroom is at its best when paired with ingredients that won't mask its exceptional flavor.

Look for exceedingly firm porcinis with a pale, dry underside on the gills. They should have a mild scent similar to sourdough bread. Thick stems should be halved to check for insect infestation. After checking the stems, wipe the mushroom with a clean, damp cloth.

Pack Size: By the pound or kilogram
Shelf Life: 2 to 3 days
Storage Conditions: 34°F/1°C
Season: Available year-round frozen. Available fresh year-round except for August.

CHANTERELLES

Chanterelles are very popular wild mushrooms that are available most readily in the market in both summer and winter. This mushroom is cornet- or trumpet-shaped and most commonly range in color from golden yellow to a bronze/orange hue. There are also varieties of chanterelle that can be red, gray, and nearly white or beige in color. The underside of the cup-shaped cap will have wrinkles, not the typical gills, and the cap should be tender and sweet/spicy smelling with a nutty to almost stone fruit-like aroma. The texture when cooked is tender yet still crisp.

FIGURE **4.8** Cepes/Porcini Mushrooms

FIGURE **4.9** Chanterelles

The white chanterelle looks less inviting when raw and can be quite fragile, and therefore commands a lower price, but they cook up very similarly and can provide a better value. The red variety is beautiful in appearance and has a rich fruity scent, but this chanterelle is rarely available in North America. There is also a black trumpet mushroom that is related to the chanterelle; this funnel-shaped species is smaller and hollow through the stem, rarer, and quite delicious.

The flavor of the chanterelle is often compared to apricots and complements almost any flavor, which helps account for its great popularity. The texture lends itself to roasting, sautéing, or braising. It can also be sliced and simmered into soup to season and scent the broth. Choose smaller, very dry chanterelles with a rich sweet aroma; the stronger the scent, the fuller the flavor. Avoid wet or shriveled mushrooms, those showing signs of mold and decay at the tips, or those with a sour odor. Chanterelles should be rinsed carefully to extract all dirt from the wrinkles under the caps. Dry thoroughly on towels prior to use.

Pack Size: By the pound or kilogram
Shelf Life: 2 to 3 days
Storage Conditions: 34°F/1°C
Season: Available year-round with the exception of May and June

CHICKEN OF THE WOODS

The Chicken of the Woods mushroom is yellow to gold in color and grows in clusters. The caps are fan-shaped and overlap one another. They have distinctive pores in lieu of gills on the underside of the caps. This mushroom, in time, can grow to be quite large, but from a culinary standpoint, the younger, smaller mushrooms are much more desirable. The older specimens can become unpalatably bitter, fibrous, difficult to digest, and have been known to cause allergic reactions.

The sought-after smaller mushrooms are tender and savory and actually do have a chicken-like flavor. The texture should be soft and pliable and the mushroom should be cool to the touch. The protruding caps or fingers should be moist and give to pressure without crumbling. When cooking, the smaller fans can be cut off of the base and quickly sautéed. The heavier, dense base, however, responds better to the slow-cooked braising technique. The two can be combined in the stock and garnish a vegetarian risotto.

As discussed, avoid large or dry mushrooms when receiving. Look for small, tender, moist product with no signs of mold or decay.

Pack Size: By the pound
Shelf Life: 3 to 4 days
Storage Conditions: 34°F/1°C
Season: May through October

LOBSTER MUSHROOM

The lobster mushroom is a fungus, not a true mushroom, as it is a parasitic growth that grows over and feeds off of a host mushroom. The lobster mushroom gets its name from its orange/red outer coloring and the mild to peppery seafood flavor it exhibits. This is a large, very dense fungus with a meaty texture; the base is quite thick and the cap folds back. The dense texture makes this mushroom well suited for roasting, braising, deep-frying, and sautéing. It is excellent on its own, or paired with seafood or eggs.

Avoid any product that is slimy, with soft or wet spots, or exhibiting mold or decay at the edges. If the cap is cracked, there could be dirt deeply imbedded in the meat that

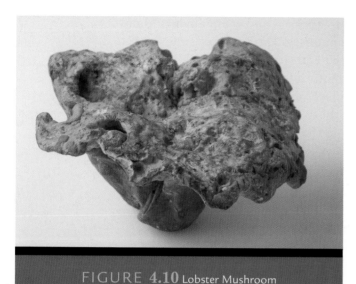

FIGURE **4.10** Lobster Mushroom

FIGURE **4.11** Morel Mushrooms

will be difficult to clean away and cause more rapid spoilage. They should be firm, dry, and exhibit a mild scent. These can be cleaned by simply wiping away any foreign material with a damp cloth.

> **Pack Size:** By the pound
> **Shelf Life:** 3 to 4 days
> **Storage Conditions:** 34°F/1°C
> **Season:** July, August, and September

MORELS

The morel is one of the true harbingers and gifts of springtime. These mushrooms have distinctive honeycomb-like pointed caps and are hollow. The mushroom can be a light tawny brown to almost black-brown in color. All of these are good but the fairer colored morels should be superior in flavor and are said to be easier to digest. The hollow bodies are excellent places for dirt and soil to get stuck and for bugs to hide. Be sure to split the morel in half or slice it into rings when cleaning.

The earthy, woodsy to smoky flavor and soft yet crunchy texture is what makes these mushrooms so prized by chefs when in season. These flavors combine well with other springtime treats such as asparagus, peas, and fiddlehead ferns. Morels are wonderful in risotto, pasta, or a frittata, or any preparation that showcases their delicious spring flavor. Cultivated morels were found to be lacking in flavor.

Morels should be dry and tender with a sweet forest aroma. Anything sour or pungent should be avoided. As previously noted, check morels thoroughly for any signs of critters that have taken up residence inside. If relatively clean, the outer shell can be brushed clean, if not, rinse thoroughly and dry on towels prior to use. There is a mushroom called a "false morel" that is somewhat similar in appearance and poisonous so be sure to purchase morels from an approved source.

> **Pack Size:** By the pound or kilogram
> **Shelf Life:** 2 to 3 days
> **Storage Conditions:** 34°F/1°C
> **Season:** Available fresh from March to August

TRUFFLES

The truffle is the gem of the forest. No fungi are more prized for their flavor and aroma, and their cost can be as expensive as jewels. The best black truffles come from the Perigord region of France, but are also found in Umbria, Italy, in the winter. The best white truffles come out of the Piedmont, Alba region of Italy. There are varieties of black French truffles that are lesser in quality and price in the summer and fall that can still be delicious. There are also truffles with white centers from Oregon that can be good, but they are not equal to the French truffles. Chinese truffles are a cheaper strain usually available frozen, and although they are not comparable to the fresh truffles, they may be preferred to the canned variety. Weather is a huge factor in determining the quality of the truffle. In some years an area prized for their product may yield mediocre results and lesser regions can yield excellent ones. You will need to learn from and rely on your sense of smell and taste to be certain of the quality you seek.

The truffle grows underground on the roots of various trees, most commonly the oak. They can only be found by scent and this task is usually performed by trained dogs. Pigs were originally utilized for this, but they badly wanted the truffles for themselves once they were located. Trained dogs are much more manageable in this endeavor. The painstaking way in which these jewels are found and handled afterward is much of what drives the prices so high.

The truffle does not have an appearance that matches its wonderful flavor and aroma. They are gnarly and bumpy little balls that look anything but appetizing. The black truffle is the most pungent in aroma and flavor and must be peeled prior to use; save the truffle peelings to flavor soups and broths. White truffles are actually pale brown and do not need to be peeled. Their aroma and flavor is less assertive and has a garlicky edge to it, which make this truffle ideal for shaving over warm pasta and risotto. Truffles should be used quickly once purchased as the aroma and flavor fade in a few days; many chefs store their truffles in rice or with eggs so that the aroma will permeate those foods until the truffle is used, but viewpoints on this vary.

Black winter truffles from Perigord come into the market in November, but usually improve for a few weeks or more before achieving their best quality. These should be very firm and dry with a very pungent odor; no smell indicates that the truffle has no flavor. It will have very dark gray flesh ideally with widely spaced white veins. These truffles pair well with poultry, duck liver and fat, eggs, pasta, and seafood.

White truffles from Alba should also be dry and firm with no wet or soft spots and must have that exciting aroma. These can be incredibly expensive so you must be sure of the quality when receiving. The truffle will have a tan interior with white veins; a pink blush is very desirable. This truffle is best when sourced in mid or late fall when the weather and ground are cool.

Summer truffles have a pale putty-colored interior and their flavor and aroma are much less noticeable than the winter truffles. They also have a considerably lower price point. These fungi, while lacking the desired pungency of a winter truffle, are not without their advantages. They have a full woodsy mushroom flavor and a desirable crisp texture. These improve with size and the mushrooms should not appear to be dehydrated. These truffles are found in France and in the Pacific Northwest of the United States.

FIGURE **4.12** Black Truffle

In the fall, the Burgundy truffle from Italy is often available. This truffle has a black rind with a brown interior flecked with white veins. This outwardly appears very similar to the winter black truffle but has a milder aroma and flavor. This truffle should be used raw because its milder flavor will dissipate quickly when cooked. Shaving over pasta or risotto or soft-cooked eggs are ideal uses for these fungi. The burgundy truffle does not have as hefty a price tag as winter truffles and certainly nothing like the Italian whites, but it can still be an excellent choice and its popularity is growing.

Relatively new to the market is the Chinese black truffle. Outwardly, the fungi can look similar to the true black truffle and it can be purchased for far less money, but beware as the quality is not at all similar. When cut open, the flesh will be dark gray to nearly black with little or no white vein. The aroma is chemical in nature and they will have little to no true truffle flavor. Buyers must be well aware of what they are purchasing and receiving. Once shaved and tossed with truffle oil these may have their place when mixed into some dishes, but given the difference in value, be sure you are getting what you pay for. There is no real comparison in the quality.

Pack Size: By the ounce
Shelf Life: 3 or 4 days in the refrigerator in a paper bag. Several months in the freezer.
Storage Conditions: 34°F/1°C
Season: Available year round except for April

STALKS

This chapter addresses a small group of vegetables that in some way defy classification in other categories or culinary applications. Stalks refer to those vegetables that grow heavy fibrous and edible stalks. Celery is the most obvious and commonly used member of this group. Rhubarb is similar in appearance to celery stalks that have been removed from the bunch, except for its bright red color, but its applications are completely different. Botanically, celery and fennel are related to carrots, but from the culinary perspective they share little in common. Fennel has long stalks and frilly fronds on a heavy bulb, and is nearly 100 percent edible.

Also included in this grouping is asparagus. Artichokes are in the thistle family and have no culinary equal or relative other than the cardoon, which has not yet gained popularity in the United States. Fiddlehead ferns are a wild and foraged item that come into season for only a few weeks each spring and, again, have no similarity to other culinary vegetables, although some compare the flavor to asparagus. However, you could say they all do have a common thread; all of these are wonderful, delicious, nutritious, and unique.

FIGURE **5.1** Celery

CELERY

Few vegetables are as well known and commonly used as celery. Several varieties exist, though in foodservice Pascal is the most prevalent variety. Other varieties include Giant Red, which is hardy and strongly flavored; Victoria, which is used raw and is very crunchy; and Loretta, which is white and very juicy. These would more commonly be found in regional farm markets. Celery and the heavy bulbous root, celeriac, are of the same family, but we will address celery root in Chapter 7 on page 95.

Celery's unique salty, sweet, and earthy flavor is indispensable in so many cuisines and dishes. Raw and cold, it adds flavor and crunch to salads and crudités and there is the ever-popular celery sticks and peanut butter. Celery grows and is sold in bunches of long stringy stalks with bright green leaves at the ends. Celery is packed by counts of bunches per case—24, 30, 36, or 48. Look for celery that is very firm and heavy for its size. Avoid browning, bruised, or dehydrating product. Be sure the leaves are vibrant with no yellow and check the ends to ensure there is no mold or rot inside the stalks. Celery is very healthy for you and is an excellent source of vitamins C and K and dietary fiber. Raw celery is also considered to have "negative calories" because eating celery burns more calories than it contains.

Pack Size: 24, 30, 36, or 48 each per carton
Shelf Life: 3 to 5 days
Storage Conditions: 35°F/2°C
Season: Available year-round

Nutritional Information

Serving Size:	3-1/2 oz/100 g
Water:	95.43 g
Calories:	16
Protein:	0.69 g
Fat:	0.17 g
Saturated Fat:	0.042 g
Fiber:	1.6 g
Sodium:	80 mg
Iron:	0.20 mg
Potassium:	260 mg
Vitamin C:	3.1 mg

RHUBARB

Rhubarb is one of those confusing plants that begs the question, "Is it a vegetable or a fruit?" That's because it is a vegetable related to buckwheat that normally is cooked and eaten like a fruit. Rhubarb is extremely tart and generally requires substantial sweetening to be palatable. It is also a "love it or hate it" vegetable with many devoted fans and others that simply abhor its bitterness.

Rhubarb has long thick stalks that range in color from bright red to speckled pink to green. All are suitable for cooking, but in this country the red is most prized for its visual appeal. The green stalks are somewhat more pungent in flavor. Be sure to only utilize the stalks because the leaves and roots contain so much oxalic acid that they are poisonous and potentially deadly. Look for stalks that are firm, hefty, and lie flat, without dehydration or cracking. This plant was originally cultivated for medicinal purposes but culinary rhubarb became popular in Europe and Asia back in the 1700s.

Still widely considered a spring vegetable, hothouse rhubarb is now available much of the year. Winter to spring is generally the best season for the hothouse; field grown is found from early spring into summer. Chefs' opinions will vary, as they usually do, on whether hothouse is better than field grown, winter beats summer, or which color stalk is preferred. Sampling the various options will reveal what will work best for your taste and application.

Rhubarb can be stewed slowly in a sauce, either highly seasoned or left fairly tart, and works well with richly flavored foods such as game and the more oily fish. It is most famous as a pie filling either solo or with strawberries, but is also used in strudels, muffins, biscuits, and tarts. Raw, the stalks can be sliced and marinated with honey, herbs, and aromatics as a dessert compote or even to accompany fish. Rhubarb can even be juiced and combined with currant juice and sweetened with honey for a very refreshing beverage. Look for straight firm and crisp stalks. Avoid any bruising, dark spots or mold, especially on the ends.

Pack Size: 10 lb/4.54 kg box
Shelf Life: 3 to 5 days
Storage Conditions: 35°F/2°C
Season: Available year-round but best from April to September

Nutritional Information

Serving Size:	3-1/2 oz/100 g
Water:	93.61 g
Calories:	21
Protein:	0.9 g
Fat:	0.2 g
Saturated Fat:	0.053 g
Fiber:	1.8 g
Sodium:	4 mg
Iron:	0.22 mg
Potassium:	288 mg
Vitamin C:	8 mg

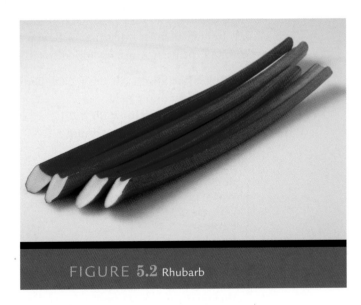

FIGURE **5.2** Rhubarb

FENNEL

FIGURE **5.3** Fennel

Formerly thought of as somewhat exotic, this lush wonderful vegetable is now commonly found on both supermarket shelves and restaurant menus. It is no surprise as this versatile and beautiful vegetable is delicious, fragrant with the mild aroma and flavor of anise, and almost completely edible. The variety almost exclusively used in foodservice is known as Florence fennel, and also Finocchio from its Italian heritage. This variety has a large, heavy white bulb with long, dark green stalks and lush frilly fronds, and each part of the fennel has its own culinary purpose. Because of its bright anise aroma and flavor this product is often, and incorrectly, referred to as sweet anise or anise fennel. Anise is a separate plant whose only culinary purpose is its seeds which are used as a spice. The anise flavor of fennel has a more subdued and sublime flavor than true anise, which is more biting and pungent.

The bulb, which is actually the base of the stalks, is typically considered the best part for eating and, sadly, the tops are often lopped off and discarded. These fronds and stalks have enormous value in appearance, aroma, and flavor and should be utilized. The base can be slivered, lightly dressed, and eaten raw, blanched and marinated, or braised, roasted, baked, or puréed into soup. The fronds can be used as a garnish for other vegetable dishes. The key to maximizing your value is in the full utilization of the product.

Look for firm, heavy bunches with bright pearly bases; avoid browning, molding, or dehydrating product. The tops should be vibrant, brightly colored and crisp with full, lush fronds. The bulbs can be full and round or flattened in shape without loss of quality, but with some variance in flavor and texture. Fennel can be minced as a garnish, infused into vinegars, or added to salads.

Pack Size: 18, 24, 30, or 36 each per case
Shelf Life: 3 to 5 days
Storage Conditions: 35°F/2°C
Season: Available year-round

Nutritional Information

Serving Size:	3-1/2 oz/100 g
Water:	90.21 g
Calories:	31
Protein:	1.24 g
Fat:	0.2 g
Fiber:	3.1 g
Sodium:	52 mg
Iron:	0.73 mg
Potassium:	414 mg
Vitamin C:	12 mg

ASPARAGUS

This highly prized vegetable is a harbinger of spring, being one of the earliest vegetables to appear each year. In today's marketplace it is available almost year-round. Truly tender and delicious asparagus, however, is found only in the spring and is preferably grown locally or most certainly grown domestically. Generally, the season will begin in California in February and last in Michigan and the Northeast into July, depending on the weather. Asparagus comes in three varieties, green, white, and purple. Green is far and away the most popular variety in this country. White asparagus is preferred primarily in Europe but has grown more popular recently in the United States. The purple variety is scarce, although it has appeared recently in some farm stands. Asparagus is highly nutritious and is a member of the lily family, which also includes leeks and garlic.

Asparagus is sold by size, or thickness of the stalk. These range from Colossal to Jumbo, to Standard, and then Small or Pencil. Generally, standard and jumbo are the most commonly preferred sizes in foodservice because they can be adapted to various cooking applications. Uniformity in the pack is crucial for the cook to ensure uniform cooking times; otherwise each case needs to be hand-sorted. Look for asparagus with tight closed tips and nothing open or seeding. Avoid shriveling stalks or excessive woodiness at the base. Preferences vary as to whether asparagus should be peeled but generally that is only needed with the thicker stalks. Asparagus is delicious steamed or simmered and served with hollandaise, grilled, roasted, or marinated cold in salad. This is a delightful vegetable for a creamy delicate spring soup. For brunch, serve roasted asparagus on grilled country bread, topped with a lightly poached or sunny side up egg, freshly grated Parmesan cheese, and ground black pepper.

FIGURE 5.4 Left to right: Standard Green Asparagus, Purple Asparagus, White Asparagus, Jumbo Green Asparagus

White asparagus is much more costly than green due to the labor-intensive method of farming. They must be kept covered in dirt as they grow to prevent photosynthesis from occurring and bringing out the green color. The flavor is milder, a bit sweeter, and nuttier than the green variety. Some consider it more akin to salsify or hearts of palm, and the thicker European variety is usually preferred to the domestic, although improvements have been made.

Purple asparagus is, when you can find it, a wonderful choice. The texture is less fibrous and it has a rich, sweet flavor. They can be eaten raw and should never be overcooked or the purple color will fade to green. The Jumbo spears are the sweetest and most succulent. Although each variety has subtle variances in flavor and texture, they can all be used interchangeably in most recipes.

Pack Size: 11 or 30 lb/4.99 to 13.6 kg box
Shelf Life: 3 to 5 days
Storage Conditions: 38°F/3°C
Season: Available year-round but best from late February to June

Nutritional Information

Serving Size:	3-1/2 oz/100 g
Water:	93.22 g
Calories:	20
Protein:	2.2 g
Fat:	0.12 g
Saturated Fat:	0.04 g
Fiber:	2.1 g
Sodium:	2 mg
Iron:	2.14 mg
Potassium:	202 mg
Vitamin C:	5.6 mg

ARTICHOKE

There is an old line that says the first man to eat a raw oyster had to be hungry indeed because of its forbidding appearance. The same could be said of the artichoke, with its pointy-tipped and leathery petals; it is a daunting and unwelcoming culinary adventure to the uninitiated. This vegetable is actually the flower bud of the artichoke plant and has been popular in the Mediterranean for centuries. In the United States, virtually every artichoke, mostly of the Globe variety, is grown in California. Artichokes are packed by size count per case. The so-called baby choke is actually full-grown; it simply comes from the base of the plant where it receives less sunlight for growth. The artichoke is very closely related to the relatively unappreciated cardoon.

When eating, only the fleshy lower part of each scale (or petal or bract) is consumed as well as the meaty, lower part of the base called the heart. The stem is too often discarded but it can be peeled and cooked like the heart. The thistly fibrous material in the center of the artichoke is called the choke and is inedible; this is not an issue with the small or baby artichokes because it has not yet developed in the baby chokes and need not be extracted. Place cut artichokes in acidulated water to prevent browning before cooking.

When receiving this product, make sure they are hefty and have a dense feel that squeaks when squeezed. The size of the stalk should correspond with the size of the choke and not be dehydrated, shrunken, or limp. A blue-gray tinge on the outer petals is known as "frost kissed" and is not a negative factor if all other quality signs are good. However, even given year-round availability, the best product is found in the spring, with a smaller crop in the fall.

Artichokes are generally steamed in the United States, and can be cooked in a microwave. In Italy and Spain, they are often fried or cooked in olive oil. These are often served with lemon butter, aïoli, or mayonnaise as a dipping sauce. They can also be stuffed and baked and small ones can be quartered and cooked in sauces or stews.

FIGURE **5.5** Left to right: Baby Artichoke and Standard Artichoke

Pack Size: Cases usually weigh about 20 lb/ 9.07 kg and will be designated by the number of artichokes in each case—12, 18, 24, 30, 36, or 48. Also baby artichokes will be designated as SL (small loose) or LL (large loose).
Shelf Life: 4 to 7 days
Storage Conditions: 35°F/2°C
Season: Available year-round but best from March to May

CARDOONS

Think of celery with fuzz and nasty sharp edges and you have the cardoon. Also a thistle and closely related to the artichoke, the stalk of this vegetable is consumed rather than the flower bud. When cooked, the flavor is very similar to the artichoke, with a touch of celery. Nevertheless, in this country this delicious vegetable has limited popularity and is usually only found around the Christmas holidays, despite year-round availability from California.

Look for pale slender stalks that are firm and not hollow or wilting. Browning along the edges is not a quality issue. Cardoons, if young and small, can be served raw. They are delightful battered, fried, and served with a dipping sauce; otherwise, they can be stewed into a purée or soup, creamed, steamed, and baked or stewed with a variety of meats and vegetables. They are hard to find outside California for much of the year, but they are well worth the pursuit.

Pack Size: 50 lb/22.68 kg box
Shelf Life: 3 to 5 days
Storage Conditions: 35°F/2°C
Season: Fall into winter

FIDDLEHEAD FERNS

Fiddlehead ferns are a delicacy only found for a few weeks at most in early spring. Their name comes from the coiled head of the Ostrich fern that looks like the upper neck of a stringed instrument. Other varieties of ferns have this same type scroll and are edible, but most authorities recommend the Ostrich as it is safest and most commonly found. This fern grows primarily in Maine and in the Northeast and blooms briefly as spring comes into these areas. Fiddleheads must be cooked—do not eat raw. They are usually boiled or steamed and served with butter or chilled and served with onions and vinaigrette. Asian flavors also work well with the flavor of this vegetable. Choose firm, tight, springy, dark green ferns; avoid wilting or limp ones, and use them quickly to assure freshness. If the ferns have a fuzzy brown coating, it needs to be rubbed off prior to cooking.

Pack Size: by the pound
Shelf Life: 2 to 3 days
Storage Conditions: 35°F/2°C
Season: Spring

Nutritional Information

Serving Size:	3-1/2 oz/100 g
Water:	88.68 g
Calories:	34
Protein:	4.55 g
Fat:	0.40 g
Sodium:	1 mg
Iron:	1.31 mg
Potassium:	370 mg
Vitamin C:	26.6 mg

FIGURE **5.6** Fiddlehead Ferns

ONION AND GARLIC

Both onions and garlic are members of the *Allium* genus and are related to the lily. These items are prevalent in nearly all of the major cuisines in the world and provide much of the oomph in the flavor of myriad dishes. Onions and garlic have been utilized for many centuries and in ancient times were believed to give powers of healing, strength, and longevity.

When raw or lightly sautéed, both onions and garlic provide a sharpness that some find objectionable, but diners in many cultures adore. In contrast, when they are roasted or slowly cooked until soft and golden, both onions and garlic can supply a succulent sweetness that enriches the flavor of the recipe in which they are included. Consider how many dishes utilize one or several members of the *Allium* group and then imagine how lacking they would be without that additional flavor.

Onions are divided into two main categories, dry and green. Dry onions are the round or flat bulbs of the *Allium cepa* species. These are the mature bulb of the onion with tight layers of flesh and a dry, papery skin that can be white, red, or yellow. Dry onions are also divided into two categories: sweet (spring/summer) and storage (fall/winter). The storage onion is not as sweet, with a stronger, more pungent aroma and flavor. As their name indicates, these onions will keep for long periods of time when properly stored. Commonly available varieties of the storage onion include yellow or Spanish, white, boiling, shallots, and red onions.

Sweet onions are generally flatter in shape and have a much milder and sweeter flavor. Sweet onions typically have a much shorter shelf life and need to be utilized quickly. Vidalia, Maui, Texas 1015s, and Walla Walla are all well-known sweet onions; they are named for their growing region but are available nationally depending on the season. The varieties of sweet onions being developed and coming into the market continue to expand.

Onions are a good source of antioxidants, making them a healthy nutrition source. The quercetin and sulfur compound inherent in onions are widely believed to make the body's cell walls stronger and better able to defend against diseases such as cancer. They are also believed to be a factor in improving HDL cholesterol levels in the blood.

DRY ONIONS

When purchasing any of the dry onions, look for a dry, tight, shiny skin and onions that feel heavy for their size. Avoid onions with strong or off odors, sprouting onions, or any with dark or soft spots. Onions are always available but are best in the late summer and fall. The sulfur compound in onions permeates the air in a fine mist as the onions are cut. When this mist contacts the moisture of the eyes, it forms a mild sulfuric acid that causes the irritation and tearing so familiar to anyone who has handled onions. The age, size, and type of onion can all affect how strong the irritation will be. Many theories exist as to how to best lessen the caustic effects; these include trying to peel and cut onions under water, washing the onion after peeling and before slicing, leaving the root end intact while dicing or slicing, and refrigerating the onions before dicing. Because these compounds are released when cutting through the onion's cell structure, the best tool in lessening how forcefully they are released into the air is a very sharp knife.

STORAGE ONIONS

FIGURE **6.1** Top row, left to right: Spanish, Vidalia, Red; Middle row: Yellow, Shallots, Cippoline; Bottom row: Garlic, Red Pearl Onions, White Pearl Onions

CIPPOLINE ONIONS

The cippoline onion is not widely utilized outside of Mediterranean cuisine, but is a very delicious onion, especially roasted and glazed in a sweet and sour preparation. This onion is small, about 1 to 2 inches/2.5 to 5 centimeters in diameter, and flat with a sweet and pungent flavor. These onions can be used in many of the same ways as the small white boiling onions, but use them where their pungent sweet flavor can be appreciated, as they can be expensive. Their high sugar content does make them more perishable, so only purchase them as needed. Only accept very firm onions with a tight shiny skin. Avoid any that are soft, discolored, showing signs of mold, or have a strong odor.

Besides roasting, cippolines can be served boiled and sautéed, as agrodolce, in stews, with roasts, or in a warm salad with tomatoes over white beans.

Pack Size: 5 lb/2.27 kg bag
Shelf Life: 3 to 4 days
Storage Conditions: 40° to 60°F/4° to 16°C
Season: Available year-round

RED ONIONS

Red onions are a cultivar of the *Allium cepa* species named for their red to dark purple skin and the red tinge to an otherwise white flesh. The onions range in size from fairly small to medium, although some can be as large as a good-sized yellow onion or anywhere from 2 to 4 inches/5 to 10 centimeters in diameter. Beyond color, red onions also differ from yellow onions in flavor, as they are milder and sweeter by comparison.

Red onions are best when utilized raw in salads, sandwiches, and salsa cruda; really anywhere that a milder flavor and enhanced visual appeal would have a better impact. They are excellent when sliced thin and then pickled by soaking in vinegar. Red onions can also be cooked into marmalade to accompany pâtés, terrines, and other charcuterie items.

As with yellow onions, look for a shiny tight skin and onions that heavy feel for their size. Avoid those that are beginning to sprout, shrivel, stink, or that have dark spots.

Pack Size: 25 lb/11.34 kg bag
Shelf Life: 3 to 4 days
Storage Conditions: 40° to 60°F/4° to 16°C
Season: Available year-round

FIGURE **6.3** Red Onions

SHALLOTS

Shallots are in the same genus as the other bulb onions. However, like garlic, the shallot grows in a bunch or head composed of

FIGURE **6.4** Red Pearl Onions

FIGURE 6.5 Shallots

individual cloves. The cloves are sold separated from the head, usually in 10 lb/4.54 kg mesh bags. There are two types of shallot utilized in the foodservice. The Jersey shallot is a larger, round type and more pungent in flavor and the most prevalent in U.S. markets. The French shallot, considered to be the true shallot, is long and slender and has a softer, more nuanced, and prized flavor. Look for this type at farmers markets and from specialty vendors as it is not frequently found in commercial American markets. This flavor is reminiscent of both garlic and onion, well-pronounced, and cherished by chefs in many cultures.

Shallots are usually a pale reddish-purple with hues of green but can also be gold to copper in color. Like onions, they should be firm and plump with shiny skins and a clean aroma. Avoid shriveled, sprouting, and discolored or moldy shallots or those with a pungent aroma.

Shallots are used as an aromatic in a variety of recipes and can also be roasted and used whole as an accompaniment. Sautéed shallots are great with a burger or steak or tossed with a variety of vegetables.

Pack Size: 10 lb/4.54 kg bag
Shelf Life: 3 to 4 days
Storage Conditions: 40° to 60°F/4° to 16°C
Season: Available year-round

Nutritional Information

Serving Size:	3-1/2 oz/100 g
Water:	79.8 g
Calories:	72
Protein:	2.5 g
Fat:	0.1 g
Saturated Fat:	0.017 g
Sodium:	12 mg
Iron:	1.2 mg
Potassium:	334 mg
Vitamin C:	8 mg

WHITE ONIONS

The white onion has a higher water content than the yellow onion and a cleaner, tangier flavor. The high water content will lead them to spoil more quickly so care in purchasing is required. That tangy flavor has made this onion popular in many Latin American dishes as the flavors of the cuisine pairs well with white onions. The snowy white color also gives a nice appearance to dishes when they are diced and sprinkled over the top.

These onions come in all sizes but the smaller ones are more frequently seen in foodservice. The smaller varieties of this onion, about 1 inch/2.5 centimeters in diameter, are well utilized on kebabs or roasted with meats as well as creamed and

FIGURE **6.6** White Onions

FIGURE **6.7** White Pearl Onions

served as a side dish. The golf ball-sized white onions are often referred to as boiling onions, but a boiling onion can also be yellow or red in color. Much smaller varieties are known as pearl onions and are available in all three colors; these are called pearls as they are only about a half-inch in diameter. The white onion has a very small share of the American market, but its light tangy flavor is worth trying.

Due to their perishability, avoid white onions showing any sign of discoloration or mold. Look for firm, white, clean-smelling onions with no sprouting or soft spots. The thin, papery skin should be white with no discoloration or evidence of mold.

> **Pack Size:** Pearl onions—10 oz/284 g bags; Larger onions—5, 10, 25, or 50 lb/2.27, 4.54, 11.34, or 22.7 kg bags
> **Shelf Life:** 3 to 4 days
> **Storage Conditions:** 40° to 60°F/4° to 16°C
> **Season:** Available year-round

YELLOW/SPANISH ONIONS

The yellow onion is by far the most commonly grown and utilized onion of the species, accounting for over 90 percent of the total onion production. In foodservice, the larger yellow onions, those about 4 inches/10 centimeters in diameter and larger, are sorted and given the Spanish onion designation, and the smaller of this species are simply referred to as yellow onions, and are roughly 2 to 3-1/2 inches/5 to 8.75 centimeters in diameter. Although they are the same species, the larger onions are often somewhat milder and sweeter in flavor.

These are storage onions and can be held for quite a bit of time, but it is best to only purchase what is needed for a few days as you cannot determine how long these onions have already been in storage or how well they have been maintained. Store the onions with ample air circulation, and be sure there are no strong or strange aromas or sprouting. If holding them in storage for more than a few days, re-check your stock on occasion to cull out any onions that may start to turn. Yellow onions should feel very heavy for their size.

This onion is one of the true workhorses of the food pantry and is believed to be utilized more than any other vegetable. It is one of the three items in mirepoix, the foundation of most classical cooking. In Latin cuisine it is a major component of sofrito,

FIGURE **6.8** Gold Pearl Onions

FIGURE **6.9** Yellow Onions

which is a flavoring staple in many types of dishes. Creole cooking also relies on the "trinity" made up of onions, celery, and bell peppers as the foundation for most dishes. Most Indian curries utilize slowly cooked yellow onions as their bases. Deep-fried onion rings and "flowers" are staple side dishes on many American menus and are an excellent accompaniment to a broiled steak. Long slow cooking to completely soften and caramelize the onions will give them a full, rich, strong flavor, which can then be used as the basis for French Onion Soup. Raw yellow onions will vary in their sharpness but all will be fairly assertive.

Pack Size: 50 lb/22.7 kg bag
Shelf Life: 3 to 4 days
Storage Conditions: 40° to 60°F/4° to 16°C
Season: Available year-round

Nutritional Information

Water:	89.11 g
Calories:	40
Protein:	1.1 g
Fat:	0.1 g
Saturated Fat:	0.042 g
Fiber:	1.7 g
Sodium:	4 mg
Iron:	0.21 mg
Potassium:	146 mg
Vitamin C:	7.4 mg

SWEET ONIONS

The sweet onion is similar in appearance to a storage onion but has a paler papery husk or skin, and is generally more oblate in shape rather than round. Sweet onions also usually have a small tag on the skin identifying the type. They have a higher sugar and water content than yellow onions and a lower ratio of irritating sulfur compounds, and therefore a milder aroma. They take longer to grow, which helps develop the sugar content, but due to the higher moisture content they also have a much shorter shelf life. However, improved climate control methods have lengthened that storage time considerably.

Vidalia onions from Georgia are among the first to arrive in the market in spring and were once gone by early summer; now, with the improved storage, they may last into fall. New seasons for more sweet varieties open during the year moving west all the way to Hawaii and then south to Chile in the new year. These new crops and improved storage now mean that sweet onions can be purchased and enjoyed year-round.

Sweet onions are best enjoyed lightly cooked or raw to get their full sweetness and lighter flavor profile. They are excellent on sandwiches and burgers, tossed in salads, or diced and added to salsas and relishes. Onions retain higher levels of their healthy antioxidants if consumed raw, making these sweet varieties a better and sweeter way to promote good health.

The following are some common varieties in the market:

MAUI

This Hawaiian onion is a hybrid developed from a Texas variety of sweet onion. This onion arrives in markets in the spring and is available into December.

OSO SWEETS

This Chilean onion is relatively new on the market but the first to arrive each year in January. The climate along the Andes in Chile is perfect for growing this onion, and it has the highest sugar content of all the sweet onions. The Oso Sweet will last in the market into the month of March.

SPRING SWEETS OR TEXAS SWEET 1015S

The Spring Sweet is the first domestic sweet onion into market each year followed by the Sweet 1015s. The number is indicative of the onion's planting date in Texas. This onion is available in the market from March into June.

SWEET IMPERIAL

The Sweet Imperial is grown in California, globe-shaped rather than oblate, and will be a minimum of 2-1/2 inches/6.25 centimeters in diameter. This onion has approximately the same season as the Vidalia.

VIDALIA

The Vidalia onion, from the Vidalia area in Georgia, was the first sweet onion to be marketed and receive wide acclaim on a national level. This familiar sweet onion comes to market in early April until June. If properly stored in a controlled atmosphere (marked CA), they will last into the fall.

FIGURE **6.10** Vidalia Onion

WALLA WALLA

The seed from this onion came from Italy to Walla Walla County in Oregon during the 1800s and rapidly found a great appreciation there, which has now spread nationally. This delicious sweet onion comes into market around June and will last into the late summer or fall.

Pack Size: 40 lb/18.14 kg box or by the pound
Shelf Life: 3 to 4 days
Storage Conditions: 40° to 60°F/4° to 16°C
Season: See individual onion listings for seasonal information

GREEN ONIONS

A green onion is simply an onion that has been pulled from the ground when the shoots are still vibrant and green and before the bulb has begun to fully develop. Green onions are separated into three categories, but each is very similar and interchangeable with the other. A scallion is considered to be youngest of the three classes because they should only have a short white tip with no bulb growth at all. A green onion has started to mature further and the bulb is just beginning to become more pronounced.

The spring onion has developed a small bulb, approximately 1 inch/2.5 centimeters in diameter. Scallions are available year-round from commercial produce vendors; green and spring onions are generally only found from spring into summer.

The entirety of the onion is edible except the root. Be sure to thoroughly clean under running water and remove any withered outer layers and tough green parts. Green onions are most commonly eaten raw but are excellent sautéed or grilled. Grilled spring onions make an outstanding accompaniment to grilled poultry and steaks. The green shoots of these onions have a delightful, mild, grassy flavor that is a terrific addition to the salsas and relishes that are used as delicious garnishes for many dishes. Scallions are also stir-fried with pork and chicken in spicy Asian preparations.

Because the green shoots are what are most often prized with green onions, be sure to only accept those with vibrant, brightly colored greens. Avoid those that are slimy, shriveled, or wilted and very dark or coarse, indicating dehydration. The tips or bulbs should be clean and white with no browning, slime, or mold. Green onions are sold in bunches by the count per case.

FIGURE **6.11** Green Onions

Pack Size: 48 count boxes
Shelf Life: 2 to 3 days
Storage Conditions: 32°F/0°C
Season: Available year-round

Nutritional Information

Serving Size:	3-1/2 oz/100 g
Water:	89.83 g
Calories:	32
Protein:	1.83 g
Fat:	0.19 g
Saturated Fat:	0.032 g
Fiber:	2.6 g
Sodium:	16 mg
Iron:	1.48 mg
Potassium:	276 mg
Vitamin C:	18.8 mg

LEEKS

The leek is a member of the *Allium porrum* family and is related to onions and garlic, but it is not a large green onion, for which some mistake it. Instead of forming a bulb, the leek forms concentric rings of flesh that grow in long stalks. The root end is bleached white by piling dirt around the plant. This practice is labor intensive and can drive the price much higher. The white portion and the tender pale green portions of the leek are primarily what are utilized in cooking, so the ratio of white to green portions of the stalk is important to consider when purchasing. More of the pale green portion can be found in the center of the leek by stripping away the coarse outer green leaves instead of merely lopping off the leek where the green and white portions meet. This may be more time consuming but it will yield more of the valued tender leek.

Because of the nature of the plant, as it grows through the soil, dirt is forced and trapped into the crevices between the leek's rings. Therefore it is important to thoroughly clean each leek prior to use. Make a slit down the side of each leek and open the leek up so that all the dirt can be rinsed away under running water.

Leeks have a rich onion flavor without the pungency and are indispensable ingredients in some classic soups such as Vichyssoise,

FIGURE **6.12** Scallions

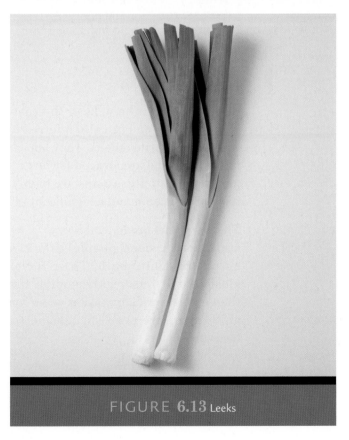

FIGURE **6.13** Leeks

Cock-A-Leekie, and Potage Parmentier. Leeks can also be fried until crisp, braised in stock, or shredded into a raw salad with vinaigrette. They are a highly prized vegetable in the food service industry.

Relatively new to the market is a leek grown using the hydroponic method. In this method, leeks are grown in a soil-like substance called perlite, which allows much more air to circulate around the roots and promotes drainage of water away from the roots. They tend to run much larger than leeks grown traditionally and have a much higher ratio of white to dark green. These leeks are more expensive by the case or bunch, but the higher yield and value should more than offset the price difference.

Pack Size: 11 or 20 lb/4.99 kg or 9.07 kg crates
Shelf Life: 3 to 4 days
Storage Conditions: 32°F/0°C
Season: Available year-round but best when purchased at your local farm stand from mid summer into fall

Nutritional Information

Serving Size:	3-1/2 oz/100 g
Water:	83 g
Calories:	61
Protein:	1.5 g
Fat:	0.3 g
Saturated Fat:	0.04 g
Fiber:	1.8 g
Sodium:	20 mg
Iron:	2.1 mg
Potassium:	180 mg
Vitamin C:	12 mg

RAMPS

Ramps grow in the wild in the eastern United States and are also referred to as wild leeks or wild onions. They appear in late winter and are foraged for just a few months; due to this ramps are highly esteemed and command a significant price.

The ramp has broad oval leaves, a white stalk with a deep purple streak, and an oblong white bulb. Their flavor is most like a musty garlic-onion flavor that inspires much passion when available; there are even springtime ramp festivals.

When purchasing ramps, only buy what you can consume in a day or two as they are highly perishable. For optimum storage and shelf life, wrap the bulbs in a

FIGURE **6.14** Ramps

damp paper towel and refrigerate them without washing. Avoid shriveled or sliming leaves when buying ramps.

Traditionally ramps are fried with bacon and potatoes but they are also great sautéed with chicken or used as the greens in a salad. Ramps can also be quickly grilled and served with a steak or stuffed into the cavity of a fish and grilled or baked.

> **Pack Size:** by the pound
> **Shelf Life:** 2 to 3 days
> **Storage Conditions:** 32°F/0°C
> **Season:** Available April and May

GARLIC

Garlic is the most pungent and flavorful member of the *Allium* family and is known as the "stinking rose." Garlic grows in a head of individual cloves covered by a white or purplish papery husk. There are two main classifications of garlic: soft neck, with a pliable papery center core, and hard neck, with a stiff wooden center core. The hard neck variety is easier to peel and is fragrant with a bright intense flavor. Within these two categories there are numerous specific types of garlic. Elephant garlic is not true garlic and grows in bigger heads with larger cloves. The flavor is much less pronounced and assertive. Green garlic is the tender young shoots that come up before the individual heads are formed. Green garlic is much less pungent with a mild herbal flavor and can used in salads, whipped into soft cheese, or used as a garnish for grilled meats.

Raw and lightly cooked garlic is very assertive and pungent with a strong aroma. When slowly roasted with a bit of olive oil and salt, the garlic becomes meltingly sweet and rich in flavor. Virtually every cuisine utilizes garlic to some extent and benefits from it, except possibly Northern Europe. The number of dishes utilizing garlic would be too numerous to list but the flavor complements every kind of meat, fish, beans, salads, tomato sauces, vegetable dishes, and so on.

Only purchase rock-hard heads of garlic with no sprouts. The green sprouts will be bitter. Avoid garlic that is soft, shriveled, has dark spots, or a sour edge to the nose.

> **Pack Size:** by the pound or 30 lb/13.6 kg box
> **Shelf Life:** 4 to 5 days
> **Storage Conditions:** 40° to 60°F/4° to 16°C
> **Season:** Available year-round

Nutritional Information

Serving Size:	3-1/2 oz/100 g
Water:	58.58 g
Calories:	149
Protein:	6.36 g
Fat:	0.5 g
Saturated Fat:	0.089 g
Fiber:	2.1 g
Sodium:	17 mg
Iron:	1.7 mg
Potassium:	401 mg
Vitamin C:	31.2 mg

FIGURE **6.15** Garlic

SCAPES

FIGURE **6.16** Scapes

Scapes, or garlic scapes, are the long, pliable, green tendrils that will grow out of the bulb of garlic once it forms. Leaving this tendril attached to the bulb will inhibit the full development of the garlic bulb and the scape will wither into something akin to the white papery husk around the bulb. These are not readily available but can be utilized if you grow garlic. Fully utilizing this added benefit of young garlic is therefore recommended when available in spring and early summer. Try them minced in scrambled eggs, pounded into pesto, or minced and sautéed with vegetables. Scapes should be bright green, tender, and not woody.

Pack Size: by the pound
Shelf Life: 2 to 3 days
Storage Conditions: 32°F/0°C
Season: Available May and June

ROOTS AND TUBERS

Both roots and tubers grow underground and are frequently referred to as root vegetables. A true root is the actual root portion of a plant that stores the plant's nutrition in a swollen bulb. Often, the tops or greens of these roots, such as beet greens, are also a valuable food source. A tuber is the stem of that plant that grows underground and swells as that plant's means to store nutrition. Both of these plants have significant importance in the world's food chain. In parts of the Pacific, West Africa, and South America, they are the basic food staple sustaining those cultures.

In ancient cultures, the ability to simply leave these foodstuffs in place until they were needed for consumption was part of the reason why these crops were essential. Nothing needed be harvested or stored until precisely the right moment and, if the native people ventured out to hunt or had to flee their enemies, their food staples would be where they had left them. Also, if they lived in a cool environment, many of these vegetables could be stored for long periods of time. Their good nutritional value, varied flavors, textures, tradition, and relatively low food costs are also why these play such an important role in foodservice today.

ROOTS

BEETS

The beet is actually closely related to chard and spinach and its nutritious greens can be utilized and enjoyed in the same manner as their leafy relatives. However, when most consumers think of beets, they think only about the root. Beets coming out of storage and those most commonly seen in supermarkets and from produce wholesalers, are generally just the bulb roots with the greens lopped off. Beets with tops are commonly only found in season at farm stands and green markets. However, baby beets with the tops attached are now commonly available to the foodservice industry year-round from good produce wholesalers and from farm markets when in season.

Beets are the sweetest vegetable available, with a very high sugar content. Up until recently, only red beets were commonly found for purchasing in foodservice but beets can now be found in shades of red, gold, white, and striped. These are all related to the sugar beet, which is raised strictly for the production of sugar, not for culinary applications.

Beets are a storage crop and therefore available year-round. However, summer through early fall is the best time to find them and is when you will get the added value and enjoyment of the beet tops or greens. Full-grown beets that measure up to 3 inches/ 7.5 centimeters in diameter are best for cooking. Very large beets can lose sweetness and develop a woody texture. Baby beets with globes smaller than 1-1/2 inches/3.81 centimeters in diameter are now very popular because they are tender and cook quickly. These will also come with young tender greens attached.

Look for beets that are heavy for their size, well colored, and of the appropriate size. Avoid discolored or scaling beets or those with a soft and sagging skin as these are indicators that the beets have been stored too long. Whenever possible, purchase beets with greens and utilize the tops quickly as they are highly perishable. Look for vibrantly colored bright red and green tops without any slime or discoloration.

Beets are often boiled, but roasting gives them a sweeter, more robust flavor. They can be pickled, creamed, grated raw on a salad, or puréed into soup such as the famous borscht, which can be served hot or cold.

The beet's color comes from compounds called betalain pigments. The type and combination of these pigments determines the color the beets will be. However, the flavor and cooking application of each of these beets is the same. Visual appeal, contrast, the end use, the desire to eliminate the red juice from bleeding out onto the plate or into other foods are the primary reasons for opting for one color beet over another. The options are as follows:

CHIOGGIA

Originally from Italy, this beet has a red skin and flesh with concentric pale white to yellow rings running through the flesh. It makes an attractive plate presentation when sliced to accentuate its multi-colored rings. This is available in both the full-sized or the mini-sized root bulb, but the baby chioggia is more prevalent in the market.

GOLD

The gold beet will appear with yellow to copper-colored flesh and the skin will be reddish in hue. This beet is milder in flavor than its red cousin, almost carrot-like, and has the advantage of not bleeding red into other items on the plate. These run a bit higher in price, but many chefs and consumers enjoy the variety that the added cost brings.

RED

The red beet is the most common beet in the market and the most well known. Commonly found varieties in the American market are Detroit Dark Red which is mild in flavor, the Lutz Greenleaf which stores well, and the Red Ace which is appreciated for its bright red color and the appearance of its red and green leaves.

WHITE

The white or Albino beet has a dull gray skin and pure white flesh. This is not a commonly found beet, and despite its total lack of color the Albino cooks and eats the same as a red beet. This variety is great for applications when no bleeding of color is desired.

Pack Size: Large-topped beets—25 lb/ 11.34 kg bag; Baby beets—24 bunches per carton (about 12 lb/5.4 kg per carton)

Shelf Life: up to 2 weeks for topped beets, 4 to 6 days for beets with tops

Storage Conditions: 32° to 34°F/0° to 1°C

Season: Available year-round but best in late summer and fall

FIGURE **7.1** Baby Chioggia Beets

FIGURE **7.2** Gold Beets

FIGURE **7.3** Red Beets

Nutritional Information

Serving Size:	3-1/2 oz/100 g
Water:	87.58 g
Calories:	43
Protein:	1.61 g
Fat:	0.17 g
Saturated Fat:	0.027 g
Fiber:	2.8 g
Sodium:	78 mg
Iron:	0.8 mg
Potassium:	325 mg
Vitamin C:	4.9 mg

CARROTS

The carrot is related to the herb parsley. The greens of the carrot are considered edible but are generally not used for culinary purposes. Most commonly, carrots are known as the long orange, tapering, or horn-shaped root vegetable so prized by Bugs Bunny. Carrots can also be white, reddish-purple, cylindrical, round, wedge-shaped, large, or baby-sized. Carrots are most commonly found with the tops removed and packaged in plastic bags. Buying carrots with the tops attached, however, can be an excellent determination of freshness. Carrots with tops are sold bunched and, if the clearly visible tops are fresh, you can be sure the carrots are fresh because the greens have a very short shelf life. Be sure to remove the tops once purchased however, as they will absorb the moisture from the carrot and ruin the product in short order.

The carrot's color comes from beta carotene, which the body converts to vitamin A, making this a very nutritious vegetable and an excellent source of fiber. Carrots, besides their nutritional benefits, are prized for their rich, sweet and savory flavors. They are frequently enjoyed raw, either as a snack or grated into salads. The peel is edible but not usually desired for aesthetic reasons; it is typically removed prior to consumption. Carrots can be cooked by boiling, steaming, pan-glazing, roasting, or stir-frying. Along with celery and onions, they comprise mirepoix, the vegetable medley used as the base for stocks, soups, sauces, and to flavor roasts. Due to its sweetness, the carrot is also frequently utilized in baked goods such as carrot cake.

Look for fresh, shiny-looking carrots with no whiting, molding, sprouting at the tips, or cracks. Carrots should be crunchy and firm; avoid soft or limp product. As noted, buy with the greens attached if available, but only when these are bright and fresh in appearance. Carrots are best from fall into winter, but they are available year-round. Carrots with tops are most prevalent in spring but can be found year-round, including baby carrots with tops.

FIGURE **7.4** Baby Carrots

BABY CARROTS

True baby carrots are fully developed carrots that are bred to stay small, tender, and sweet. These are generally found bunched with their tops, but can also be found in a cello pack. Caution must be used to assure you are purchasing true baby carrots and not larger, older carrots that have been peeled, cut into small carrot shapes and packaged as snack food; the quality difference is marked. Be sure they have a natural carrot shape and not a barrel or man-made appearance. Cooks like to use baby carrots because they make a beautiful presentation on the plate without requiring much labor or effort.

Pack Size: 24 bunches per carton (about 12 lb/5.4 kg per carton)
Shelf Life: 3 to 5 days under refrigeration
Storage Conditions: 32° to 34°F/0° to 1°C
Season: Available year-round but best in fall and early winter when purchased at your local farm stand

Nutritional Information

Serving Size:	3-1/2 oz/100 g
Water:	90.35 g
Calories:	35
Protein:	0.64 g
Fat:	0.13 g
Saturated Fat:	0.023 g
Fiber:	2.9 g
Sodium:	78 mg
Iron:	0.89 mg
Potassium:	237 mg
Vitamin C:	2.6 mg

FIGURE **7.5** Round Carrots

ROUND CARROTS

There are several varieties of carrots that grow in small spherical shapes and usually about 1 to 2 inches/2.5 to 5 cm in diameter. These are generally grown in dense soil more suitable for their shape and are characterized by a rich, sweet flavor. Their unique shape also makes for an interesting visual appeal when presenting on the plate. Common varieties on the market include Thumbelina and French Round. These carrots can be utilized in any recipe or cooking method in which their long tapered cousins are used. Look for well colored very firm and well shaped carrots.

Pack Size: 24 bunches per case
Shelf Life: 4 to 5 days
Storage Conditions: 32 to 34°F/0 to 1°C
Season: Available year round but best when purchased at your local farmstand

BUNCHED CARROTS

A bunched carrot will have essentially the same end use as the cello carrot. It should only be a fresher product, not one out of

FIGURE **7.6** Bunched Carrots

storage. Bunched carrots retain their greens and they are the quality check to inspect. Look for bright green color and avoid any yellowing or black coloration. This should be the freshest and sweetest tasting of the full-grown carrots but be advised the fresher quality will often cost a bit more money.

FIGURE **7.7** Cello Carrots

Pack Size: 20 lb/9.07 kg crate
Shelf Life: 3 to 6 days under refrigeration
Storage Conditions: 32° to 34°F/0° to 1°C
Season: Available year-round but best in the fall and early winter. Look for these at farmers markets and farm stands.

CELLO CARROTS

Cello carrots are full grown but will be thinner and crisper than the horse carrot. These should be the same quality as the bunched carrots, but without the tops. Cello carrots should be crisp and have a bright color with no discoloration. This carrot is the all-purpose vegetable in the kitchen and is used raw in salads, as a side vegetable, in soups and stews, roasted or glazed, and in cakes and other desserts.

Pack Size: Forty-eight 1 lb/454 g bags per case
Shelf Life: 5 to 10 days under refrigeration
Storage Conditions: 32° to 34°F/0° to 1°C
Season: Available year-round but best in fall to winter

HORSE CARROTS

Horse carrots are larger and older than carrots desired for eating out of hand or in any application where sweetness and tenderness is desired. These are usually somewhat woody and may be tougher than other carrots. Their size and age make them more appropriate for long, slow cooking and flavoring in stocks or soups, or feeding horses! Not surprisingly, these carrots should command a lower price point.

Pack Size: 50 lb/22.68 kg bag
Shelf Life: 5 to 10 days under refrigeration
Storage Conditions: 32° to 34°F/0° to 1°C
Season: Available year-round but best in fall to winter

FIGURE **7.8** Horse Carrots

Nutritional Information

Serving Size:	3-1/2 oz/100 g
Water:	88.29 g
Calories:	41
Protein:	0.93 g
Fat:	0.24 g
Saturated Fat:	0.037 g
Fiber:	2.8 g
Sodium:	69 mg
Iron:	0.3 mg
Potassium:	320 mg
Vitamin C:	5.9 mg

CELERIAC, CELERY ROOT, CELERY KNOB

This root is in the same family as stalk celery; however it is the underground bulb that is desired, not the tops. This vegetable has a rich but mild herbal celery flavor that is prized both as a raw vegetable finely julienned in salad or cooked in a variety of applications. The appearance of celery root is not very appetizing and there is some waste and effort required in utilizing it; all of these factors may keep the uninitiated from experimenting with celery root. Tasting is believing, however, and the flavor of celeriac is excellent enjoyed raw or cooked, alone or in combination with other vegetables.

Try this vegetable shredded or as a fine julienne tossed with lemon and rémoulade dressing. Dice, boil, and purée it as a side dish or in combination with mashed potatoes and roasted garlic. Celeriac can also be braised slowly with various cuts of meat, served in a gratin or made into a great soup. If purchased with the tops, remove the stalks before storing. These tops can be used as an aromatic in making stocks and broths, but they are assertive and not recommended for use like stalk celery would be. However, a fresh vibrant top on the root will be indicative of the product's freshness.

Look for good-sized heavy bulbs that have a somewhat even outer layer to make them easier to peel and thereby lessen the trim loss. A clean celery scent indicates freshness; nothing should smell dull or sour. Be sure the entire root is hard and firm; a spongy texture at the stalk end is to be avoided. Look for celeriac from fall well into spring, as it may be difficult to find quality specimen by summer.

Pack Size: 20 lb/9.07 kg carton
Shelf Life: Up to 1 week under refrigeration
Storage Conditions: 34° to 36°F/1° to 2°C
Season: Fall to early summer for the best quality

Nutritional Information

Serving Size:	3-1/2 oz/100 g
Water:	88 g
Calories:	42
Protein:	1.5 g
Saturated Fat:	0.079 g
Fiber:	1.8 g
Sodium:	100 mg
Iron:	0.7 mg
Potassium:	300 mg
Vitamin C:	8 mg

FIGURE **7.9** Celeriac

HORSERADISH

The horseradish, a large, unattractive root in the *Brassica* family known for its pungent flavor, can serve as an accent to enliven other foods. This vegetable is only used in cooking as a condiment. Horseradish is commonly found in the cuisines of central Europe, where it is believed to have originated, and is related to mustard and cabbage. This root can be 1 foot/30.5 centimeters long with a bulbous end and coarse, tan skin. The pungency of the flesh will not be noticeable until the root is cut or grated at which time it can bring tears to your eyes and clear the sinuses. When purchased commercially grated, it is generally mixed with vinegar to stabilize the flavor, which otherwise fades quickly. Mixing the grated root with vinegar also mutes the aroma's bite.

As with other root vegetables, only buy horseradish roots that are very firm with no soft spots or flabbiness. Very large roots may be woody and have less flavor. Fresh horseradish comes into the market in the spring and again in the fall, but is often available throughout the year. Horseradish works well with roast and boiled beef, on sandwiches, with asparagus, in Bloody Mary cocktails, and in the ubiquitous cocktail sauce served with raw seafood.

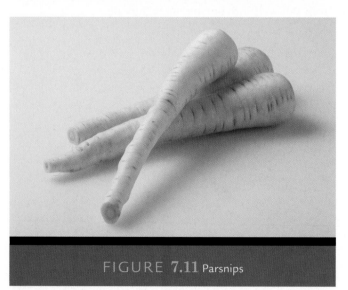

FIGURE **7.10** Horseradish

Pack Size: by the pound
Shelf Life: 1 to 2 weeks
Storage Conditions: 35°F/1.6°C
Season: Available year-round

Nutritional Information

Serving Size:	3-1/2 oz/100 g
Water:	88.2 g
Calories:	37
Protein:	2.1 g
Fat:	0.2 g
Saturated Fat:	0.033 g
Fiber:	3.2 g
Sodium:	42 mg
Iron:	0.36 mg
Potassium:	461 mg
Vitamin C:	141 mg

PARSNIPS

Parsnips look like a white carrot, with a similar size and tapering shape, and they are related to the orange root vegetable. Their flavor will also be sweet but more assertive than the carrot. Parsnips have a creamy white flesh and beige skin. They should be harvested after the first frost to ensure a higher level of sugar and sweetness; therefore autumn is the best season for this root

FIGURE **7.11** Parsnips

vegetable. Avoid limp and shriveled parsnips; they should be very firm and heavy. Parsnips are best medium sized as very thin ones will have poor yield and can be stringy. Large, fat parsnips will have a good yield if young, but check the center as some are apt to have a woody core when they age. Parsnips can be eaten raw but are most often fried, boiled, roasted, or puréed.

Pack Size: 20 lb/9.07 kg bag
Shelf Life: 3 to 5 days
Storage Conditions: 32°F/0°C
Season: Available year-round but much better in the fall

Nutritional Information

Serving Size:	3-1/2 oz/100 g
Water:	79.53 g
Calories:	75
Protein:	1.2 g
Fat:	0.3 g
Saturated Fat:	0.05 g
Fiber:	4.9 g
Sodium:	10 mg
Iron:	0.59 mg
Potassium:	375 mg
Vitamin C:	17 mg

FIGURE **7.12** Round Red Radish

RADISHES

Radishes are also members of the *Brassica* family and related to cabbage and mustard. Like other members of this family, these roots are characterized by their crisp flavor and pungent bite. There are a variety of radishes in the market, mostly identified by their color and shape. These range from the most common red globe to green, white icicle and the large, elongated, white daikon so prized in Asian cuisines. Typically served raw, radishes can also be served lightly boiled or sautéed.

Black radishes are the size of turnips with a dark brown skin; these are more pungent than most other types with a drier white flesh. Readily available from winter into spring, these radishes come packed in a 10 lb/4.54 kg box.

The French Breakfast radish is a beautiful addition on a plate with its slim, elongated shape that starts out bright red and fades to white at the tip. This radish has a more subdued and sweeter flavor than other more pungent radishes. These are best when available in the spring because they are smaller in size with a sweeter, milder flavor. They can, however, be sourced most of the year. As with other bunched radishes, French Breakfast radishes are sold in a case of 24 bunches. This radish is best eaten raw as an accompaniment to other items or utilized on crudités, or simply served with good butter and sea salt.

Other less-common radishes include the White Icicle radishes, which are thin and tapering with a white skin and flesh that is mild and sweet. There is a watermelon radish which, not surprisingly, is larger with a green outside and dark red center flesh. This radish is sweet in flavor and very crunchy. All of these specialty radishes are prized for their appearance as well as their flavor. Be sure when receiving that they do not appear dull or dehydrated and that they have bright even color.

The most-well-known and commonly found radish is the red globe which is small, round, and has red skin surrounding a white flesh. These are commonly found bunched with their tops attached or with their tops removed in cello bags. The topped form store in better condition, but it is more difficult to ascertain their freshness. These can be used in crudités, sliced in salads, or cooked as a side vegetable. The flavor of this radish is generally mildly pungent with a clean, crisp taste, but they can be quite assertive.

All radishes should be purchased with a clean, bright color. Avoid slimy tips, discolorations, and dried out or cracked radishes. Radishes are available year-round but are usually best in the spring and summer.

Pack Size: Bagged—Thirty 8 oz/227 g bags per case; Bunched—Twenty-four 12 oz/340 g bunches per case
Shelf Life: 3 to 4 days
Storage Conditions: 32°F/0°C
Season: Available year-round but best when purchased locally
Red Radish

Nutritional Information

Serving Size:	3-1/2 oz/100 g
Water:	95.27 g
Calories:	16
Protein:	0.68 g
Fat:	0.10 g
Saturated Fat:	0.032 g
Fiber:	1.6 g
Sodium:	39 mg
Iron:	0.34 mg
Potassium:	233 mg
Vitamin C:	14.8 mg

DAIKON

The Asian daikon has white skin and flesh and is less pungent to mild in flavor. These can be the size of a large cucumber or grow considerably larger and be shaped like a big white carrot. Although unusual, there are daikons that have a more bulbous or turnip-like shape and size with a pink hue in the flesh. Daikons can be used raw in grated form or sliced into chips and are also good stir-fried with other vegetables. Look for clean, white, firm daikons that are heavy for their size. Avoid those sallow in color and showing signs of dehydration or discoloration. Daikons are usually sold in a 40 lb/18.14 kg box. Daikon matures later and is best in the fall.

Pack Size: 40 lbs/18.14 kg box
Shelf Life: 4 to 5 days
Storage Conditions: 33°F/.5°C
Season: Available year-round

Nutritional Information

Serving Size:	3-1/2 oz/100 g
Water:	94.62 g
Calories:	18
Protein:	0.6 g
Fat:	0.1 g
Saturated Fat:	0.03 g
Fiber:	1.6 g
Sodium:	21 mg
Iron:	0.4 mg
Potassium:	227 mg
Vitamin C:	22 mg

RUTABAGA

The rutabaga is also known as a yellow turnip even though it is actually a different species than a true turnip. The rutabaga is similar to the turnip in flavor and texture but is usually a bit sweeter in flavor and yellow to orange in color. A rutabaga is a large, round, heavy root, generally over 3 inches/7.5 centimeters in diameter with a dark purple to brownish rind. Choose rutabagas with no blemishes, mold, or cracking that have a shiny rind and are very heavy for their size. Their shininess is often preserved with a waxy coating used to preserve the vegetable through winter and well into the spring. Rutabagas come on the market in the fall and are best used by early summer, but should be available year-round.

Rutabagas can be cooked much in the same way as other root vegetables. They can be diced and roasted with meat, or simmered in soups and stews. They can also be boiled and puréed either plain or whipped with cream, or combined with puréed carrots or potatoes.

Pack Size: 50 lb/22.68 kg box
Shelf Life: up to 3 months
Storage Conditions: 32°F/0°C
Season: Available year-round

FIGURE **7.16** Salsify

Nutritional Information

Serving Size:	3-1/2 oz/100 g
Water:	89.66 g
Calories:	36
Protein:	1.2 g
Fat:	0.2 g
Saturated Fat:	0.027 g
Fiber:	2.5 g
Sodium:	20 mg
Iron:	0.52 mg
Potassium:	337 mg
Vitamin C:	25 mg

SALSIFY, OYSTER PLANT

The salsify root is a long, tapering, cylindrical-shaped root with a tan to brown skin and off-white flesh, most closely resembling a gnarly parsnip with a straggly rootlet beard. These roots have a mild flavor and break down quickly when cooked, so either prepare them by simmering gently or quickly roasting them. When purchasing, look for heavy, solidly firm roots, and avoid anything limp or flabby in texture. Look for a medium-sized root because small ones will mostly be wasted once trimmed and peeled and larger ones can be overgrown and woody in texture. If the salsify roots are very coarse or gnarled, peeling can be facilitated by blanching first and slipping the skin off. If salsify is purchased with its tops attached, the young tender shoots can be consumed in a salad.

SCORZONERA

Scorzonera is also called black salsify and cooks and eats in much the same way as white salsify. This root has a darker brown, mottled skin with white flesh and a straighter, more evenly formed, cylindrical root shape. The skin can feel sticky and it is not normally sold with the tops. Scorzonera was once rarely seen in U.S. markets, being most heavily grown in Belgium, but it is now more commonly found. For culinary purposes, the white and black salsify are virtually interchangeable.

These plants are also referred to as oyster plants or black oyster plants as the flavor is thought to be somewhat similar to oysters, although some think that it is similar to artichokes. These roots can be used simply as a stand-alone side in a vinaigrette, are excellent creamed, and work well in a variety of soups. When preparing, place the peeled vegetable in acidulated water to prevent it from oxidizing. As with the white variety of salsify, look for firm, heavy roots with no indication of limpness or signs of mold.

Pack Size: 11 lb/4.99 kg carton
Shelf Life: Up to 1 week under refrigeration
Storage Conditions: 32° to 34°F/0° to 1°C
Season: Available year-round but best August through April

Nutritional Information

Serving Size:	3-1/2 oz/100 g
Water:	77 g
Calories:	82
Protein:	3.3 g
Fat:	0.2 g
Fiber:	3.3 g
Sodium:	20 mg
Iron:	0.7 mg
Potassium:	380 mg
Vitamin C:	8 mg

TURNIPS

The turnip, also known as white turnip or purple top turnip, is smaller than the rutabaga, generally 2 to 3 inches/5 to 7.5 centimeter in diameter with a white base and purplish ring at the stem end. When small and young, the turnip can be tender and quite sweet, but becomes harder, almost woody, and stronger in flavor as they grow larger. Therefore the younger, smaller turnips are recommended. The young turnips may also have their greens attached which can be utilized much the same as other braising greens. Turnips can be cooked in a variety of ways: simmered into soups and stews, mashed, roasted with meats, and even grated into a salad if young and sweet.

FIGURE **7.17** White Turnip/Purple Top Turnip

Look for a smooth skin with good color, no cracking or mold, and good heft for their size. The greens, if still attached, are a good gauge of freshness and should be vibrant and fully green. Turnips are available from late summer through the winter but are best in the fall. Young turnips with greens will be available in late spring and into the summer.

Pack Size: 25 lb/11.34 kg bag
Shelf Life: up to 1 week
Storage Conditions: 32°F/0°C
Season: Available year-round but best in late summer and early fall

Nutritional Information

Serving Size:	3-1/2 oz/100 g
Water:	91.87 g
Calories:	28
Protein:	0.9 g
Fat:	0.1 g
Saturated Fat:	0.011 g
Fiber:	1.8 g
Sodium:	67 mg
Iron:	0.3 mg
Potassium:	191 mg
Vitamin C:	21 mg

TUBERS

Beyond the many types and sizes of potatoes in the market are other highly desirable tubers. As with the potato, look for products with good weight for their size, no molding or shriveling of the skin, and no soft or discolored areas. Aromas should be consistent with the product and avoid any sour, strong, or other strange odors.

CASSAVA OR MANIOC

There are several species of this tuber but all are considered to be either the sweet or bitter variety. Those species consumed as a vegetable staple are all of the sweet variety. The bitter variety is most often found in the form of tapioca pearls. Cassava should always be consumed fully cooked as the raw form can be poisonous, especially the bitter variety.

This tuber is native to South and Central America and is now grown extensively in Africa as a staple crop. This tuber is also widely used in the Caribbean and Indonesia and is the world's third largest source of carbohydrates. The cassava has a dark brown skin, a hard white to very pale yellow flesh, and grows in a horn like shape up to a foot/30.5 centimeters in length.

FIGURE **7.18** Cassava

When fully cooked, the flesh will have a thick, creamy texture and a sweet, nut-like flavor. This flesh can be boiled or steamed and used instead of potatoes in soups or stews or puréed and used in dumplings, soups, and sauces. The steamed flesh can also be deep fried into chips or French fries. The flesh can be milled into flour and used instead of wheat flour in a thick, rich cake or for flat bread. The starch from the cassava is also formed into pearls which can be boiled, sweetened, and flavored with vanilla to make into tapioca pudding.

> **Pack Size:** 40 lb/18.14 kg crate
> **Shelf Life:** One week
> **Storage Conditions:** 33°F/.5°C
> **Season:** Available year-round

GINGER

Very few things can add more snap and zest to dishes than the rhizome ginger. This tuber originated in Southeast Asia and is a major flavor component of most every cuisine in that part of the world. It has now spread globally from there and is very popular in U.S. markets. Ginger combines very

FIGURE **7.19** Ginger

well with the other aromatics such as garlic, green onion, chiles, and lemongrass. Ginger is also prized in Southeast Asian cultures for its reputed health benefits. Ginger has a yellow to tan skin and ivory to gold flesh that has peppery sweet pungency and is quite juicy. When purchasing, avoid ginger that has a puckered or wrinkled complexion as it has lost much of its juice and succulence and will also be quite stringy in texture. Only purchase what can be utilized quickly. When this tuber is cooked or grated, ginger should emit a pronounced and delicious spicy aroma.

As noted, ginger is an integral part of many Asian dishes, as an aromatic in stir-fries, pickled as a condiment, as a base ingredient in curries, pickles, chutneys, and in the fiery spice mixture used in pickling cabbage

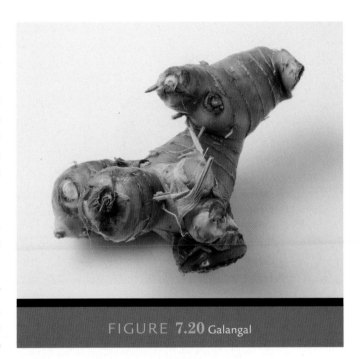

FIGURE **7.20** Galangal

for kimchee. In western cuisines, ginger takes a bigger role in sweet dishes such as puddings, jams, cakes, and cookies and beverages such as teas and soda. Ginger root comes in hands and should have a healthy sheen and sweet aroma. Avoid anything appearing to be shriveled, desiccated, or molding at the tips.

Other members of the ginger rhizome family include cardamom, galangal, and turmeric. Galangal root is prevalent in Thai cooking. Most of the roots look similar but the higher-quality, younger roots will have a moist pinkish-white hue and the flesh will be white and creamy. The flavor is quite spicy but also has piney, sour, and bitter tones that give it an interesting complexity. Fresh galangal is not yet commonly found in many American markets. Galangal is highly perishable; only buy what you will use within a day or two, or freeze the remainder in small chunks.

Pack Size: Ginger is available in 30 lb/13.6 kg box; Galangal is available in 10 lb/4.54 kg box
Shelf Life: 3 to 5 days
Storage Conditions: 50°F/10°C
Season: Available year-round

Nutritional Information

Serving Size:	3-1/2 oz/100 g
Water:	78.89 g
Calories:	80
Protein:	1.82 g
Fat:	0.75 g
Saturated Fat:	0.203 g
Fiber:	2 g
Sodium:	13 mg
Iron:	0.6 mg
Potassium:	415 mg
Vitamin C:	5 mg

JÍCAMA

The jícama is a member of the legume or bean family and the thick bulbous tuber above the root is the only part of the plant that can be consumed. Also called the Mexican potato or the yam bean, this tuber is turnip-shaped with a papery, dry, light brown skin covering a white, crisp, juicy flesh. The bulb can grow to be quite large but are best for eating when still relatively small, about 1 to 2 pounds/454 to 907 grams or smaller, so they can retain their full sweetness. Larger specimens can be drier and lose both sweetness and texture.

FIGURE **7.21** Jícama

The flesh can be cooked in stir-fries in lieu of water chestnuts, boiled, baked, or fried. However, this vegetable is best appreciated raw, shredded in a slaw, diced in salsas, julienned in a salad with corn and black beans, or simply served diced with lime juice, salt, and chili pepper. Native to Mexico and South America, jícama is used extensively in the cuisines of those regions. The flavor is hard to describe; it is sweet but not overly so, similar to a nutty apple or pear with low sugar, or comparable to the water chestnut when cooked. In addition to use in salsas and savory salads, this tuber can also be enjoyed in a fruit salad where its flavor and texture is an excellent foil and companion to various sweet fruits.

The jícama should be well formed, heavy for its size with an unblemished skin. The skin should always be removed prior to cooking and eating. Under the skin, the flesh should be white and juicy.

Pack Size: 20 lb/9.07 kg box
Shelf Life: 3 to 5 days
Storage Conditions: 35°F/1.5°C
Season: Available year-round

Nutritional Information

Serving Size:	3-1/2 oz/100 g
Water:	90.07 g
Calories:	38
Protein:	0.72 g
Fat:	0.09 g
Saturated Fat:	0.021 g
Fiber:	4.9 g
Sodium:	4 mg
Iron:	0.6 mg
Potassium:	150 mg
Vitamin C:	20.2 mg

LOTUS ROOT

The lotus root has been used for many thousands of years, mainly in Asian cuisines. The shape of this root vegetable is reminiscent of squash or plantain and it has a pale reddish-brown skin. These usually grow to roughly 6 to 8 inches/15.25 to 20 centimeters in length and about 3 inches/7.5 centimeters in diameter but they can get well over a foot long. The flesh is creamy white and there are five to seven tunnels running through the center of flesh lengthwise. These spaces give the flesh a lace-like appearance once sliced.

The flesh has a mild almost coconut-like sweet flavor with a potato-like texture and can be used in a variety of ways once peeled. The flesh can be used raw cut into lengths and served much the same as celery on crudites. It can also be filled with dips or cheese as an appetizer. The cut flesh is best placed in acidulated water to prevent oxidation. Cooked, the root can be sliced and fried, used in stir fries, or diced into soups and stews. The lotus leaves can also be used as a wrapper in which to cook rice and meat. The seeds can be eaten out of hand and are also found in a candied form.

Look for roots with a good, firm, plump shape and no soft spots or shriveled areas in the rind. Once cut, the flesh around the spaces should be clean and white; a brown or black tint indicates the product is too old.

Pack Size: 10 lb/4.54 kg box
Shelf Life: One week
Storage Conditions: 33°F/.5°C
Season: Available year-round, but best from late summer into winter

POTATOES

The humble potato has been cultivated for thousands of years beginning with the Incas in Central and South America and then across Europe in the sixteenth century. Today, wheat, rice, and corn are the only food crops grown more extensively than the potato in the world market. This immensely popular starchy tuber is prepared in a myriad number of ways and there are an almost equal number of varieties on the market to choose from. The main categories for these varieties are russet, round white, long white, yellow round, yellow long, and red round. There are also fingerlings and purple or blue varieties; some may consider these new varieties but they are actually very old

FIGURE **7.22** Top row, left to right: Yellow A, Red B, Purple A; Bottom row, left to right: White C, Red C, Yellow Fingerlings

heirloom types that are enjoying a resurgence. A "new potato" is a relatively freshly dug potato that hasn't been put into storage; these are characterized by a thin, more tender skin and finer texture to the flesh. These are generally smaller in size and red skinned, but yellow and white varieties can also be classified as "new" if freshly dug and not yet placed into storage.

These varieties of potatoes can usually be separated into starchy or waxy categories. Russets are starchy in nature and have a drier texture, making them most suitable for baking, roasting, and deep-frying. These are also less sweet, making them slower to caramelize during the cooking process. The waxy potatoes such as red or white round varieties are both moister and sweeter. These types are best suited to boiled and puréed applications or when you want to retain the proper cut shape of the potato during cooking. Some varieties such as fingerlings and long whites may be suitable and delicious using most any cooking method.

Potatoes are almost always cooked prior to consumption. They are sometimes peeled but often are not. Sometimes they are eaten cold such as in potato salad, but the potatoes for that preparation are typically cubed and boiled prior to cooling. Cooking methods and applications include baking or boiling whole, mashing with or without skin, frying, roasting in wedges or cubes, home fries, shredding and frying into hash browns or potato cakes, dicing and boiling into soups either as an ingredient or puréed into the base, chunked into stew, scalloped with cream and sometimes cheese, sliced and braised with onions and stock, or formed into dumplings or gnocchi. For all these methods of preparation, there exist an endless number of recipe variations as they pair well with a great variety of flavors and ingredients.

Potatoes should be firm with very little odor, the skins should be smooth and tight with no greening, sprouting, dark or soft spots, or cracks. Uniformity in shape is preferred to limit the time and product loss in peeling. Potatoes are often purchased by size as well as type; russets, or Idahoes, are sold by the count per 50 lb/22.68 kg box. Red, yellow, and white potatoes are sorted for size as A, B, and C. The "C" size or Creamer potato is a very small size approximately 1 to 1-1/2 inches/2.5 to 3.75 centimeters in diameter. A "B" size is just a little larger ranging about 2 to 2-1/2 inches/ 5 to 6.25 centimeters across and the "A" size is full grown and more than 3 inches/ 7.5 centimeters in diameter.

Greening in the skin of potatoes is seen as both a marketing and health risk and the two concerns are related. This condition is affected by light; the type, quantity, and duration will increase its effect. The green color comes from chlorophyll which in itself poses no danger. However, the same conditions that will promote the greening of the skin can cause the increase of a toxic glycoalkaloid called *solanine* in the flesh near the skin. A bitter taste in the cooked flesh is indicative of its presence. This toxin can cause symptoms similar to food poisoning or gastroenteritis if consumed in a large enough quantity.

Greening can occur in any type of potato but is more prevalent in thin-skinned types, commonly the white and yellow varieties. Even though a large amount of potatoes would likely need to be ingested to cause serious harm, it is better to be cautious. Neither greening nor solanine production will occur if refrigerated below 40°F/4°C, and peeling away all green areas of the potatoes is effective, but cooking in itself does not nullify the solanine.

BLUE/PURPLE POTATO

This South American breed of potato is gaining interest in North America but still lacks the popularity it has long had in South and Central America. This is a firm, waxy potato with a dark purplish to blue skin and purple flesh. The flesh retains this unique color throughout the cooking process. That unusual appearance is thought to be why this potato has been slow to grow in popularity. This tuber has a rich, almost nutty flavor and is best cooked by boiling or steaming.

CHEF POTATO

A *chef potato* is the term for very large, round, white potatoes used in the industry for general cooking applications and they are considered multipurpose with a fairly starchy consistency. These are generally available from fall well into spring or early summer and are an inexpensive choice for large production recipes such as potato salad, stew, or home fries. White long, or California Whites, are often used as a substitute in the summer months.

FINGERLING POTATO

The fingerling potato gets its name from its small, narrow, elongated shape. This is a very firm, very waxy, thin-skinned potato with a rich, buttery flavor. Fingerlings are excellent steamed, roasted, and grilled. Russian Banana and LaRatte are two very popular varieties of this prized tuber. The quality and labor-intensive harvesting give these potatoes a higher price point, but their flavor and appearance on the plate make them worth the cost for many chefs. Once a small seasonal crop, these potatoes are now found year-round.

RED POTATO

The red or Red Bliss potato gets its name from its distinctive red skin color which many cooks like for its visual appeal on the plate. The flesh of the potato is very white and waxy, making this a good choice for boiled potatoes, stews, or potato salad. Its relatively low price point usually means that it lends itself to

FIGURE **7.23** Purple Potatoes

FIGURE **7.24** Chef Potato

FIGURE **7.25** Russian Banana Fingerling Potatoes

FIGURE **7.26** LaRatte Fingerling Potatoes

FIGURE **7.27** Red Potato

FIGURE **7.28** Russet Potato

more rustic dishes. Because of the red skin's appeal, many cooks use this for roasted potatoes, but the flesh's consistency is not ideal for that application. These sell by the 50 lb/ 22.68 kg bag or box and should be sorted by size.

Nutritional Information

Serving Size:	3-1/2 oz/100 g
Water:	80.96 g
Calories:	70
Protein:	1.89 g
Fat:	0.14 g
Saturated Fat:	0.034 g
Fiber:	1.7 g
Sodium:	6 mg
Iron:	0.73 mg
Potassium:	455 mg
Vitamin C:	8.6 mg

RUSSET, IDAHO

The Russet is also referred to as an Idaho potato as that state is so prolific in production as to be synonymous with this potato. Idaho potatoes are always available and their yield, versatility, and popularity make them a good value. This is your choice for a baking potato as its starchy texture bakes up dry and fluffy with a full rich flavor. Russets are also a great choice for French fries, Rösti potatoes, and hash browns. Russet is not a good choice for boiled applications or for use when you want a cut piece of potato to retain its shape once cooked. Sold by the count per case, 100 count is a commonly used size in the foodservice.

Nutritional Information

Serving Size:	3-1/2 oz/100 g
Water:	78.58 g
Calories:	79
Protein:	2.14 g
Fat:	0.08 g
Saturated Fat:	0.02 g
Fiber:	1.3 g
Sodium:	5 mg
Iron:	0.86 mg
Potassium:	417 mg
Vitamin C:	5.7 mg

WHITE POTATO

The white or California white potato is most commonly found in the summer and is a long, thin-skinned, waxy variety that works well in several applications. There are round whites as well that have virtually the same uses as the red potato varieties, but lack the eye appeal of the red skin. These are commonly known as boiling potatoes and also sold and sorted by size.

Nutritional Information

Serving Size:	3-1/2 oz/100 g
Water:	81.58 g
Calories:	69
Protein:	1.68 g
Fat:	0.1 g
Saturated Fat:	0.025 g
Fiber:	2.4 g
Sodium:	6 mg
Iron:	0.53 mg
Potassium:	407 mg
Vitamin C:	19.7 mg

FIGURE **7.29** White Potatoes

YELLOW POTATO

Yellow, Yellow Finn, or Yukon Gold potatoes have a brown skin and a warm yellow to golden hue in the flesh. Yellow potatoes are available year-round but are best in late summer into fall. Yukon Golds are the most prevalent of the yellow potatoes. These are an all-purpose potato but they are not considered ideal for baking. They will work in fried applications, and with their rich, creamy texture are excellent in potato salad and mashed potato recipes. The texture combines with a color that looks pre-buttered to make this a highly appreciated variety. As with the red varieties, these potatoes come in a 50 lb/22.68 kg box or bag and should be sorted by size.

FIGURE **7.30** Yellow Potatoes

Pack Size: 50 lb/22.68 kg box or bag
Shelf Life: up to 1 week
Storage Conditions: 50F/10°C
Season: Best in late summer into fall but available year round

SUNCHOKE, JERUSALEM ARTICHOKE

This tuber became known as the sunchoke because of the confusion stemming from the original moniker of Jerusalem artichoke. The latter is confusing in that this vegetable is related to the sunflower, not the artichoke, and its origins are not in Jerusalem but in the Americas. The sunchoke is small, like a knobby golf ball, similar to ginger in appearance and has a dry crackled skin and a nutty sweet flavor somewhat reminiscent of jícama, sunflower seeds, or the artichoke. The texture of the flesh should be crunchy. Sunchokes may be eaten raw in salad or salsa or cooked by gentle, moist heat techniques, such as simmered in a soup. Like some other tubers, this vegetable can also be baked, roasted, or sliced and deep-fried into chips.

The skin is often removed when preparing the sunchoke, but it is quite nutritious and if it is thin, it can be left on provided the choke is well scrubbed. Look for smooth, plump tubers with an even surface, especially if peeling. Avoid bruised, wrinkled, limp, or molding sunchokes. Look for soft spots and handle gently as this tuber bruises easily.

> **Pack Size:** by the pound
> **Shelf Life:** 3 to 4 days
> **Storage Conditions:** 35°F/1.5°C
> **Season:** Summer into late winter

SWEET POTATO

Although the sweet potato originated in the Americas and can be cooked in many of the same ways as the potato, they are not botanically related. Sweet potatoes are also often referred to as yams, but that too is a different species. A yam is darker, drier, and less sweet than the true sweet potato and so it is often cooked with other ingredients and spices to make it more appetizing. The sweet potato will have a rich, moist texture and a sweet flavor that can stand alone. This tuber can be served baked, deep-fried, mashed, in casseroles, boiled, or in pies, much like the pumpkin. Many southern U.S. farmers market the Beauregard sweet potato as yams. Garnets and Jewels are other popular southern types of sweet potatoes and are known for their moist texture and deep orange color. Sweet potatoes grown in more northerly climates will be paler in color and drier in texture in comparison.

FIGURE **7.32** Sweet Potato

A reddish skinned variety of sweet potato with white flesh is known as the boniato. This sweet potato enjoys great popularity in Latin American and Asian markets. The boniato has a dry, fluffy texture and mild, yet rich flavor.

> **Pack Size:** 40 lb/18.14 kg burlap bag
> **Shelf Life:** up to 1 week
> **Storage Conditions:** 50°F/10°C
> **Season:** Available year-round but best in late summer into fall

FIGURE **7.33** Boniato Sweet Potato

Nutritional Information

Serving Size:	3-1/2 oz/100 g
Water:	77.28 g
Calories:	86
Protein:	1.57 g
Fat:	0.05 g
Saturated Fat:	0.018 g
Fiber:	3 g
Sodium:	55 mg
Iron:	0.61 mg
Potassium:	337 mg
Vitamin C:	2.4 mg

TARO, YAUTIA, OR MALANGA

The taro and yautia (or malanga) tubers are very closely related and used in similar fashion. Taro originated in Asia many thousands of years ago in what is now India and it is still popular there; it spread from there into the islands of the Pacific where it is now a staple food. The yautia species is native to South and Central America and used in much the same manner.

Taro can get fairly large and is oblong or oval in shape with brown tufted skin; the flesh can be white or yellowish to pink in hue with flecks of purple or red. The flesh will turn a grayish hue when cooked and have a somewhat nutty flavor. In Hawaii, the flesh is mashed and puréed for the dish poi. Poi is a dietary and spiritual staple in the Hawaiian culture. Hawaiians also boil the leaves in coconut milk and serve this at outdoor celebrations. Both the party and drink are referred to as lu'au. Larger taro leaves are called callaloo and consumed as a vegetable green and in soup in the Caribbean.

Care must be taken to fully cook the taro before serving to mitigate the toxic effect on the tongue and throat of the calcium oxalate in the tuber's sap. Taro can also be fried and baked. Malanga or Yautia is more elongated and bumpy with a scaly brown rind. The flesh is also mild to nutty in flavor and golden in hue. The flesh can also be boiled, baked or fried. Look for firm heavy tubers with no soft or molding spots and a clean natural odor.

FIGURE **7.34** Taro Root

Pack Size: 10 lb/4.54 kg box
Shelf Life: One week
Storage Conditions: Store at room temperature if using quickly or hold under refrigeration
Season: Generally available year round

PODS AND SEED VEGETABLES

The vegetables in this chapter are mainly legumes, or vegetables in the seed and bean families. In each of these families, the seed of the vegetable is enclosed in a pod; some pods are tender and edible and others require the seed to be shelled from their tough inedible pod casing. This chapter also includes corn and okra because they have many seeds that are encased by the outer covering of the plant. The common culinary factor between these vegetables is that they should all be picked, purchased, and consumed when very young and while still very fresh. Corn and peas may be the most sensitive to this, but freshness is a key quality factor for all of these vegetables. As a general rule, this dependence on freshness and the need to go quickly to market make these vegetables highly seasonal. You may be able to source fresh corn throughout much of the year, but it is only truly at its peak when grown close by, picked at its peak, and sold and consumed within a few days. Locally grown pod and seed vegetables will almost always be the best option.

Snap beans, shell beans, edible and non-edible pod peas, soy and Chinese long beans are all included in this group as well as sweet corn and okra. As noted, freshness is the key, so carefully examine the pod or outer shell of each, even those that are inedible. They are often, but not always, an indicator of how these vegetables have been handled and how long they have been in transit or storage. When there is any doubt, open the pod and sample the seed or pea within or snap and sample those with edible pods. They must be tender and sweet with good moisture content. Sweet corn kernels should be plump, bursting with juice, and very sweet. Poor product at this stage may improve when cooked, but will never achieve the quality desired.

SNAP BEANS, GREEN BEANS, AND WAX BEANS

There is a group of beans that fit in this category, all considered common beans, and this includes the most commonly known green bean. The term *string bean* is still used to describe green beans, but this is now a misnomer as the long fibrous filament that was found along one side was bred out long ago.

FIGURE 8.1 Left: Fava; Top row, left to right: Green Beans, French Green Beans, Wax Beans; Bottom row: Snow Peas, Sugar Snaps, Cranberry Beans; Right: Chinese Long Beans

CHINESE LONG BEANS, YARD-LONG BEANS

The long bean looks much like a pliable green bean and can extend more than 18 inches/45.75 centimeters in length. This bean is actually more closely related to black-eyed peas and is not a snap bean. The yard-long bean is very flexible and dense, not crisp (so there is no snap), and the flavor lacks sweetness but otherwise it tastes somewhat similar to the green bean. Long beans can be grown to maturity to obtain and dry the seeds, but are best and most often utilized when young before the seeds mature and the pods are still tender.

These are best when stir-fried, deep-fried, or seared and then braised in liquid. These beans can also be cooked and cut into lengths and added to salads, often with citrus or green papaya. They should be chewy and firm when eaten and the flavor will become somewhat nutty in nature. Their texture and flavor lend them to spirited seasoning and they will complement highly flavored dishes. When purchasing, look for smaller, thinner beans with no bulging from mature seeds. They should be pliable but not withered, dehydrated, or limp. These beans can be pale or dark green but rust or other discoloration is not preferred. Only purchase what you can use quickly as the long bean has a short shelf life.

Pack Size: 10 lb/4.54 kg carton
Shelf Life: 2 to 3 days
Storage Conditions: 40° to 45°F/4° to 7°C
Season: Available year-round but best in summer and early fall at your local farm stand

FIGURE 8.2 Chinese Long Beans

FRENCH BEANS, HARICOTS VERT

The haricots vert is also a green snap bean, but is much more refined. This bean is smaller and thinner than a green bean, which makes for a more impressive appearance on the plate. The pod will be a dull and darker green than a green bean with an almost velvety feel, and there should be no bulging from the seeds within. These beans should be comparably sized and very straight. Avoid any beans that are withered, indicating dehydration, or showing signs of rust or mold.

Because their cultivation is more labor intensive and they are highly desired, this bean generally commands a much higher price than ordinary green beans, depending on the season and market conditions. The finer texture and shape dictates a more precise hand in cooking so the value is not lost to a flabby, overcooked dish. Other than this precaution, the haricots vert is cooked in virtually all the same ways as other snap beans; they should have a slightly richer depth of flavor.

FIGURE 8.3 French Beans/Haricots Vert

> **Pack Size:** 5 lb/2.27 kg carton
> **Shelf Life:** 2 to 3 days
> **Storage Conditions:** 40° to 45°F/4° to 7°C
> **Season:** Available year-round but best in summer and early fall

GREEN BEANS

The assortment of green beans ranges somewhat in size and color, such as Blue Lake and Kentucky, but from a culinary standpoint they all are handled and cooked the same and taste similar. The outer edible pod should always be fresh and brightly colored, firm, flat, tender, and sweet. There should be no visible sign of shriveling, russeting, or molding decay at the tips. The seeds inside should still be small and tender and not showing or bulging through the outer pod. When purchasing these in bulk, look for a very dry product with no signs of moisture as this may adversely affect the shelf life.

FIGURE 8.4 Green Beans

FIGURE 8.5 Wax Beans

Green beans can be prepared using a wide range of methods, but it is important to allow them to cook through enough for the sweetness to develop but not so long as to become flabby and washed out. Most commonly these beans are prepared by boiling or steaming and then quickly sauteing in butter or olive oil and aromatics just prior to service. They are also delicious roasted under high heat and they pair well with walnuts and almonds. Battered and deep-fried, green beans are often used as a side dish or for "bar food" served with a garlic aïoli or horseradish cream.

Besides the green bean there is also the yellow snap bean, commonly known as the wax bean. These have essentially the same qualities as the green bean in terms of consistency, quality standards, and cooking method. Good clean color with no rust or discoloration is critical when accepting this bean. There is also a burgundy or purple snap bean that looks really interesting paired with the others when raw. Sadly, this bean turns green once cooked, thereby removing the wonderful eye appeal one would hope for. These beans are more commonly found in the marketplace during the warmer months, especially at farmers' markets.

Pack Size: 10 or 25 lb/4.54 to 11.34 kg crate
Shelf Life: 3 to 4 days
Storage Conditions: 40° to 45°F/4° to 7°C
Season: Available year-round but best in summer and early fall when purchased at your local farm stand

ROMANO FLAT BEANS

The Romano or Italian flat green bean is related to the common green snap bean, but tends to be shorter, broader, and quite flat in shape. These beans should be meaty and full of moisture and will have a mild flavor that works well with many other foods. Like the common snap bean, the Romano is most often green in color, but is also often found in yellow and purple as well. Look for beans with good color and moisture that snap with crispness. Avoid flabby beans that look withered or dry, are limp, and have russet spots or signs of mold at the tips.

The Romano bean's unique shape increases visual interest when served with other beans. The mild flavor and chewy texture makes them a nice addition to braised dishes and soups, especially when sliced on the bias to form interesting shapes. The yellow and the purple flat beans should be sweet but are very mild in flavor; the green ones are also mild but will be the most flavorful.

Dragon's Tongue and Tongue of Fire beans are most often found dried; however, when found young and tender, these two heirloom beans have an edible pod and are quite delicious. In order to yield any benefit from their interesting coloration, they must be found when extremely young in order to be thinly sliced and eaten raw. Once cooked, these beans, like their cousins the purple snap beans, lose their bright red to purple hues. However, even when a dull and commonplace green, these are a delicious addition to the plate. These beans are not common in the market but look for them in the summer at your local farm stand. They should have a vibrant color and firm pod with no wilting or mold.

Pack Size: 10 or 25 lb/4.54 kg to 11.34 kg crate
Shelf Life: 3 to 4 days
Storage Conditions: 40° to 45°F/4° to 7°C
Season: Summer to early fall at your local farm stand

SNOW PEAS, MANGE TOUT

The snow pea is an almost completely edible pod pea that should be a vibrant green color. This pea's pod should be very firm and crisp-crunchy, full of moisture; the peas inside should be very tiny with virtually no bulging. The flavor should be very bright, sweet, and spring-like. The only preparation required before cooking this vegetable is that it be washed and each tip pinched off, unless a side string is evident and it can be pulled away.

These peas are edible raw in salad, but are excellent stir-fried, or served in a light broth. Snow peas are essential to many Chinese and Japanese dishes even though they originated in Holland. Freshness is essential so only accept snow peas that are vibrant with no wilting or loss of moisture and that can be fully utilized with a day or two. Examine the pods to be sure the peas inside are very small. Larger peas are too mature and the consistency and sweetness will be diminished.

Pack Size: 10 lb/4.54 kg carton
Shelf Life: 2 to 3 days
Storage Conditions: 33° to 35°F/0.5° to 1.5°C
Season: Available year-round but best in late spring and early summer at your local farm stand

Nutritional Information

Serving Size:	3-1/2 oz/100 g
Water:	88.89 g
Calories:	42
Protein:	2.8 g
Fat:	0.2 g
Saturated Fat:	0.039 g
Fiber:	2.6 g
Sodium:	4 mg
Iron:	2.08 mg
Potassium:	200 mg
Vitamin C:	60 mg

FIGURE 8.6 Snow Peas

FIGURE **8.7** Sugar Snap Peas

SUGAR SNAP PEAS

Like the snow pea, the sugar snap is a small, bright green pea in an edible pod. It is different in that it is much smaller but it is full and plump like an English pea pod. The peas inside will be more fully developed than a snow pea's and the pod should be crisp and full of moisture. As the name indicates, these peas should be very sweet and succulent. The sugar snap pea may be quickly roasted with herbs, served in stir-fries and salads as well as simply blanched and buttered as a side dish.

When cooking the sugar snap pea, brevity is crucial; overcooking quickly destroys the texture and flavor of this little vegetable. As with the snow pea, you will likely need to remove the string from these little pods to eliminate the tougher piece of fiber along the outside of the pod. This can be done prior to cooking, but some suggest that it can be easier to remove after an initial blanching. If you happen to be working with a local farmer, request a stringless variety. Purchase only bright green vibrant pods with no discoloration, mold, or flabbiness. Only purchase what you can fully utilize in a few days.

Pack Size: 10 lb/4.54 kg case
Shelf Life: 3 to 4 days
Storage Conditions: 33° to 35°F/0.5° to 1.5°C
Season: Available year-round but best in late spring to early summer at your local farm stand

Nutritional Information

Serving Size:	3-1/2 oz/100 g
Water:	90.27 g
Calories:	31
Protein:	1.82 g
Fat:	0.12 g
Saturated Fat:	0.026 g
Fiber:	3.4 g
Sodium:	6 mg
Iron:	1.04 mg
Potassium:	209 mg
Vitamin C:	16.3 mg

SHELL BEANS AND PEAS

The following legumes have an inedible shell surrounding the pea or bean inside. These require the pod be shucked or removed prior to cooking. This does increase the labor required but yields a delicious and nutritious vegetable.

CRANBERRY BEANS, BORLOTTI

The cranberry bean is a gorgeous cream and red-violet streaked bean that comes in an inedible but beautiful red and tan pod. Sadly, once these beans are cooked, they turn a less attractive dull beige color and some will have flecks of brown or dull purple. There are other beans that are similar and related to these beans; they vary slightly in color but are usually marketed fresh as Borlottis. When purchasing, open a few pods because even if the pod itself looks wilted or discolored, the beans may still be fine. The beans should be plump and show no withering or mold.

These beans are very popular in Italy and Spain and are mild in flavor, but are sweet and have a rich creamy texture that chefs value. They make a delicious rich soup, meld wonderfully with escarole braised with garlic and chicken stock, can be puréed with rosemary, or served in a salad.

Pack Size: 10 or 25 lb/4.54 to 11.34 kg crate
Shelf Life: 3 to 4 days
Storage Conditions: 39° to 40°F/3.5° to 4°C
Season: Late summer into fall

Nutritional Information

Serving Size:	3-1/2 oz/100 g
Water:	12.39 g
Calories:	335
Protein:	23.03 g
Fat:	1.23 g
Saturated Fat:	0.316 g
Fiber:	24.7 g
Sodium:	6 mg
Iron:	5 mg
Potassium:	1,332 mg

FIGURE 8.8 Cranberry Beans

ENGLISH PEAS, GARDEN PEAS

The garden or English pea must be shelled, as the pod is too tough and stringy to eat. These are best when young and the peas are small and sweet. Upon receipt, pop open a pod and sample the pea inside. The best test for this product is taste; look for a bright sweetness and avoid anything that is chalky. The pod should be well formed, bright green, and smooth to the touch. The peas should be small and just fill out the pod. Avoid those with overdeveloped starchy peas that are jammed together in the pod and those that are immature with flat pods containing few visible peas. Also avoid discoloration, be it gray or yellow, and any sign of mold or withered decay.

Peas are excellent boiled with a bit of onion and sautéed in butter, braised with butter and shredded lettuce, chilled in a salad, or in soup. Introduce these to your menu in early to late spring and serve them as long as they are sweet and succulent. Frozen peas work better once the fresh peas become too starchy.

Pack Size: 10 or 25 lb/4.54 to 11.34 kg case
Shelf Life: 3 to 4 days
Storage Conditions: 33° to 35°F/0.5° to 1.5°C
Season: Best in late spring and early summer at your local farm stand

Nutritional Information

Serving Size:	3-1/2 oz/100 g
Water:	78.86 g
Calories:	81
Protein:	5.42 g
Fat:	0.40 g
Saturated Fat:	0.071 g
Fiber:	5.1 g
Sodium:	5 mg
Iron:	1.47 mg
Potassium:	244 mg
Vitamin C:	40 mg

FAVA BEANS, ENGLISH BEANS, BROAD BEANS

The fava bean is favored in many of the world's cultures; it was a staple in American cuisine many years ago, lost favor, and is now coming back in wide demand again. Favas are large, flat, meaty beans with a rich bean flavor that is prized throughout the Mediterranean, Middle Eastern, and European cooking. The bean comes in a large, spongy, inedible pod and each bean inside has an outer skin that should also be removed prior to final preparation and service. This additional step makes the fava bean much more labor intensive in preparation than other beans, but the flavor and texture makes it well worth the effort.

FIGURE 8.9 Fava Beans/English Beans/Broad Beans

Look for fava beans with no yellowing or withering on the pod and avoid them if the pod has shrunken over the beans inside. However, the pods can show some dark spots without affecting the quality of the beans inside. Look for pods that are full of pale and plump beans.

When preparing fava beans, remove the beans from the pod, drop the beans into boiling salted water briefly, and then shock in ice water. Remove the outer skin by nipping it open at one end and squeezing out the bean from the other end. At this point the bean can be enjoyed with no further cooking or can be further utilized by puréeing into a paste with garlic and olive oil, in soups, risotto, marinated in a salad, or braised with other vegetables.

Pack Size: 10 or 25 lb/4.54 to 11.34 kg crates
Shelf Life: 3 to 4 days
Storage Conditions: 39° to 40°F/3.5° to 4°C
Season: Available from late spring into the early fall

Nutritional Information (raw)

Serving size:	3-1/2 ounces/100 grams
Water:	10.98 g
Calories:	341
Protein:	26.12 g
Fat:	1.53 g
Saturated fat:	0.254 g
Fiber:	25 g
Sodium:	13 mg
Iron:	6.70 mg
Potassium:	1,062 mg
Vitamin C:	1.4 mg

LIMA BEANS

The lima bean gets its name from its South American derivation and is also known as a butter bean. The lima has a large dark green pod that holds the kidney-shaped beans inside. There are two varieties of this bean in the market, the baby Lima and the Fordhook, which is much larger, meatier, and more pronounced in flavor. The beans are pale green when they are very young and mature into a pale yellow shade. The older beans work best in dishes with a long braise to tenderize and soften the texture; the young greener beans are suitable for quick preparations. The pod is opened by pulling the string that runs down the side of the pod, or cutting it open if it is tough, and extracting the beans. The beans are then blanched in boiling salted water; they should not be consumed raw because lima beans contain a cyanide compound that is nullified in cooking.

These are rich, fully flavored, and succulent beans that compare most closely to the fava bean. Try limas sautéed with butter and corn to make the famous succotash. They are also delicious in soups, paired with shellfish, sautéed with lemon and aromatics, and creamed. If you have only had frozen beans, give fresh limas a try; the difference in flavor and texture will amaze you. As with all shell beans, avoid pods that are shriveled and showing signs of decay or mold. The pod should be full of plump beans.

Pack Size: 10 or 25 lb/4.54 to 11.34 kg crate
Shelf Life: 3 to 4 days
Storage Conditions: 39° to 40°F/3.5° to 4°C
Season: Summer through fall if fresh

FIGURE **8.10** Lima Beans

FIGURE **8.11** Black-eyed Peas

Nutritional Information (raw)

Serving Size:	3-1/2 oz/100 g
Water:	10.17 g
Calories:	338
Protein:	21.46 g
Fat:	0.69 g
Saturated Fat:	0.161 g
Fiber:	19 g
Sodium:	18 mg
Iron:	7.51 mg
Potassium:	1,724 mg
Vitamin C:	0.0 mg

BLACK-EYED PEAS

The black-eyed pea is a small tan or beige colored pea that gets its name from the small black ring in the concave hollow on one side. They are available in fresh and dried form and are also known as a cowpea as they were originally grown for feeding livestock. The pods of these peas are inedible, long, and thin, and can be found in shades of purple, cream, yellow, green, or a mottled mix. The purple-hulled bean will usually have a more assertive flavor and are better suited for more pronounced seasoning than the milder peas found in the pale cream to yellow pod, also referred to as cream peas. These unusually colored varieties are not commonly found in commercial markets. The more typical black-eyed pea is found in the yellow and green pod and has an earthy flavor. The varieties and variances in flavor of these peas make them difficult to pinpoint exactly so it is best to taste them and determine the optimal dish and seasoning.

These peas have deep southern heritage and combine well with assertive seasoning and pork and rice, as in the classic dish Hoppin' John. Their clean, earthy flavors combine well with the most basic ingredients such as rice to the sublime such as foie gras and squab. Cowpeas are commonly used in the Caribbean and in many Asian dishes as well as in the Mediterranean. These beans make a great accompaniment in braised vegetable dishes, salads, soups, and ragouts. Look for well-formed pods that are well filled out with the peas inside; avoid anything looking wilted or dehydrated.

Pack Size: 10 or 25 lb/4.54 to 11.34 kg crates
Shelf Life: 3 to 4 days
Storage Conditions: 39° to 40°F/3.8° to 4°C
Season: Summer into fall

EDAMAME, SOYBEANS

Edamame are fresh green soybeans that are related to the common soybean so widely utilized in a variety of ways such as tofu and tempeh. These beans are incredibly healthy and offer a complete protein such as in meat and eggs.

They are very popular in Asia, particularly in Japan, and have finally been gaining great acceptance in the United States as well. These beans are most commonly found frozen in American markets, but can now often be found fresh at farmers' markets and from specialty produce vendors when in season.

The inedible pod is dark green, flattened, and appears to be hairy. The beans inside are a bright olive green and similar to a small fava or lime bean in shape. They are eaten cooked and have a very green pea-like flavor and buttery texture that responds well to boiling or roasting in the pod.

FIGURE 8.12 Edamame/Soybeans

These delicious peas are served as a snack and in sushi bars. They can also be puréed into a sauce for fish or marinated in a salad with other vegetables and seafood. As noted, they also make a great snack simply cooked and served with coarse salt. Like all the other shell beans, look for firm, well-formed, and brightly colored pods with no sign of wilting, dehydration, or decay.

Pack Size: by the pound
Shelf Life: 2 to 3 days
Storage Conditions: 39° to 40°F/3.8° to 4°C
Season: Available frozen year-round but best in the summer months when purchased fresh at your local farm stand

Nutritional Information

Serving Size:	3-1/2 oz/100 g
Water:	75.17 g
Calories:	110
Protein:	10.25 g
Fat:	4.73 g
Fiber:	4.8 g
Sodium:	6 mg
Iron:	2.11 mg
Potassium:	482 mg
Vitamin C:	9.7 mg

CORN

Corn is one the world's biggest staple crops and is utilized in a huge variety of applications from sweeteners to oils, flours, bourbon whiskey, dried in cereals, posole, and masa for tortillas and tamales and of course, eating fresh. Corn originated in the Americas and remains the number-one food crop there. There are a number of cultivars from the original species used in these varied applications but for the purposes of this book, the focus will be on sweet corn.

An ear of corn consists of the core or cob, which is covered by rows of kernels in shades of pale off-white to bright yellow. In sweet corn, the varieties are bred to contain a much higher ratio of sugar to starch, making it more palatable as a table vegetable; hence the origin of the term *sweet corn*. The kernels are protected by a wrapping or husk of green outer leaves which should be bright and tightly adhere to the cob. There is also a tuft of fibers or corn silk at the tip of each ear, which can range from light to very dark brown.

FIGURE **8.13** Left to right: White, Yellow, and Bi-color Sweet Corn

When receiving, corn should be heavy with full straight rows of plump kernels. These kernels should burst with a milky sweetness if pressed with the thumbnail. When inspecting corn, look for insect damage on the tips and the sides of the ear where a small borer hole will be visible. Also peek at the tip to be sure that the kernels are full. An ear that is dehydrated will display dented kernels.

Corn's sweetness begins to convert to starch when first picked, so quick utilization is a key in reaping all its sweet goodness. This is why locally grown corn picked in season will almost invariably be preferable to corn grown cross-country and shipped and held in storage for days. Nothing compares to the just-picked, sweet flavor corn has when it is harvested in season and used within a day or two at most. Many advances have been made with sweet corn varieties to improve shelf life. The "super sweet" varieties now available have a shelf life of up to a week but there is a sacrifice of flavor for this. SE or "sugar enhanced" varieties have a much better flavor but need to be used within a few days. There are three types of sweet corn available: yellow, white, and bi-color, which is yellow and white kernels combined on the same ear. Some good yellow varieties are Bodacious and Sugar Buns. White varieties include Argent and Silver King. Some bi-color varieties are Lancelot and Delectable. Some of the older varieties such as Gentleman Jim, Golden Bantam, and Silver Queen have great flavor but only if they are utilized within a few hours of harvest; otherwise the sugar turns to starch.

Corn can be cooked directly on the cob, either husked and boiled or grilled in its husk for a smoky flavor. Corn is also cut off the cob before cooking in many applications. After slicing the corn kernels from the cob, scrape down the cob with the back of your knife to "milk" out the flavorful juices that adhere.

Pack Size: 50 count crate or bag
Shelf Life: 2 to 3 days is optimum
Storage Conditions: 34° to 38°F/1° to 2°C
Season: Best when available locally

Nutritional Information

Serving Size:	3-1/2 oz/100 g
Water:	75.96 g
Calories:	86
Protein:	3.22 g
Fat:	1.18 g
Saturated Fat:	0.182 g
Fiber:	2.7 g
Sodium:	15 mg
Iron:	0.52 mg
Potassium:	270 mg
Vitamin C:	6.8 mg

OKRA

Okra originated in Africa and is not a hugely popular vegetable across the United States. However, it is essential in Cajun or Creole cooking, and especially in gumbo. Okra is very popular in parts of the Caribbean, India, Pakistan, and Asia. Okra is a green tapering pod, several inches in length with a ridged skin. Okra can be found year-round in some areas of the southern reaches of the United States, but typically is only found fresh in the warmer months of the year. Avoid okra exceeding 4 inches/10 centimeters in length as it may be tough and fibrous. Look for pods with a bright color and firm texture; it should not be pale or limp.

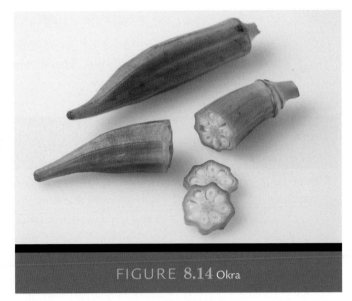

FIGURE 8.14 Okra

Okra is used in soups and, can be pickled and also deep-fried. The okra will yield a thick viscous liquid which some find objectionable, but this adds body to dishes such as gumbo.

Pack Size: 10 or 25 lb/4.54 or 11.34 kg box
Shelf Life: 2 to 3 days
Storage Conditions: 34° to 38°F/1° to 2°C
Season: Best in summer but usually available year-round

Nutritional Information

Serving Size:	3-1/2 oz/100 g
Water:	90.17 g
Calories:	31
Protein:	2 g
Fat:	0.1 g
Saturated Fat:	0.026 g
Fiber:	3.2 g
Sodium:	8 mg
Iron:	0.8 mg
Potassium:	303 mg
Vitamin C:	21.1 mg

DRIED LEGUMES

Many beans are available year round in their dried form. Worldwide these are used in most cultures and in a wide variety of forms and recipes. They are prized not only for the delicious contribution they make to many dishes but also because they provide an inexpensive source of nutrition that is very shelf stable.

Care should be taken to sift through dried beans to remove pebbles and/or other foreign objects. Many dried beans benefit from presoaking to expedite cooking time and soften the texture. They should have a good color and no signs of dust or mold; always wash your beans prior to cooking or soaking to remove any dirt. These continue to dry and harden over time so try and utilize your inventory within a few months of purchase.

COMMON DRIED LEGUMES

These beans are used in great numbers in many diverse cultures and cuisines and are readily available. These represent an economical, diverse, and economical dietary staple.

COMMON DRIED LEGUMES		
NAME	**DESCRIPTION**	**CULINARY USES**
Black Bean, Turtle Bean	Medium sized and shiny black in color. Full, earthy flavors that complement strong spices and aromatics.	Latin American dishes, sides, soups, refried, salsas.
Cannelini Bean	Elongated white bean. Smooth texture with a nutty flavor.	Works well in soups, salads, and braised with escarole.
Cranberry/Borlotti Bean	Speckled purple, pink, and ivory colored. Medium-sized bean with Italian origin.	Nutty flavored beans work well in soups and stews.
Fava/Haba Bean	Large, pale, pinkish-brown bean with very meaty texture and assertive flavor. This bean is best when fresh.	Used as a side dish and for purées.
Flagelot	Thin, oblong, greenish-white European bean. Very creamy in texture.	Excellent braised with aromatics and herbs, complements lamb very well.
Garbanzo/Chick Pea	Round, tan colored bean with a nutty flavor. Also can be found in red, white, and green hues.	Heavily used in Middle Eastern cuisine such as hummus and falafel. Also delicious with garlic and pasta.
Great Northern	Fat oblong white bean. Very mild in flavor.	Works well in soups, paste, or cassoulet.
Kidney/Red Kidney	Found in varying sizes and shades of red.	Popular bean used for chili, refried, and salad.
Lentil	Very small commonly used bean found in shades of brown, green, red, yellow, and black, depending on European or Egyptian origins. Rich earthy flavors.	Common in Northern European and Middle eastern cuisines. Well used in soups, purées, dals, and salads.
Lima/Butter Bean	Large white bean with a prized buttery texture and flavor.	Used in soups and stews or a stand-alone side dish.
Navy/Yankee Bean	Small white, but hard to digest bean that is very mild in flavor.	Popular in baked beans, soups, and bean paste.
Pinto Bean	Fat, speckled pale brown to dark red bean that cooks to a pale pink color.	Popular in Southwestern American dishes. Used commonly for refried beans and chili.
Rice Bean	Very small thin white bean that resembles pasta.	Cooks quickly and used in soups or instead of a starch-like rice.
Black-eyed Pea	Small kidney-shaped tan bean with black ring on concave hollow.	Mild earthy flavor popular in southern cooking such as Hoppin' John.
Pigeon Pea	Small, round, beige and orange colored bean.	Very popular in Caribbean and African cuisines.
Split Pea	Small, round peas in shades of dull green or yellow. Rich, strong earthy flavor.	Popular in soups with smoked pork.

HEIRLOOM DRIED LEGUMES

These varieties are not as commonly found in the market as the preceding list. However, their unique appearance and fine texture and flavor make them worth looking for and justify the additional cost.

HEIRLOOM DRIED LEGUMES		
NAME	**DESCRIPTION**	**CULINARY USES**
Anasazi	Oblong, red and white colored with a smooth creamy texture.	Mexican dishes
Appaloosa	Slender, curved, purple and white bean with an herbal flavor	Good used in southwestern dishes such as refried beans.
Christmas Limas	Large burgundy/brown and white bean with a meaty texture, nutty flavor.	Good in soups or as a side simply dressed.
Corona (Sweet White Runner)	Large, white, half moon-shaped bean.	Roast or marinate in oil, vinegar, and garlic.
Marrow	Round plump white bean.	Purées smoothly, good for baking, bacon-like flavor.
Mark	Unusual speckled black and purple to lavender in color with a rich flavor.	Use in salads or bake them. They are very versatile in use.
Peruano	Oblong shape, yellow color. Holds shape in cooking.	Works great in spicy Latin stews and soups as they absorb flavor of cooking liquid very well.
Rattlesnake	Slender oval shape with a light and dark brown in color. Tastes like a pinto but more robust.	Great in stews and chilies.
Scarlet Runners	Beautiful large purple and black to lilac color beans. They are European in origin.	Good with roasted root vegetables and aromatics.
Tiger Eye	Unusual light and dark orange/brown hues with a smooth texture.	Works well in baked dishes such as cassoulet.
Tongues of Fire	Similar in heritage and appearance to the Cranberry or Borlotti bean. Attractive speckled purple.	Bakes well with pork or sausages.
Vaquero	Interesting black and white mottled look. Related to the Anasazi. Mild in flavor.	Good in chilies and stews.

TOMATOES

Is the tomato a fruit or a vegetable? The battle rages on. Botanically it's the former, but it cooks and eats like the latter. There are literally hundreds of varieties of tomatoes and few things in the culinary world spark as much passionate discourse. The two leading condiments in the United States, catsup and salsa, are tomato based, as are many pizza and pasta sauces. Tomatoes are baked, stuffed, fried green, puréed, juiced, concentrated, you name it. They are sliced raw for sandwiches, diced in salad, concassed, chopped into salsa cruda, sliced with fresh mozzarella and basil, and so on . . . there simply isn't anything more beloved for so many delicious reasons.

Sadly, that passion for this fruit isn't justly addressed or satisfied during the proper season when tomatoes are in a plentiful and varied supply and really taste bright and sharp with acidic flavor. They are still consumed by the tons year-round even though the only true similarity to tomatoes in season is a paler color.

For many years in the foodservice industry, there were three basic tomatoes: the slicing tomato, the plum tomato, and the cherry tomato. In today's market those still represent the general categories but a multitude of variations, flavors, and colors challenge the chef and the palate and enhance presentation. Commercially, outside of certain heirlooms, tomatoes are not sold by the specific variety but rather the type. In this chapter the tomatoes will be separated into these three basic categories: round, plum, and small (which include cherry, grape, currant, and pear). The hybrid varieties common to the market are addressed as well as some of the more popular heirloom varieties, which gain more recognition each year. There are literally hundreds of heirloom varieties. This chapter touches on some of the more common to provide a sense of the wonderful options that exist.

ROUND TOMATOES

FIGURE **9.1** Clockwise from top left: Plum, Slicing, Grape, and Cherry Tomatoes

SLICING TOMATOES, GLOBE TOMATO

These are generally the pale pink, hard, round tomatoes so commonly found in foodservice and the supermarket. They are bred to grow fast and survive long travel and prolonged shelf life. They are picked when still fully green and undeveloped, shipped all over the country, and then gassed in ethylene chambers to develop a somewhat red, tomato-like appearance. Sadly, full tomato flavor isn't considered a necessary marketing point. Diners, schools, quick service restaurant chains, hospitals, and families purchase, serve, and consume this type of tomato daily. For a great many people in the United States, this is what a tomato looks, smells, and tastes like.

These pack in 25 pound/11.34 kilogram cases by size, generally identified as 5 × 6 or 6 × 6, which indicates how many tomatoes fit across and lengthwise in a case. They are available year-round with most grown in Florida, California, and Mexico.

Relatively new to the market is the hydroponic tomato. It is a marked improvement from the standard slicing tomato in color, texture, and somewhat in flavor, These tomatoes are hothouse grown in a nutrient-rich water system without soil. Although still inferior in flavor to a seasonally grown farm-raised product, hydroponic tomatoes have improved substantially over time and are a much better choice than the typical commercially grown and packed slicing variety. If price is not the primary consideration, this is a viable option. Beefsteak tomatoes, which are a type of tomato, not a variety, are not always available commercially. However, larger hydroponic tomatoes are sometimes marketed as such, especially in the colder months.

A tomato grown in Israel, but developed 50 years ago in New Jersey, is being re-introduced to the market gradually. Known as the Ramapo, this tomato brings back the flavor and texture of New Jersey tomatoes long prized for their balance of acid and sugar. Sized approximately the same as the slicing tomato, this brings hope that a commercially viable tomato with homegrown taste will once again be on the market. If this succeeds in marketing tests, these tomatoes could be available nationally in the near future.

FIGURE **9.2** Slicing/Globe Tomatoes

Pack Size: 10 to 15 lb/4.54 to 6.8 kg flats or 25 lb/11.34 kg lugs
Shelf Life: 3 or 4 days
Storage Conditions: 62° to 68°F/16° to 20°C
Season: Available year-round but best July through the end of September

Nutritional Information

Serving Size:	3-1/2 oz/100 g
Water:	94.50 g
Calories:	18
Protein:	0.88 g
Fat:	0.2 g
Saturated Fat:	0.028 g
Fiber:	1.2 g
Sodium:	5 mg
Iron:	0.27 mg
Potassium:	237 mg
Vitamin C:	12.7 mg

YELLOW ROUND

These tomatoes are roughly the same size as slicing tomatoes and are bright yellow in color rather than red. Typically lower in acid than their red counterparts, these tomatoes are prized for offering contrast on the plate to please the eye and a milder, sweet flavor that offsets the acid expected in a quality red tomato. Carolina Gold is the most notable hybrid on the commercial market and known for its bright full color. Other excellent yellow choices include Dr. Wyche's Yellow, which is a large, heavy heirloom tomato (like a beefsteak) known for its meatiness and full flavor.

The Gold Medal tomato is yellow with streaks of red and is prized for its eye appeal as well as being very sweet. There are also several orange-colored tomatoes that have similar applications.

Yellow tomatoes are beautiful in salads, especially those utilizing a spectrum of tomatoes to visually showcase the variety of colors, shapes, and sizes available. Very little is needed to improve upon the flavor combination in such a salad. These tomatoes also make beautiful and smooth, tasty soups, hot or cold. Many recipes traditionally made with red tomatoes can accommodate yellows, which will give a lighter, sweet flavor in dishes such as a chicken pizza and curries. Look for firm, plump, well-colored tomatoes with a sweet fragrance. Avoid anything rock hard, cracking, or showing soft, spongy spots.

Pack Size: 10 or 25 lb/4.54 to 11.34 kg
Shelf Life: 3 or 4 days
Storage Conditions: 62° to 68°F/16° to 20°C
Season: Available year-round but best in late July through late September

TOMATOES ON THE VINE

Available in both red and yellow, these tomatoes have gained considerable popularity in recent years, especially for the home cook. Developed in Europe (most in the market still come from there), these tomatoes are prized for their texture, shelf life, good color, and aroma. That aroma, however, is almost completely generated by the vine not the fruit, and these carry a higher price per usable pound. Tomatoes improve in flavor as they ripen on the vine, and shipping these in clusters on the vine does allow for further ripening than the Globe varieties. Usage of these tomatoes should be predicated on assessing whether their appearance and the somewhat enhanced flavor are worth the additional cost. There may well be options available that match the flavor and cost less. When local farm-grown product is not available, conduct cuttings of the different tomato types that are available to ascertain what will best meet your needs while considering the value of quality versus cost. Or consider doing without fresh tomatoes when the lack of quality warrants. These tomatoes should be vibrantly fully red, firm, and attached to the vine. Avoid anything soft or very hard.

Pack Size: 10 lb/4.54 kg
Shelf Life: 3 to 4 days
Storage Conditions: 62° to 68°F/16° to 20°C
Season: Available year-round

FIGURE **9.3** Tomatoes on the Vine

LOCAL AND HEIRLOOM VARIETIES

During the local growing season there are a great multitude of medium-sized red slicing hybrid tomatoes with many different attributes and variances. Almost all are certain to be preferable to the mass-marketed varieties listed previously. Getting to know which farmers in your area grow what and learning which tomatoes are most appropriate to your tastes and needs is the best way to determine where to buy tomatoes. Look for tomatoes that have good acid and flavor, an appropriate size, a bright even color, are not prone to scarring and cracking, and have a shelf life sufficient to your delivery schedule. These are generally a more expensive product compared with commercially grown slicing tomatoes but their value is in the vastly improved flavor and texture.

The following are some prominent round heirloom tomato varieties to consider. Please be open to the many other varieties that exist and may have better availability in your particular market. They won't always be as consistent in appearance (some can be downright ugly), nor have as good a shelf life because they are picked ripe, but they taste the way tomatoes should. Use them whenever they are available because good rich flavor is a top priority in whatever dishes you serve.

AUNT RUBY'S GERMAN GREEN

These are a large beefsteak-sized green tomato meant to be eaten when ripe and soft to the touch. They're not pretty but are very juicy with a sweet and spicy flavor.

BLACK KRIM

This is a large 4 to 5 inch/10 to 13 centimeter tomato that has green/black shoulders. In the high heat of the summer, this tomato is almost reddish-black in color with a full rich taste, making it a very good option for a tomato sampler salad plate.

FIGURE **9.4** Aunt Ruby's German Green

FIGURE **9.5** Black Krim

FIGURE **9.6** Brandywine

FIGURE **9.7** Cherokee Purple

BRANDYWINE

This tomato is one of the most widely known and appreciated heirloom varieties. Its popularity stems from its incredibly rich flavor and large, pink beefsteak appearance. Very meaty and dense, some Brandywines exceed two pounds in size.

CHEROKEE PURPLE

Another very popular tomato that is mid-sized with a rose-purple cast, this tomato has excellent flavor and sweetness. This fruit rivals the aforementioned Brandywine in how well it is regarded and loved.

GERMAN PINK

Another excellent large beefsteak-sized tomato, this variety is well liked by growers because it is resistant to cracking and scarring which makes it easier to market. This variety has a very good sweet flavor and relatively few seeds. There is also a German Yellow variety with similar attributes.

STRIPED GERMAN

Similar to the Gold Medal tomato, this large heirloom is a beautiful yellow-and-red striped variety that will add tremendous visual appeal to any plate. The interior is marbled,

FIGURE **9.8** German Pink

FIGURE **9.9** Striped German

which only enhances the appeal. It has an unusually complex and rich flavor the matches its attractiveness.

GREEN ZEBRA

This is a cultivar, not a true heirloom, but is marketed and utilized in the same way. This is a small tomato with a wonderfully bright, zestful flavor. The name comes from its bright green color and beautiful yellowish to pale green stripes. This is an excellent choice when offering a variety of types and flavors.

STRIPED CAVERN

This is an unusual tomato. At first glance it can almost resemble a large red pepper with yellow stripes. The walls of this tomato are very thick, also like the pepper, making it an excellent choice as a salad or light luncheon option when stuffed with cheese or a fish or poultry salad. It offers a creative chef a new option to explore.

> **Pack Size:** 10 to 15 lb/4.54 to 6.8 kg flats
> **Shelf Life:** 3 to 4 days
> **Storage Conditions:** 62° to 68°F/16° to 20°C
> **Season:** July to late September

PLUM TOMATOES

These are the small- to medium-sized oblong or barrel-shaped tomatoes that are the workhorse of cooking tomatoes in the kitchen and in the canning industry. They are denser with fewer seeds and less water by weight than round tomatoes, which give them a better flavor and consistency when they are cooked down for sauce. This is why they are also referred to as a *paste tomato*. Also, the thicker, meatier body and smaller seed cavities make this the ideal choice for drying. It greatly heightens and concentrates the tomato flavor. Sun-dried and oven-dried tomatoes have enjoyed huge success and popularity for several decades now. They are available in the dried form or dried and then packed in olive oil.

FIGURE **9.10** Green Zebras

FIGURE **9.11** Striped Cavern

FIGURE **9.12** Plum Tomatoes

Originally from Italy, the true San Marzano variety is still widely considered the best canned plum tomato. The fresh plum tomatoes grown in the United States mostly come from California, Mexico, or Florida, with Roma being the most prevalent variety. In winter months the quality of this tomato slips, as one would expect, but the flavor when raw may still be superior to the generic slicing tomatoes found at that time. Still, many chefs prefer to switch over to the canned Italian tomatoes at that time of year for all other purposes.

Look for tomatoes with a full color, a firm feel that has some give to pressure, and a hefty weight for their size. Avoid those tomatoes that will not ripen fully before use, or are discolored, cracked, or shriveled.

SUPER MARZANO

A large, pear-shaped tomato with fruit exceeding 5 inches/13 centimeters in length. This is a hybrid of the famed San Marzano tomato. It is prized for its fine flavor and excellent thickening qualities when cooking down for sauce.

JERSEY DEVILS

This tomato has a very long, tapered shape. Once nearly extinct, it is now making a comeback. It is very bright and sweet in flavor and excellent raw and in salsa as well as for making sauce.

HOWARD GERMAN

This is a very old variety of tomato that is also tapered and elongated in shape. At times the fruit has a definite pear shape and its appearance is often more like a pepper. Its longevity is undoubtedly linked to its excellent flavor in cooking.

AMISH PASTE

This is an heirloom variety paste tomato with an oblong, oxheart shape. It is medium sized with a deep red color and rich, sweet flavor. This is very meaty variety with few seeds.

Pack Size: 10 lb/4.54 kg flats or 25 lb/11.34 kg boxes
Shelf Life: 3 to 4 days
Storage Conditions: 62° to 68°F/16° to 20°C
Season: Available year-round but best from July to the end of September

SMALL TOMATOES

CHERRY

Available most commonly as red cherry, these are also found in a yellow variety. Cherry tomatoes are grown mostly as a salad tomato or used as garnish. Generally available year-round, these are often the sweeter and better-tasting alternative to other tomatoes on the market. The typical cherry tomato found on the supermarket and foodservice shelf is a hybrid and, not surprisingly, there are other, more interesting varieties and shapes available during the growing season. In addition to use as a salad garnish, these may be used stuffed with a flavored cream cheese, as a colorful addition to kebabs, or added at the final moments to various stir-fried vegetables for a contrast in flavor and color. Cherry tomatoes should be firm, brightly and fully colored, and have a sweet scent. Usually available by the pint basket, cherry tomatoes are also sold on the vine at a considerably higher price. Heirloom types are also often sold in mixed pints to give the buyer a greater variety of colors and shapes.

Grape tomatoes are the plum tomato version of a cherry tomato. The following are some examples of other small varieties and shapes found in the market, especially during the growing season.

CURRANT

Available in red and yellow varieties, this is the smallest type of cherry tomato on the market, sometimes the size of a large green pea. These are prized for their size and the look they can lend to the plate, rather than their flavor, which is not unusual.

PEAR

These are roughly the size of a cherry tomato, but as their name describes, they have a distinct pear shape. This tomato is also available in both red and yellow varieties. Once again, the main attraction for this tomato is its color and different shape; the flavor is nothing unusual or special.

SUN GOLD

Yellow/gold to orange in color, this tomato is not only beautiful, but widely considered to be one the best and sweetest tasting of the

FIGURE **9.13** Round, Red Cherry Tomatoes

FIGURE **9.14** Round, Yellow Cherry Tomatoes

FIGURE **9.15** Red Grape Tomatoes

FIGURE **9.16** Yellow Pear Tomatoes

cherry tomatoes. The Sun Cherry is the red variety of this and sweeter than the usual cherry tomato.

SWEET 100

The name comes from its small size and how many might grow per plant. Tender and prone to cracking, these are a juicy and very sweet variety. These are delicious raw or tossed with pasta just before service.

GREEN GRAPE

This is a green variety of the grape tomato, dark green to pale translucent in color. Its unique and attractive appearance is coupled with an excellent flavor.

PECHE JAUNE

This is a very unusual variety that is pale yellow to pink in color with a soft peach like fuzz on its skin. This fruit is approximately an inch in diameter with a mild and fruity flavor.

CHOCOLATE CHERRY, BLACK CHERRY

This is a 1 inch/3 cm heirloom variety with a dark greenish-black cast to the flesh. It may well be the most delicious and full flavored of the cherry tomatoes. There are also Black and White and Black Plum varieties of this excellent fruit.

> **Pack Size:** Twelve 1-pint flats
> **Shelf Life:** 3 to 4 days
> **Storage Conditions:** 62° to 68°F/16° to 20°C
> **Season:** Available year-round but best July to the end of September

TOMATILLOS

Tomatillos are related to the tomato and widely used in Mexican and Latin American cuisines. They are easily identified by the light brown papery husk that surrounds each fruit. Most commonly, tomatillos found commercially are green in color, but they can be found in shades of yellow, red, and purple. Look for very firm and brightly colored fruit as the color is prized in salsas and sauces. These are generally 1 to 2 inches/2.5 to 5 centimeters in diameter and have a much more tart flavor than a tomato.

Pack Size: 10 lb/4.54 kg box or 40 lb/18.14 kg case
Shelf Life: 1 to 2 weeks
Storage Conditions: 40°F/4°C
Season: Year-round

Nutritional Information

Serving Size:	3-1/2 oz/100 g
Water:	91.63 g
Calories:	32
Protein:	0.96 g
Fat:	1.02 g
Saturated Fat:	0.139 g
Fiber:	1.9 g
Sodium:	1 mg
Iron:	0.62 mg
Potassium:	268 mg
Vitamin C:	11.7 mg

FIGURE **9.17** Tomatillos

PEPPERS

Peppers are members of the *Capsicum* genus and provide a good deal of sweetness as well as heat in cooking. They provide bright color to the dishes they are part of, and come in vibrantly colored hues of green, red, white, yellow, orange, brown, and purple. There is an enormous number of members in this family; but in foodservice they are divided into two main groups: sweet peppers and chile peppers. Sweet peppers, mostly of the bell variety, can provide sweet to somewhat tart flavors to a recipe. Chile peppers provide the heat in many recipes and, depending on which chile pepper is used, they can give a mild touch of heat to a very fiery burn. Generally, the rule of thumb is: the smaller the pepper, the higher the heat. The broader the shoulder, the sweeter the pepper will be. Capsaicin, the chemical that creates the level of heat in peppers, is genetically nullified in the sweet or bell varieties. Whatever pepper you opt for, it is advisable to taste it carefully before adding it to your dish; the level of sweet to tart and mild to hot can vary greatly from one pepper to the next.

Most every pepper starts off green in color and ripens into the other shades seen in the market. Peppers are prized in both stages of maturity. The flavor generally gets more complex and sweeter as it ripens. Look for peppers that have a clean, full color and shiny rind. They should be firm, full, and heavy for their size, with a clean aroma. Avoid peppers with a shriveled appearance, soft spots, or signs of mold.

It is quite common, and preferable with many peppers, to quickly roast or char them and remove the shiny outer skin, which can be tough and bitter. Peppers are roasted by blistering or charring the skin over an open flame or in a broiler, placing the pepper in a brown paper bag to steam, and then simply pulling off the skin. This gives the peppers a more unctuous and delicious flavor, especially when bathed in olive oil and vinegar. Do not remove the skin under running water or you will dilute the smoky flavor and wash away the essential oils of the pepper. Typically, the stem is also removed along with the seeds and white connective pith, unless your aim is to maximize the heat the pepper provides. In that case, leave the seeds and connective pith on the pepper. Smaller peppers are the hottest primarily because the ratio of seeds and connective pith to flesh is much higher in them. Exercise caution when handling peppers because your skin can react painfully to the capsaicin.

Be very careful not to touch tender areas of the body such as your eyes after you have handled peppers. These precautionary notes should not impede your desire to learn about and utilize the incredible array of peppers available. They are simply meant to encourage you to take preventative measures when handling them.

FIGURE 10.1 Top row, left to right: Green Sweet Pepper, Red Sweet Pepper, Yellow Sweet Pepper, Poblano, Anaheim; Bottom row: Red Fresno, Jalapeno, Serrano, Padron, Thai Bird Chiles

SWEET BELL PEPPERS

Bell peppers are the large sweet peppers so common in the market and in many cuisines. Depending on the color and its state of ripeness, the flavor of this pepper will range from tart in the under-ripened, green variety to quite sweet for a fully-ripened red bell. These peppers will generally have three or four straight sides and the latter is usually block shaped. They are sometimes tapered, with rounded ridges along the top and bottom. Most commonly this pepper is either green or red in color; the red results from the green pepper ripening fully. However, the bell pepper is also found in shades of yellow, orange, brown, white, and violet. Be aware that the violet peppers will likely turn green once cooked. The green bell pepper is the most under-ripe and will have the tartest flavor. The red will generally be the sweetest, with the other colors also being more sweet than tart as a rule. The eye appeal and higher sweetness gives the red, yellow, and orange peppers a higher price point than the green bell.

Other than the color, all bell peppers will have common characteristics to look for when purchasing. The size will either be medium or jumbo; starting at about 3 to 4 inches/8 to 10 centimeters in height and width and going up to nearly 5 inches/

12.5 centimeters. Sweet peppers are also highly nutritious with high levels of vitamin C and other minerals. They should have good, solid color, a bright sheen to the skin, thick walls, and good heft for their size. Avoid multi-colored skin, those with shriveled or soft spots, cracking, and deeply bent or crooked peppers, especially if roasting them. Expect to pay 10 to 50 percent more for colored peppers as compared to green bell peppers.

For culinary purposes the bell varieties will not substitute for various chile peppers as the flavor profiles and how they match with other foods will be completely different. This type of pepper is completely different in appearance, flavor, and usage. Green bell peppers are part of the Cajun trinity along with celery and onions. Bell peppers are often cored or halved and stuffed before baking and are sometimes served with a tomato sauce. Roasting these peppers is also very popular, especially for the red bell peppers, yielding sweet and tender flesh. Bell peppers can also provide flavor, crunch, and color to crudités and salads when used raw.

Orange bell peppers will run smaller than either the green or red peppers. These are fruity, sweet, and make a great addition to salads and salsas with their bright flavor and color. Cooked, these work well in pasta sauces, stews, and soups. They are also an excellent roasting pepper. Look for nice thick walls, and a bright, even texture and color. Yellow bell peppers will run as big as the green peppers and should be selected and used as you would the orange bells. The violet and white, or blond, bells are more decorative as they lose their color when cooked and will not be quite as sweet as the more colorful choices.

> **Pack Size:** 10, 11, or 15 lb/4.54, 5, or 6.8 kg box
> **Shelf Life:** 4 to 7 days
> **Storage Conditions:** 50°F/10°C
> **Season:** Available year-round but best in the summer into fall at your local farm stand

CHILE PEPPERS

These peppers have a much different flavor profile than the bell peppers and generally are not interchangeable in recipes. These chiles offer a broad range of color and sweet to great heat in your dishes, so choose what is most appropriate for your recipe and for your dining customer.

ANAHEIM, LONG GREEN

This common, widely available chile pepper is also known as the California chile and is widely used because of its good color and mild flavor. The Anaheim is generally about 6 inches/15 centimeters in length and about 2 inches/5 centimeters at most in diameter at the shoulders, tapering down to a rounded point. It has a pale to bright green color and is fairly mild. This is a good cooking chile for sauces and stews and makes a wonderful Relleno when stuffed and fried or baked. Anaheim peppers will ripen into a vivid red color and develop a richer, sweet flavor that is great in sauces and other applications.

Look for a good even color and a warm pepper aroma. Avoid Anaheim chiles with soft spots, shriveling, cracks, or signs of mold.

FIGURE **10.4** Anaheim

Pack Size: 10 lb/4.54 kg box
Shelf Life: 4 to 7 days
Storage Conditions: 45°F/7°C
Season: Available year-round but best when purchased at your local farm stand

FRESNO

The Fresno looks like a red jalapeño but is its own chile; it should be wider at the shoulders, a bit shorter, and supply more heat. The flavor will also have sweetness coupled with its heat and is delicious pickled in vinegar. The Fresno works well in salsas, sauces, breads, and is appetizing when roasted. As with other chiles, look for firm, brightly colored peppers with no shriveling or soft spots.

FIGURE **10.5** Fresno

Pack Size: 10 lb/4.54 kg box
Shelf Life: 4 to 7 days
Storage Conditions: 45°F/7°C
Season: Available year-round but best when purchased at your local farm stand

HABAÑERO

The habañero chile pepper is a cute, 1 inch/2.5 centimeter lantern-shaped pepper that comes in pretty shades of red, orange, yellow, and green. However, there is nothing charming about its heat. The habañero is considered to be possibly the hottest chile in the world and certainly the hottest grown in the Western hemisphere. This pepper can literally be fifty times hotter than a jalapeño; it can irritate the mouth when eaten and burn the skin if not handled with gloves. Despite the dangers fraught with preparing and eating this chile, the habañero is delicious and mixes well with foods that are sweet and acidic. As with other chiles, the redder peppers will be sweeter and work well in ceviche and salsa as well as marinades. This pepper has become very popular in bottled hot sauces sold in the United States. Look for smooth skin that is free of any blemishes or wrinkles. Habañero peppers freeze very well for a few months. Simply wrap in an airtight plastic bag and they will be available when you need them.

Pack Size: 10 lb/4.54 kg box or by the pound
Shelf Life: 4 to 7 days in refrigeration and 2 to 3 months in the freezer
Storage Conditions: 45°F/7°C
Season: Available year-round but best when purchased at your local farm stand

FIGURE **10.6** Habañero

JALAPEÑO

The jalapeño pepper is the very familiar, small, bright green chile that is usually 3 to 4 inches/7.5 to 10 centimeters in length and about 1 inch/2.5 centimeters in diameter from the bottom to the top. Jalapeños should be firm and thick walled and exhibit a warm vegetable aroma and heat. They are the biggest selling of the hot chiles sold in the United States. It is difficult to list the myriad ways this chile is enjoyed. Jalapeños can be eaten raw or roasted, stuffed and fried, put on salads and tacos, and added to soups, stews, and sauces to give some additional heat and kick.

Jalapeño chiles will also ripen to a bright red color; it looks like the Fresno chile but is a different milder and sweet pepper. Red jalapeños have a sweet rich heat that complements tamales, sauces, and salsas. When dried and smoked this pepper becomes the chipotle, which is sold dried or canned and packed in adobo sauce. Look for a firm

FIGURE **10.7** Jalapeño

solid pepper with no decay, especially near the stem or tip. If there are what appear to be small cracks or lines in the skin, this is not a bad quality indicator, just a natural part of the growth. Jalapeños freeze well for short periods of time.

Pack Size: 10 lb/4.54 kg box
Shelf Life: 4 to 7 days under refrigeration or 2 to 3 months in the freezer
Storage Conditions: 45°F/7°C
Season: Available year-round but best when purchased at your local farm stand

Nutritional Information

Serving Size:	3-1/2 oz/100 g
Water:	91.69 g
Calories:	30
Protein:	1.35 g
Fat:	0.62 g
Saturated Fat:	0.062 g
Fiber:	2.8 g
Sodium:	1 mg
Iron:	0.70 mg
Potassium:	215 mg
Vitamin C:	44.3 mg

MALAGUETA

Rarely found fresh in North American markets, the Malagueta chiles are thin, roughly 2 inches/5 centimeters long, and found in green and red varieties. This pepper is intensely hot and used mainly in the dishes of Brazil where it is grown. It can be found jarred in brine in other markets.

MANZANA

The Manzana chile is a brightly colored chile that is several inches long and almost as wide. This chile has an intense heat, thick walls, and unusual black seeds. This pepper is not common in American markets and, due its thick walls, is rarely seen in a dried form. Use the Manzana chile for fiery salsas and relishes.

FIGURE **10.8** Padróns

PADRÓN

The Padrón pepper is a small green chile that is generally sweet and rich in flavor. However, be aware that about ten percent of any box will carry a fairly intense kick of heat. This pepper is commonly found in tapas bars served simply by frying in hot oil and sprinkling with coarse salt.

PIQUILLO

The Piquillo is a red sweet chile, similar to a pimiento in size and shape, but with a rich smooth flavor. True Piquillos are only from a specific region in Spain and usually found canned in the market, but even canned these are a delicious and popular pepper.

POBLANO

The poblano is another popular cooking chile, but will have more oomph than the Anaheim. They are wedge-shaped, wide at the stem end, tapering down to a point, and usually 4 to 5 inches/10 to 12.5 centimeters long and 2 to 3 inches/5 to 7.5 centimeters in diameter. This chile is very dark green in color, almost purple-black. Poblanos should be sampled before adding to dishes as the heat may range from medium to mild or quite hot. The poblano is always cooked.

The poblano's shape and flavor make it a great choice for Rellenos and is delicious roasted. It is also a good choice for moles. The poblano can be purchased after it has ripened and turned red in color. Poblanos should be firm, thick walled, and darkly colored; avoid those that are shriveled, dehydrated, or beginning to show signs of mold. When dried, the poblano is known as the ancho and is the most popular dried chile sold.

FIGURE **10.9** Poblanos

> **Pack Size:** 10 lb/4.54 kg box
> **Shelf Life:** 4 to 7 days
> **Storage Conditions:** 45°F/7°C
> **Season:** Available year-round but best when purchased at your local farm stand

SERRANO

The serrano is another chile that can be mistaken for a jalapeño, but it lacks the full vegetable flavor of the jalapeño and provides a more intense and acidic heat. The serrano is also considerably smaller in length, usually just 1 1/2 to 2 inches/3.75 to 5 centimeters long, as well as smaller in width with small, rounder shoulders. This chile works well in sauces, ceviche, salsas, and pickled in vinegar. Serranos are used interchangeably whether green or ripened to red. The red will be sweeter, but the heat makes that difference less noticeable. These are thick walled and should be firm and brightly colored with a biting hot aroma.

FIGURE **10.10** Serrano

> **Pack Size:** 10 lb/4.54 kg box
> **Shelf Life:** 4 to 7 days
> **Storage Conditions:** 45°F/7°C
> **Season:** Available year-round but best when purchased at your local farm stand

Nutritional Information

Serving Size:	3-1/2 oz/100 g
Water:	90.25 g
Calories:	32
Protein:	3.7 g
Fat:	0.44 g
Saturated Fat:	0.059 g
Fiber:	3.7 g
Sodium:	10 mg
Iron:	0.86 mg
Potassium:	305 mg
Vitamin C:	44.9 mg

SCOTCH BONNET

The Scotch bonnet is of Caribbean origin, closely related to the habañero, and similar in appearance and heat. They are often used interchangeably. The Scotch bonnet will be a bit smaller in size and are usually bright yellow to pale orange in color. Very hot with a smoky fruitier flavor, this is an essential ingredient in many Caribbean dishes such as Jamaican Jerk. Use precautions such as wearing gloves when handling the chile, as it can irritate or burn the skin if mishandled.

Pack Size: 10 lb/4.54 kg box or by the pound
Shelf Life: 4 to 7 days under refrigeration or 2 to 3 months in the freezer
Storage Conditions: 45°F/7°C
Season: Available year-round but best when purchased at your local farm stand

FIGURE **10.11** Scotch Bonnet

THAI BIRD

The Thai bird chile, whether red or green, is grown and used almost exclusively in Southeast Asian cooking, as the name suggests. These supply an intense heat and are used cooked or, more rarely, raw as a garnish. The tiny body is about an inch in length, thin walled, and packed with seeds. Use this pepper sparingly due to its fiery nature, but use it in stir-fries and soups to add that authentic Southeast Asia flavor and kick. Avoid chiles that are withered and showing signs of mold.

Pack Size: by the pound
Shelf Life: 3 to 6 days
Storage Conditions: 45°F/7°C
Season: Available year-round but best when purchased at your local farm stand

FIGURE **10.12** Thai Bird

SQUASH

The family of squashes is a large and varied group that is broken down into the hard skin, or winter squash, category; and the soft skin category, which consists of summer squash, cucumbers, and eggplant. The latter category is not generally thought of as squash, but it does fall into this grouping.

The winter and summer designation came from a time when those were the only seasons that such squash were available. Winter squashes grew into the autumn of the year and with their hard shells could last far into the winter if stored properly. Summer squash, such as zucchini, only grew in the warmer months and had a very short shelf life. These days summer squash is in the market year-round and many winter squashes can generally be found all year as well, although the quality is not the same as when they are in season.

Because the seeds of a squash are contained within them, squashes are truly a fruit. However, due to their almost universal savory applications, they are regarded and discussed here as a vegetable.

WINTER, HARD-SKINNED SQUASH

Winter squash arrive in the market from late summer to late fall but generally are available year-round or until late spring. Winter squashes all pack in 40-pound cases and should be held around 50° to 55°F/10° to 13°C. They come in an amazing array of colors and shapes on the outside and have light to deep orange flesh on the inside. The seeds are edible in all of the winter squashes, even though people usually only think of eating pumpkin seeds. Generally, the flesh of any of these squashes can be steamed, baked, or roasted. It can be removed from the rind before cooking and in some cases cooked and served in the rind. Each of these squashes has its own specific characteristic and flavor, but they are all similar enough to be used interchangeably. They are low-cost sources of good nutrition that add sweetness and color to the plate.

ACORN SQUASH

The acorn squash is so named because it is shaped like a large acorn, only with deep ridges that run from the stem to its tapered end. Most commonly seen in the market with a deep, dark green rind, they can also be found with yellow-orange to gold and multi-colored or even white rinds. This squash typically weighs 2 pounds/907 grams and is usually prepared by cutting it in half or quarters, scooping away the stringy fibers and seeds, and then roasting in the rind with butter and often spices. Other cooking options include steaming or sautéing the flesh once it has been removed from the rind. The flesh is sweet and fibrous, and darkens and softens as it cooks. The acorn squash is fairly popular, but is a bit less flavorful then many of the other winter squashes. These squashes should be heavy for their size, indicating high water content.

Pack Size: 40 lb/18.14 kg crates
Shelf Life: 1 to 2 months
Storage Conditions: 50° to 55°F/10° to 13°C
Season: Mostly available year-round but always better in the late fall to early winter

FIGURE **11.1** Acorn Squash

BUTTERNUT SQUASH

Butternut squash is a beige or dun-colored squash with a bulbous end and heavy, thick neck. The rind is tough, but not very hard and the squash can be cooked by baking with the rind on or in chunks after paring the rind off. The flesh is fine grained and sweet and almost has a sweet potato or nutty flavor. The consistency of the flesh can be a bit watery if the butternut was picked young; the older the squash the darker, drier, and sweeter the flesh will be. If the squash was picked too young there will be tinges of green at the stem end and running down its length in thin streaks; a squash that is too old will be beginning to dehydrate and lose its water weight. Look for good, firm, heavy squash with more neck than bulbous seed end to improve yield. Avoid squash with soft spots, greening, or that are lightweight indicating moisture loss.

Butternut squash can be roasted in the rind with butter and spices. The flesh can also be steamed and puréed to use in a gratin, to make a luscious sweet soup, or in breads and muffins. Slow roasting or baking will richen and enhance the sweetness of the flesh as compared to steaming.

Pack Size: 40 lb/18.14 kg crates
Shelf Life: 2 to 3 months
Storage Conditions: 50° to 55°F/10° to 13°C
Season: Mostly available year-round but always better in the late fall to early winter

FIGURE **11.2** Butternut Squash

Nutritional Information

Serving Size:	3-1/2 oz/100 g
Water:	86.41 g
Calories:	45
Protein:	1 g
Fat:	0.1 g
Saturated Fat:	0.021 g
Fiber:	2 g
Sodium:	4 mg
Iron:	0.7 mg
Potassium:	352 mg
Vitamin C:	21 mg

CARNIVAL

The carnival squash is similar in size and shape to the acorn variety with ridges running from stem to base. The hard inedible rind can either be a fairly pale green hue with flecks and stripes of dark green, or very pale yellow with orange splotches. Some rinds have areas of both colors.

FIGURE **11.3** Carnival Squash

The flesh of this squash is yellow with a rich sweet flavor, but it can be somewhat stringy. The carnival squash can be steamed but is better baked or used in soup. As with the acorn squash, look for heavy, firm product with no cracking or soft spots.

Pack Size: 40 lb/18.14 kg crates
Shelf Life: 1 to 2 months
Storage Conditions: 50° to 55°F/10° to 13°C
Season: Mostly available in the late fall to early winter

DELICATA

Delicata squash is a very delicious heirloom variety. It is also known as the peanut squash, due to its crinkled rind and shape, or the sweet potato squash because of the similarity in flavor. The sweet, tasty flesh is creamy in texture and can be cooked by baking or steaming. The skin is more tender and delicate than many other winter squashes, and is actually edible, but not commonly eaten. The more delicate nature of this squash's texture may be the reason this heirloom squash at one time almost disappeared from the market, but the quality of its flavor is surely why it has come back. That more fragile constitution is why this squash is best used from late summer until early to mid-autumn when it is available at your local farm market. Look for good firm squash with no soft areas or mold and no signs of dehydration.

> **Pack size:** 40 lb/18.14 kg crates
> **Shelf life:** up to 1 month
> **Storage Conditions:** 50° to 55°F/10° to 13°C
> **Season:** Mostly available year-round but always better in the late fall to early winter

HUBBARD

The Hubbard is a monster winter squash that can grow from fairly large to massive in size, with a blue-gray, mottled, and warty rind. These squashes will often be sold cut in pieces as they can reach well over 20 lb/9.07 kg. There is also a relatively scarce golden variety, but the ugly, gray one eats much better, having a richer sweet flavor. That heavy rind also gives the Hubbard an excellent, long shelf life. The size of this squash can make it cumbersome to handle and lengthen its cooking times. The rind, stringy center, and seeds are inedible.

Despite the effort it takes to break down this big squash, the Hubbard's flesh is well worth the trouble. The sweet, dense, dark orange meat can be cubed and steamed or baked, puréed into a soup, or made into a great "pumpkin" pie. The flesh also freezes well. The pie is reputed to be better than the much more famous pumpkin alternative. Don't let this squash's looks or size scare you; when cooking for a crowd it is a good choice.

> **Pack Size:** 40 lb/18.14 kg crates
> **Shelf Life:** up to 6 months
> **Storage Conditions:** 50° to 55°F/10° to 13°C
> **Season:** Mostly available year-round but always better in the late fall to early winter

Nutritional Information

Serving Size:	3-1/2 oz/100 g
Water:	88 g
Calories:	40
Protein:	2 g
Fat:	0.5 g
Saturated Fat:	0.103 g
Sodium:	7 mg
Iron:	0.4 mg
Potassium:	320 mg
Vitamin C:	11 mg

FIGURE **11.4** Hubbard Squash

KABOCHA, BUTTERCUP

Kabocha is Japanese in origin and closely related to the Buttercup squash, both of which are in the Turban family of winter squashes. Both squashes have very hard rinds, are dark green/gray in color, and are squat and dense in nature. The flesh is drier than most other winter squashes, dark orange and very sweet; the buttercup's flesh will be creamier than the kabocha's, which is dense and dry enough to be flaky. Both varieties can be cooked in any manner from poached to baked to steamed and puréed and can be used in lieu of sweet potatoes in certain applications. Always look for good heavy specimens with no soft spots.

Pack Size: 40 lb/18.14 kg crates
Shelf Life: up to 6 months
Storage Conditions: 50° to 55°F/10° to 13°C
Season: Mostly available year-round but
always better in the late fall to early winter

PUMPKIN

The pumpkin is a large, gourd-like winter squash. The most commonly found are large, round, bright orange pumpkins and are not meant to be eaten. They have watery, stringy flesh and are best used for their most common purpose: decorative carving. These can be fairly small to extremely large in size and very round or the traditional "jack-o'-lantern" shape. Enjoy the seasonal look, but don't eat them.

Sugar pumpkins are typically 5 lb/2.27 kg and are about the size of a small bowling ball. These have a thicker, less stringy flesh with a creamier texture. They have a thin, paler orange rind and are a good choice for cooking.

Mini pumpkins are about 4 inches/10 centimeters in diameter and 3 inches/ 7.5 centimeters tall. These can be utilized by hollowing them out and baking the shell to serve as soup bowls for a festive autumnal occasion, but are really simply decorative.

Cheese pumpkins are the best pumpkin for making pies as they have a dark orange, sweet, thick flesh. This is a buff-colored pumpkin that weighs about 6 to 10 lb/2.72 kg to 4.54 kg and is a cultivar of the heirloom Long Island cheese pumpkin.

All pumpkins should be very heavy for their size, with the stem intact. Avoid anything still green, cracked, or with any soft spots.

SPAGHETTI SQUASH

The spaghetti squash is a pale yellow, football- or watermelon-shaped squash that gets its name from the way the yellow flesh comes out of the rind in long thin strands once it is cooked. Look for the most yellow rind possible as the flesh will be sweeter, nuttier, and flavorful. Whitish, pale yellow rinds indicate the squash is not mature enough. A newer variety to the market called the Orangetti has a gold to

orange rind, orange-yellow flesh, and is sweeter and higher in beta carotene than its paler cousin.

Cook the squash by halving it, removing the seeds, and then boiling or baking until fully tender. The flesh can then be raked out of the rind with a fork into long pasta-like strands. Like spaghetti, this is delicious tossed in butter or olive oil, garlic, and tossed with grated cheese. Spaghetti squash should be quite heavy for its size with good color and no soft spots that penetrate the rind.

Pack Size: 40 lb/18.14 kg crates
Shelf Life: up to 1 month
Storage Conditions: 50° to 55°F/10° to 13°C
Season: Mostly available year-round but always better in the late fall to early winter

Nutritional Information

Serving Size:	3-1/2 oz/100 g
Water:	91.60 g
Calories:	31
Protein:	0.64 g
Fat:	0.57 g
Saturated Fat:	0.117 g
Sodium:	17 mg
Iron:	0.31 mg
Potassium:	108 mg
Vitamin C:	2.1 mg

SWEET DUMPLING

The sweet dumpling squash is a small winter squash, suitable for a single-serving size. They have a yellow- to cream-colored rind with a green stripe between the ribs, making them a treat for the eyes as well as delicious to eat. The orange flesh is mild and sweet. These are delightful roasted and served whole or consider using the roasted, hollowed-out shell as a vessel for squash soup.

SUMMER SQUASH

The classification of squash designated as summer squash are those that are picked when immature so that they are tender with a soft and edible rind. These are at their peak when very young and small, and need to be consumed fairly soon after harvest as they have a short shelf life. Such squash should be small, firm, and unblemished with no puckering, scarring, or soft spots. The summer squash designation refers to when these were only available during the warmer months; availability is generally year-round now. The entire squash, except either tip, can be eaten. The following are all classified as summer squashes.

CHAYOTE, MIRLITON

The chayote is a major influence in Mexican cuisine, although most commercially available chayote comes from Central America. Chayotes most commonly found in the market look like a slightly flattened, light green pear with deep wrinkles. This squash has one large seed, which is commonly discarded despite being edible and nutty in flavor. Chayote tastes like a cross between a cucumber and an apple. The flesh of the chayote can be consumed raw, pickled, puréed, roasted, or stuffed and baked. When stuffing a chayote, the cooked seed may be mashed and mixed into the stuffing for a complementary and nutty flavor. The skin may be left on and is edible. The chayote can also be used in a spicy soup made with onions, garlic, chiles, and cilantro. Avoid purchasing chayotes that have a sticky and discolored rind.

FIGURE **11.6** Chayotes

Pack Size: 14 to 15 lb/6.35 to 6.8 kg flats
Shelf Life: 7 to 10 days
Storage Conditions: 45° to 50°F/7° to 10°C
Season: Available year-round

Nutritional Information

Serving Size:	3-1/2 oz/100 g
Water:	94.24 g
Calories:	19
Protein:	0.82 g
Fat:	0.13 g
Saturated Fat:	0.028 g
Fiber:	1.7 g
Sodium:	2 mg
Iron:	0.34 mg
Potassium:	125 mg
Vitamin C:	7.7 mg

PATTYPAN

The pattypan is a small, round summer squash with a scalloped edge. This vegetable should be eaten when very young and tender or not at all. Pattypans are found with pale green, yellow, or white rinds. This squash can be cooked whole, quartered, roasted, and sautéed, or halved, scooped out, and stuffed. Look for squash that are only 1 to 1-1/2

FIGURE **11.7** Pattypan Squash

inches/3 to 4 centimeters across with no softening or mold at the stem or browning and cracking along the scalloped rim. When not in season locally, most pattypans are imported from Central America. This is mainly due to high labor cost in harvesting such tiny squashes. As winter deepens, the prices tend to soar. Careful inspection for quality is essential when receiving due to their perishable nature.

Pack Size: 10 lb/4.54 kg box
Shelf Life: 3 to 5 days
Storage Conditions: 40° to 50°F/4° to 10°C
Season: Available year-round

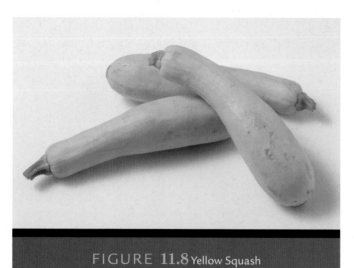

FIGURE **11.8** Yellow Squash

YELLOW SQUASH

Yellow summer squash comes as straight neck, which looks like a yellow zucchini, and crookneck, which tapers and is bent on the stem end. These have dull yellow and bumpy rinds. Beware of excessive bumping and pitting as this may mean the squash is drying out like a gourd. Essentially the yellow squash can be used in many of the same ways as the zucchini and, when combined, give a contrast in color on the plate. Although very similar, the zucchini is a bit more assertive in flavor than the blander yellow squash, and you may prefer to use the gold or yellow zucchini instead when that is available.

Pack Size: 1/2 bushel (18 to 20 lb/8.16 to 9.07 kg)
Shelf Life: 3 to 5 days
Storage Conditions: 40° to 50°F/4° to 10°C
Season: Available year-round but best in the summer months

ZUCCHINI

The zucchini is the most popular of the summer squashes. Most commonly available with a dark green rind, zucchini is also available at certain times of the year with a striking bright yellow to gold rind, referred to as Gold Bar squash. The gold variety taste and cook exactly the same but add excellent contrast and eye appeal to the plate. Zucchini is best between 6 to 8 inches/15 to 20 centimeters in length with smooth straight sides. In the summer, many chefs seek out the tiny baby zucchini (courgettes), especially with the beautiful blossom still attached.

FIGURE **11.9** Green and Yellow Zucchini

Squash blossoms are also sold separately and have become more popular in recent years. These are delicate orange flowers that can be filled with cheese, battered and fried, or cooked into a frittata. These can also be eaten raw or added to a soup. These blossoms are incredibly fragile and have a very short shelf life, so buy only what you can use within a day or two. Once these were only available from your local farmer, but blossoms imported from Israel can now be sourced for most of the year.

Zucchini is a relatively inexpensive, readily available, and exceptionally versatile squash. It is excellent for stuffing, sautéing, grilling, deep-frying, or combined with other vegetables for dishes such as ratatouille. Zucchini can also be grated, combined with onions, fried into pancakes, or baked into a quick bread. Zucchini that is oversized can be stuffed and baked by splitting it in half and scooping away the seeds. Look for heavy, straight firm squash with good color; avoid those that are dimpling, shriveled, and flabby.

FIGURE **11.10** Flowering Zucchini Courgettes

Pack Size: 1/2 bushel (18 to 20 lb/8.16 to 9.07 kg)
Shelf Life: 3 to 5 days
Storage Conditions: 40° to 50°F/4° to 10°C
Season: Available year-round but best in the summer months

Nutritional Information

Serving Size:	3-1/2 oz/100 g
Water:	94.64 g
Calories:	16
Protein:	1.21 g
Fat:	0.18 g
Saturated Fat:	0.037 g
Fiber:	1.1 g
Sodium:	10 mg
Iron:	0.35 mg
Potassium:	262 mg
Vitamin C:	17 mg

CUCUMBERS

The cucumber is related to the squash family and, as such, is technically a fruit, but in culinary terms is considered a vegetable due to its mild, bitter/sour flavor. Cucumbers are eaten when immature and dark green in color. They ripen to a yellow color but are far too sour for any culinary purpose at that point. Full-size cucumbers are referred to as slicers and smaller varieties are for pickling. Cucumbers can be served raw, pickled, or cooked into sauces. Look for firm cucumbers with good color that are heavy for their size, with no puckering, shriveled skin, or soft spots.

SEEDLESS, EUROPEAN, OR DUTCH CUCUMBERS

These cucumbers are longer (12 to 15 inches/30 to 37.5 centimeters) and narrower than the standard cucumber. They have thin, ridged, dark green skin and taper at both ends. These are usually grown in hothouses and come wrapped in cellophane to retain their moisture. The term *seedless* is used, but they do have a lesser amount of small, immature seeds. The European cucumber is often referred to as "burpless" as many people find them easier to digest. These are generally preferred for their long uniform shape, the lack of seeds, and their milder, less bitter flavor. The seedless or European cucumber can be used in all the same culinary applications as the standard cucumber. They do command a higher price, but have an excellent yield. Check the cucumbers on receipt for any withered or softening tissue; only accept firm, solid cucumbers with no dehydration or signs of mold.

FIGURE **11.11** Seedless Cucumber

Pack Size: Usually packed 12 to a box
Shelf Life: 5 to 10 days
Storage Conditions: 50° to 55°F/10° to 13°C
Season: Available year-round

SLICING OR STANDARD CUCUMBERS

The slicing cucumber can be any one of several varieties of cucumbers and are the types commonly found in the supermarket. These cucumbers will range from 6 to 8 inches/15 to 20 centimeters long and taper at each end. They have a dark green skin that is usually smooth, but some types have a bumpy or warty appearance. The skin on these cucumbers is thick and dark green and ones found commercially are generally waxed to retain the moisture content. Waxed cucumbers should be peeled or heavily scrubbed prior to eating. Some yellow color in the skin is acceptable but avoid those that show much yellowing as they will be bitter. Many recipes suggest slicing, salting, and leaving cucumbers in a colander for 20 minutes to remove bitterness and extract excess moisture.

Cucumbers can be pickled or used in salads in many different ways. They are used in so many cuisines, Middle Eastern, American, Mediterranean, and Asian; the options seem endless.

FIGURE **11.12** Standard Cucumber

Pack Size: 50 lb/22.7 kg crates

Shelf Life: 5 to 8 days

Storage Conditions: 50° to 55°F/10° to 13°C

Season: Available year-round but best when purchased at a local farm stand

Nutritional Information

Serving Size:	3-1/2 oz/100 g
Water:	95.23 g
Calories:	15
Protein:	0.65 g
Fat:	0.11 g
Saturated Fat:	0.037 g
Fiber:	0.5 g
Sodium:	2 mg
Iron:	0.28 mg
Potassium:	147 mg
Vitamin C:	2.8 mg

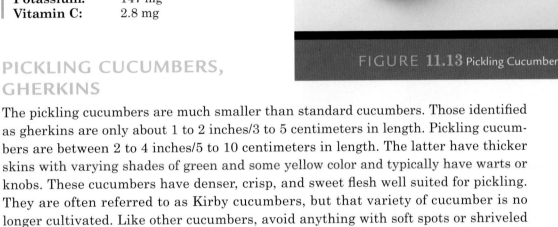

FIGURE **11.13** Pickling Cucumber

PICKLING CUCUMBERS, GHERKINS

The pickling cucumbers are much smaller than standard cucumbers. Those identified as gherkins are only about 1 to 2 inches/3 to 5 centimeters in length. Pickling cucumbers are between 2 to 4 inches/5 to 10 centimeters in length. The latter have thicker skins with varying shades of green and some yellow color and typically have warts or knobs. These cucumbers have denser, crisp, and sweet flesh well suited for pickling. They are often referred to as Kirby cucumbers, but that variety of cucumber is no longer cultivated. Like other cucumbers, avoid anything with soft spots or shriveled flesh. These should be well-colored and very firm in texture.

Pack Size: Pickling cucumber: 50 lb/22.7 kg case; Gherkins: 5 to 10 lb/2.27 to 4.54 kg case

Shelf Life: 5 to 8 days

Storage Conditions: 50° to 55°F/10° to 13°C

Season: Available year-round but best when purchased at your local farm stand

EGGPLANT, AUBERGINE, MELANZANE

The eggplant is yet another of a variety of fruits thought of and treated as vegetables because of their flavor and culinary applications. These are members of the Nightshade family that includes potatoes, chile peppers, and tomatoes. Like chile peppers, eggplants come in many sizes, shapes, and colors. They are not of Italian origin, as many assume, but date back to ancient Asia. Eggplants are identified in several varieties, but exact definitions of each are difficult to quantify. These will all have slight variations in flavor, texture, and bitterness levels. That said, once cooked they all have a spongy, white, firm flesh and a pleasantly bitter flavor that is adaptable to many cuisines and recipes.

Be sure when receiving eggplant that it is heavy for its size and firm with no soft spots or shriveling. They should have a good clean color and shine to the skin. These standards are applicable with all varieties of eggplant.

Before cooking eggplant, decide whether it is best to peel or not depending on the application. If the skin is thick and tough, it will be less appetizing to eat. If it is thin and tender, peeling is not required. If not roasting the eggplant whole, it is thought to be advantageous to salt the flesh prior to cooking. The sliced or diced flesh should be liberally salted and allowed to sit in a colander for approximately 20 minutes. This will draw much of the moisture and bitterness out. Rinse off the salt and drain it again before cooking. Doing this should make the eggplant less bitter, less able to absorb oil in cooking and less able to leach water into the dish being created. The real benefit in reducing the bitterness is often debated however as some believe the added labor has little effect on the final outcome.

FIGURE **11.14** Japanese Eggplant

FIGURE **11.15** Thai Eggplant

ASIAN EGGPLANT

These eggplants are longer and relatively thin fruits that have a tapered point instead of a heavy bulbous end. The variety referred to as Japanese is generally a heavier and denser eggplant with a deep purple skin. Those with a pale violet or lavender to almost white skin are referred to as Chinese. These tend to be sweeter, more delicate, and have a lower seed count, making them a good addition to stir-fries and a nice pair with assertive seasoning. The skin of both of these eggplants is thinner and very tender, making them good to eat. These eggplants should have a good color and firm, heavy flesh; avoid anything soft or shriveled in texture.

Pack Size: 10 lb/4.54 kg boxes
Shelf Life: 4 to 7 days
Storage Conditions: 45 to 55°F/7 to 13°C
Season: Available year-round but best when purchased at your local farm stand

THAI EGGPLANT

The Thai eggplant is a small round eggplant with a green and white skin. These eggplants are integral to cooking in both Thai and Laotian cuisines. They are generally quartered and will absorb the flavors of the stews and curries in which they are cooked. The flesh of these eggplants is crunchy and fairly bitter, which makes it pair well with the spicy foods in these cultures. Like all eggplants, these should be heavy for their size with a taut, firm flesh. Avoid any eggplants that are showing soft spots or starting to wither.

WESTERN, STANDARD, GLOBE EGGPLANT

These are the large, pear-shaped, dark purple eggplant most common in today's market. There are innumerable ways to prepare and enjoy eggplant; roasted until meltingly soft and puréed, fried, parmigiana, in caponata and other relishes, and braised with peppers, onions, and zucchini in ratatouille. Due to their large production and travel requirements for the mass market, these types of eggplant tend to have a thicker, tougher skin than other cultivars in the market. The flesh is also more fibrous than and not quite as flavorful as some of the other varieties. When selecting these, look for eggplants that are hefty for their size, firm, and shiny. Avoid those with poor color, soft and browning areas, and with a washed-out or pale appearance in the skin. The stem or calyx must be fuzzy and firmly attached with no sign of mold. The Western types of eggplant are larger than most other varieties, but avoid those that are very large in comparison as they are likely too old and bitter.

Pack Size: 25 lb/11.34 kg case
Shelf Life: 4 to 7 days
Storage Conditions: 45° to 55°F/7° to 13°C
Season: Available year-round but best when purchased at your local farm stand

Nutritional Information

Serving Size:	3-1/2 oz/100 g
Water:	92.41 g
Calories:	24
Protein:	1.01 g
Fat:	0.19 g
Saturated Fat:	0.034 g
Fiber:	3.4 g
Sodium:	2 mg
Iron:	0.24 mg
Potassium:	230 mg
Vitamin C:	2.2 mg

FIGURE **11.16** Standard Eggplant

FIGURE **11.17** Italian Eggplant

WHITE EGGPLANT

The white eggplant is not as prevalent in the market as the purple varieties, but it is believed that this was the original eggplant cultivated. The term *eggplant* reputedly comes from the shape and color of this variety. The white skin is tougher and therefore requires peeling prior to cooking. The flesh is dense, tender, and creamier with less bitterness and a delicate flavor. These are also smaller in size than the commonly found Western or standard purple eggplant. This type is usually only found in the market during the summer season. These should be very firm and heavy for their size, with no soft or discolored areas or a loose stem.

FIGURE **11.18** White Eggplant

FIGURE **11.19** Speckled Eggplant

HERBS

Herbs are the fragrant leafy parts of certain plants that have non-woody stems. They are prized for the aroma and flavor they impart to the food we cook. These differ from spices in that the latter come from the plant's bark, roots, fruits, or seeds as opposed to the leaves and foliage. Herbs have been cultivated for nearly all of recorded history and have always been held in high esteem for their aroma, flavor, and medicinal properties.

Herbs are generally found both fresh and dried but this chapter will focus on their fresh form. Fresh herbs are very fragile, have a short shelf life, and should be utilized quickly before they lose their essential oils and began to wither or mold. Fresh herbs should be added late in the cooking process to highlight the delightful yet fragile and fleeting flavor. Typically only the delicate leaves are utilized in final cooking, but the stems will supply excellent flavor to stocks, sauces, and broths and are simply strained out before service or final use.

The following herbs were once only found fresh at certain times of the season. However, due to the hydroponics growing method and the ability to fly imported product in quickly, herbs are now found year-round. As noted, these are highly perishable, so choose herbs carefully when buying; they should be clean, vibrant, and carry a full, strong aroma. When rubbed between finger and thumb, they should release their oils and the aroma should be more pronounced. Avoid anything that is wilted, turning black, and/or exhibiting an off or sour aroma. Having little or no aroma at all is a sign that an herb is past its prime, even if the appearance seems acceptable.

Herbs should be tasted before adding to the dish being prepared; even though the flavor can dissipate relatively quickly, the flavor can be quite assertive at first and dominate a dish unless utilized judiciously. These flavors are associated with the cuisine of the part of the world where the herb originated. Therefore, although experimentation is good and there are no rules, certain herbs will often best complement the cuisines where they came from originally.

BASIL, SWEET BASIL

This very popular herb originated in India and spread worldwide; it is utilized widely in the cuisines of the Mediterranean. Basil comes from the mint family, is extremely aromatic, and has a flavor that can be reminiscent of a combination of mint, oregano, and licorice or anise with a hint of pepper. The climate where the basil is grown will have an influence on its flavor profile; basil grown where it is cooler will be sweeter and that which is grown in warmer climates will have a more peppery bite.

Basil is perhaps best known for its affinity with the flavor of tomatoes, whether in sauce, in a tomato, bread, and basil panzanella, or pizza margherita. The combination is wonderful and exceptionally popular. Pesto is a rich, thick paste made from pine nuts, parmesan cheese, garlic, olive oil, and basil that is used as a flavoring or to dress pasta. Basil is also a wonderful flavor to infuse into olive oil or vinegar.

There are other forms of basil in the market as well. Lemon and cinnamon basil are so named because each has flavor undertones that evokes its given name. Purple basil is a beautiful red-purple color and, like Thai Basil, has a more pungent bite that works well with the cuisine of Southeast Asia. When cut into chiffonade and floated into a hot broth, it adds visual appeal, flavor, and an appetite-arousing aroma to the dish. Thai basil can be identified by its distinctive red stems and small dark green leaves that are more tapered than round. Look for this herb in Asian markets and from specialty produce vendors.

Basil can come in various sized leaves and hues but always look for a full bright color, vibrancy to the leaf, and warm full aroma. Avoid anything wilted, showing signs of black deterioration, badly sagging stems and leaves, or with an off aroma. The basil stems can be wrapped in moist paper towels to extend the shelf life, but it is highly perishable and best used quickly.

Pack Size: By the pound or kilogram
Shelf Life: 1 to 2 days under refrigeration. Always use as soon as possible.
Storage Conditions: 50°F/10°C
Season: Available year-round but always best fresh at your local farm stand

FIGURE **12.1** Left to right: Basil and Thai Basil

FIGURE **12.2** Purple Basil

Nutritional Information

Serving Size:	3-1/2 oz/100 g
Water:	92.06 g
Calories:	23
Protein:	3.15 g
Fat:	0.64 g
Saturated Fat:	0.041 g
Fiber:	1.6 g
Sodium:	4 mg
Iron:	3.17 mg
Potassium:	295 mg
Vitamin C:	18 mg

FIGURE **12.3** Bay Leaves

BAY LEAF, LAUREL

This is more often found dried but sometimes you will be lucky enough to find fresh bay leaf, which will have a more rich and intense flavor. This flavor lessens as the leaf dehydrates with age, so bruise or shred the herb to release more oils before adding it to the dish. The leaves should be bright, full green, glossy, approximately 2 inches/5 centimeters long, and tapered to a point at each end. The slightly bitter flavor of this spice complements many dishes such as savory soups, beef stews, tomato sauce, and even sweet custard. Bay is an integral part of the herb bundle bouquet garni, is ground with other herbs for seasoning mixes, and works well with seafood. There are several types of bay leaves, the most common being Turkish and California. The Turkish is a bit smaller and milder in flavor but both can be used interchangeably. When you do find fresh bay be sure to utilize it quickly as the leaves deteriorate and fade in flavor quickly.

Pack Size: by the pound or ounce
Shelf Life: 4 to 5 days under refrigeration
Storage Conditions: 40°F/4°C
Season: Available year-round but best when purchased at your local farm stand

CILANTRO

Cilantro is a standard in Latin American, Caribbean, and Asian cuisines where it is heavily utilized and appreciated. Outside of those cultures, this herb generates a love-it or hate-it attitude like no other. Many people find its unusual, bright pungency to be exotic and palate pleasing, while many others revile it for its soapy or chemical taste and weird smell. Whatever your viewpoint, it cannot be argued that cilantro is one of the predominate herbs used in the world.

The leaves look similar to flat-leaf parsley, but are more delicate and a paler shade of green. It has a flavor all its own but may best be described as part anise and part parsley. This is a delicate herb that will wilt and start to slime quickly, so choose carefully when you buy and use it as quickly as possible. Avoid any cilantro that looks

wilted, is exhibiting slime or mold, and has lost its distinctive aroma. Depending on your application, the more tender stems may be minced and used along with the leaves to further the flavor and yield. Again, perishability is an issue. Wrapping the cilantro in damp paper towels may help extend its life, but only purchase what you can use within a day or two if possible.

As noted, this herb is used in more ways than we can list here such as salsas, chile sauces, marinades, an unusual pesto, Indian curries and relishes, and most Southeast Asian dishes such as pad thai and pho.

Pack Size: By the pound, kilogram, or crate (usually 10 to 12 lb/4.54 to 5.44 kg)
Shelf Life: 2 to 3 days under refrigeration
Storage Conditions: 40°F/4°C
Season: Available year-round but best when purchased at your local farm stand

Nutritional Information

Serving Size:	3-1/2 oz/100 g
Water:	92.21 g
Calories:	23
Protein:	2.13 g
Fat:	0.52 g
Saturated Fat:	0.014 g
Fiber:	2.8 g
Sodium:	46 mg
Iron:	1.77 mg
Potassium:	521 mg
Vitamin C:	27 mg

CHERVIL

Chervil is a frilly, pale green, delicate herb that has a mild anise-like in flavor and looks a little like delicate curly parsley, to which it is related. The herb is utilized extensively in French cooking and is a key ingredient in fines herbes, with equal parts chopped parsley, tarragon, chervil, and chives. Due to its fragile nature, this herb is very weather dependent and becomes quite scarce in the coldest times of winter and in the heat of summer. Chervil's delicate nature also means this herb has a short shelf life and will degrade quickly, so buy carefully and use

quickly. Avoid cooking chervil as the flavor dissipates quickly under heat. It is best used as a finishing herb or in an herb-infused oil with parsley and chives to dress fish.

> **Pack Size:** By the ounce, pound, or kilogram
> **Shelf Life:** 2 days
> **Storage Conditions:** 45°F/7°C
> **Season:** Beware of gaps in the market in winter and summer but it is usually available year-round

CHIVES

The chive is an herb related to the onion family and will provide a distinctly pleasant onion-like flavor. This herb is a long, slender, hollow tube that tapers into a long, thin delicate point. As with most herbs, it is delicate in nature and the flavor comes from the juicy oils in its stalk. It is best added to dishes at the end of cooking to allow its wonderful, mild flavor to come through. Chives will produce a delicate lavender flower that is also delicious and adds eye appeal when added as a garnish to a dish. The chive is a key ingredient in fines herbes, along with equal parts of parsley, chervil, and tarragon, and also work very well scrambled into eggs, with smoked salmon, whipped into soft cheeses, and snipped over broiled fish or poultry. Beware of sliming and wilted or dehydrated stalks when purchasing and be sure to utilize it quickly.

FIGURE **12.6** Chives

> **Pack Size:** By the ounce, pound, or kilogram
> **Shelf Life:** 2 to 3 days
> **Storage Conditions:** 40°F/4°C
> **Season:** Available year-round but best when purchased from your local farm stand

Nutritional Information

Serving Size:	3-1/2 oz/100 g
Water:	90.65 g
Calories:	30
Protein:	3.27 g
Fat:	0.73 g
Saturated Fat:	0.146 g
Fiber:	2.5 g
Sodium:	3 mg
Iron:	1.6 mg
Potassium:	296 mg
Vitamin C:	58.1 mg

CURRY LEAVES

This herb is native to Southeast Asia and has a strong, pungent fragrance. The leaves are small, shiny, bright green in color, and shaped much like a lemon leaf with scalloped edges. This herb's flavor is used throughout the cooking of its native India. Avoid anything that is not fresh and vibrant or with any wilting or yellowing. The leaves tolerate freezing and drying but will yield a less pungent flavor.

> **Pack Size:** by the pound
> **Shelf Life:** 3 to 4 days
> **Storage Conditions:** 34°F/1°C
> **Season:** Available year round

FIGURE **12.7** Curry Leaves

DILL

Dill is a feathery green herb with an assertive aroma. This herb is most widely known as a flavoring in pickled vegetables, but it also accompanies salmon well, is good whipped into soft cheese, as flavoring for herring, and in vegetable salads. Dill will also produce white flowers as it grows which can add flavor to brines and marinades. Dill is available year-round but should be used quickly as the flavor will fade. Look for light feathery fronds with no sign of wilting. Wrapping the dill in damp paper towels may help extend its life, but only purchase what you can use within a day or two if possible.

> **Pack Size:** By the ounce, pound, or kilogram
> **Shelf Life:** 2 to 3 days
> **Storage Conditions:** 40°F/4°C
> **Season:** Available year-round but best when purchased from your local farm stand

Nutritional Information

Serving Size:	3-1/2 oz/100 g
Water:	85.95 g
Calories:	43
Protein:	3.46 g
Fat:	1.12 g
Saturated fat:	0.06 g
Fiber:	2.1 g
Sodium:	61 mg
Iron:	6.59 mg
Potassium:	738 mg
Vitamin C:	85 mg

FIGURE **12.8** Dill

EPAZOTE

Epazote is a very pungent herb that grows in the wild and is most commonly used in Southwestern and Mexican dishes, especially bean dishes and soups. The herb is not often found fresh in commercial markets but can usually be found in its dried form, where its flavor is more subdued.

> **Pack Size:** by the pound
> **Shelf Life:** 2 to 3 days
> **Storage Conditions:** 40°F/4°C
> **Season:** Usually available year-round

LAVENDER FLOWER

Lavender is a fragrant member of the mint family that is most often used to flavor teas or a tisane. This herb has pale violet flowers and green/gray leaves. Its flavor creates a love/hate reaction much as cilantro can inspire. Some find the floral tones pleasantly savory and others revile the soapy taste it can illicit. This herb can also be ground with other herbs in spice rubs and used to flavor baked goods.

> **Pack Size:** by the pound
> **Shelf Life:** 3 to 4 days
> **Storage Conditions:** 40°F/4°C
> **Season:** Available year-round

LEMONGRASS

Lemongrass is integral to the cuisines of Southeast Asia, especially Thailand and Vietnam. The herb has a dense, bulbous base and tightly wound leaves that extend up to over a foot in length. Lemongrass is best used sliced or cut into lengths and then crushed or bruised to release its lemony oils before adding to soups and stews. It is an excellent flavoring for seafood and poultry dishes and any dishes that are brightly spiced. Look for firm, heavy stalks that have not begun to dehydrate.

> **Pack Size:** by the pound
> **Shelf Life:** 3 to 4 days
> **Storage Conditions:** 33°F/.5°C
> **Season:** Available year round

FIGURE **12.9** Lavender Flower

FIGURE **12.10** Lemongrass

LEMON VERBENA

Lemon verbena is a long, thin, pale green leafed herb with a strong citrus lemon flavor that is best used sparingly. This works well in fruit salads and to scent cocktails and can be used as a substitute for lemongrass in Southeast Asian recipes.

Pack Size: by the ounce, pound or kilo
Shelf Life: 2 to 3 days
Storage Conditions: 40°F/4°C
Season: Available year round in the south and late spring and summer in the north

LOVAGE

Lovage is similar in scent and flavor to very potent celery. It has deep green, celery-like leaves and stalks but is much stronger in flavor. Lovage is fairly expensive when it can be found, but the flavor will go a long way. It works very well in a cream-based seafood soup. The stalks can also be cooked as a vegetable, but are not suitable for long braises; both the leaf and stem are best when quickly cooked.

Pack Size: by the ounce, pound or kilo
Shelf Life: 2 to 3 days
Storage Conditions: 40°F/4°C
Season: Late spring and summer

MARJORAM

Marjoram is akin to oregano, so much so that it is somewhat difficult to differentiate the two. Both herbs are members of the mint family. The leaves are small and round-ish with a mottled green appearance. The golden strains of marjoram will have a pale yellow blush to their upper leaves but they are used in the same manner. The flavor of this herb is strongly affected by the climate and soil where it is grown but will always have an affinity for the food of the Mediterranean, where it originated. Marjoram will be more nuanced and delicate than the assertive oregano but it also works well in Greek dishes, with lamb, tomato-based dishes, and pizza.

Marjoram's delicate nature gives it an even shorter shelf life than many other herbs. Be careful in selecting product and only buy what you can utilize quickly. Avoid wilting leaves or those exhibiting any signs of slime or decay. The scent should be bright and appetizing, not sour.

FIGURE **12.11** Marjoram

Pack Size: By the ounce, pound, or kilogram
Shelf Life: 2 to 3 days
Storage Conditions: 40°F/4°C
Season: Available year-round but best when purchased from your local farm stand

MINT

The mint family encompasses a broad variety of herbs, such as oregano, sage, and basil, and there are over 30 varieties of mint. The two most widely known and used in foodservice are peppermint and spearmint. Spearmint is the most commonly found variety in savory dishes. It has paler green and toothed leaves with a smoother, less assertive flavor that matches well with lamb, potatoes, and peas. If you muddle it with sugar and ice and add bourbon, spearmint makes for a great mint julep. There is red raripila spearmint which is rarely seen, but when available will be quite a bit more assertive. Apple spearmint has sweet, rounder, yellow-flecked leaves and will be the mildest of all. Peppermint has smoother shaped, darker green and purple leaves. Its assertive peppery flavor melds well with sweet treats and is used in oils and cordials.

Mint leaves should smell fresh and bright and the leaves should be brightly colored with no signs of deterioration such as black slimy leaves.

Pack Size: By the ounce, pound, or kilogram
Shelf Life: 2 to 3 days
Storage Conditions: 40°F/4°C
Season: Available year-round but best when purchased from your local farm stand

Nutritional Information

Serving Size:	3-1/2 oz/100 g
Water:	85.55 g
Calories:	44
Protein:	3.29 g
Fat:	0.73 g
Saturated fat:	0.191 g
Fiber:	6.8 g
Sodium:	30 mg
Iron:	11.87 mg
Potassium:	458 mg
Vitamin C:	13.3 mg

FIGURE **12.12** Spearmint

OREGANO

Oregano is the quintessential pizza herb, bright, assertive, and prized by many. Oregano is a member of the mint family and is very much like the aforementioned marjoram but with a bit more bite to it. Oregano also works very well in pasta sauces, salad dressings, and poultry and Greek dishes. Oregano has a medium green, oval-shaped leaf and exhibits an assertive aroma. Like basil, oregano is affected by the soil and climate of

FIGURE **12.13** Oregano

where it is grown, so there will be some definite fluctuation in the assertiveness of the flavor. Look for bright, vibrant leaves with an assertive aroma; avoid anything wilted or showing other signs of decay or an off odor.

Pack Size: By the ounce, pound, or kilogram
Shelf Life: 2 to 3 days
Storage Conditions: 40°F/4°C
Season: Available year-round but best when purchased from your local farm stand

BANANA LEAVES

Banana leaves are large, flat, green leaves that are used decoratively as a base to present other foods or as the plate in some cultures. They are also commonly utilized as a wrapper to steam other foods, much like corn husks function when making tamales. This use of banana leaves is quite prevalent in the cuisines of the Caribbean, Mexico, and South and Central America as well as in Southeast Asia. These leaves add not only beauty to the presentation but also a slight vegetable sweetness to the dish contained within. Used a wrapper, the banana leaf can be baked and grilled as well as steamed; when grilled, a light smoky flavor is also added to the food. These are available both fresh and frozen. If found whole, these leaves can be well over several feet in length and 2 feet wide; they also come pre-cut in single serving sized shapes. Banana leaves should have a dark shiny green color and a crisp texture.

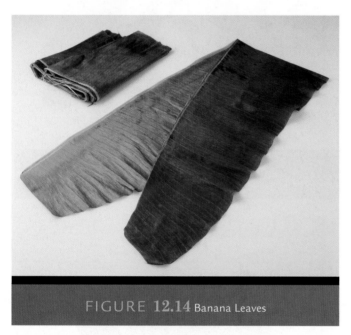

FIGURE **12.14** Banana Leaves

Pack Size: Frozen–Twenty 1 lb/454 g packs
Shelf Life: Indefinite
Storage Conditions: 32°F/0°C
Season: N/A

PANDAN LEAVES

Pandan leaf, also referred to as Pandanus and screw pine, is a leaf often used as a flavoring and food coloring in Southeast Asian cooking. These leaves have a pleasant fragrance not unlike aromatic rice which becomes more noticeable as the leaf wilts. These herbal tasting leaves are used to flavor rice, puddings, milk, and as a wrapper for food in some Thai dishes. They are long and narrow with a pointed tip. Look for a vibrant shiny leaf with various shades of green running lengthwise. Pandan is rather difficult to find fresh and is typically found in frozen packs in many Asian markets.

FIGURE **12.15** Pandan Leaves

Pack Size: 7 oz/198 g
Shelf Life: Indefinite if frozen
Storage Conditions: 32°F/0°C
Season: N/A

PARSLEY

Curly parsley is the very common, bright green, curly herb so frequently used as a garnish in foodservice. This is a nutritious and attractive herb that is unfortunately lacking in flavor, especially once cooked, which results in its most widespread use as a garnish. When using chopped parsley as an ingredient or garnish, be sure to wring the excess moisture out once it is chopped to prevent clumping and mold from forming. As appearance is everything with curly parsley, be sure the color is solid and bright, the frilly leaves are vibrant, and there is no sign of decay. There should be a bright vegetable aroma.

Flat-leaf or Italian parsley is the other common variety of parsley in foodservice. As the name suggests, this parsley has a broader flat leaf with a distinctive notched appearance. It too is dark green, but not as brightly colored as curly parsley. Italian parsley has a delicious mild vegetable flavor that holds up well during cooking and is used in too many dishes to name. It is a key component of bouquet garni, a classic seasoning tool, and is an essential part of persillade and gremolata, classic garnishes that also add great flavor to some classic dishes. The stems of flat parsley are utilized to flavor stocks and sauces when they are used in a traditional sachet. Look for firm, well-formed, and well-colored leaves when purchasing. Avoid parsley that has begun to wilt, fade, or slime. The aroma should be clean with no sour notes.

Pack Size: By the ounce, pound, or kilogram
Shelf Life: 2 to 3 days
Storage Conditions: 40°F/4°C
Season: Available year-round but best when purchased from your local farm stand

FIGURE **12.16** Curly Parsley

FIGURE **12.17** Flat Parsley

FIGURE **12.18** Rau Ram

RAU RAM

Also known as Vietnamese coriander, rau ram is a Southeast Asian herb that is very common to the cuisines in that part of the world and is not often found in American markets. This herb is greatly preferred in its fresh form and has a citrus or lemony, cilantro-like flavor. Rau ram is used raw in salads and as a flavoring in soups, stews, and spring rolls. Look for a narrow, speckled, dark green leaf on top with a deep red cast to the underside. Rau ram comes on a long stem and should be vibrant with a clean aroma. Avoid wilted or odorless product when receiving.

> **Pack Size:** By the pound
> **Shelf Life:** 2 days
> **Storage Conditions:** 40°F/4°C
> **Season:** Available year-round but may be hard to find

ROSEMARY

Rosemary is a silvery-green herb that has needle-shaped leaves and a distinctive aroma. The shape of the needle is reminiscent of pine but this herb is another member of the mint family. It has a characteristic potent flavor with undertones of both pine and lemon. Mediterranean in origin, this herb complements flavors such as olive oil and garlic well. Rosemary is used to season poultry, lamb, veal, and seafood. Small branches or skewers of rosemary are used like kabobs to hold and flavor foods such as scallops and vegetables. This herb also works really well in flavoring and perfuming roasted potatoes and garlic which makes a great side dish for roast lamb.

Rosemary should be firm and vibrant with no wilting, and redolent with its distinctive perfume. Avoid any leaves that are showing signs of mold at the tips, are parched looking, or are losing their scent.

FIGURE **12.19** Rosemary

Pack Size: By the ounce, pound, or kilogram
Shelf Life: 2 to 3 days
Storage Conditions: 40°F/4°C
Season: Available year-round but best when purchased from your local farm stand

Nutritional Information

Serving Size:	3-1/2 oz/100 g
Water:	67.77 g
Calories:	131
Protein:	3.31 g
Fat:	5.86 g
Saturated Fat:	2.838 g
Fiber:	14.1 g
Sodium:	26 mg
Iron:	6.65 mg
Potassium:	668 mg
Vitamin C:	21.8 mg

SAGE

Sage is another very aromatic herb of Mediterranean origin. The leaves are very distinctive with a silvery blue-green color, long and tapered body, and peach-like fuzz. The flavor is potent and unique and accompanies pork and organ meats very well. Lemon sage is a variety of sage with a strong, citrus scent. The full leaf can be deep-fried and added to dishes as a garnish. In the United States, sage is probably best known as a seasoning in poultry stuffing. As it ages, sage will wither and curl up, so look for flat vibrant leaves with a distinctive strong aroma and good color.

Pack Size: By the ounce, pound, or kilogram
Shelf Life: 2 to 3 days
Storage Conditions: 40°F/4°C
Season: Available year-round but best when purchased from your local farm stand

FIGURE **12.20** Sage

SAVORY

Savory is a strong, pungent-flavored herb that needs to be used sparingly so as to not dominate the other flavors in the dish. There are summer and winter varieties, both with flavors reminiscent of a blend of mint and thyme. The name of this herb alludes to the cooking term used to describe a rich and full flavor without sweetness.

The summer variety is somewhat milder but both forms are powerful. This unique combination of tastes works well in pâtés and with

FIGURE **12.21** Lemon Sage

FIGURE **12.22** Saw Leaf

members of the bean family. Try summer savory with fresh, tender varieties of green beans and the winter variety in heartier, dried bean recipes.

The summer savory will have flat, oblong leaves that are larger and rounder than the winter variety and may have small white flowers at the tip. The winter savory has a smaller, darker leaf and a coarser texture that coincides with its more pungent flavor. This herb may also have small flowers. When purchasing, avoid withered product or that which shows signs of decay, mold, or a lack of aroma.

Pack Size: By the ounce or pound
Shelf Life: 3 to 4 days
Storage Conditions: 40°F/4°C
Season: Available year-round

SAW LEAF, CULANTRO

Saw leaf is another herb from Southeast Asia and Mexico. It gets its name from the long, thin shape and serrated edges of its leaf. This herb's flavor could best be described as assertive cilantro and is best served in the spicy cuisines of Vietnam, Thailand, and India. This relative of cilantro is best fresh but also works well dried. Product should be crisp and vibrant with a pronounced aroma; avoid those with black slime or other signs of decay.

Pack Size: By the pound
Shelf Life: 2 to 3 days
Storage Conditions: 40°F/4°C
Season: Available year-round

SHISO LEAVES, PERILLA

Shiso has a spade-shaped leaf with a pronounced ridge of teeth around the upper edges and are found in either red or green colors. This herb is much better known in Asia than in the United States, but has grown in popularity here with the huge increase in popularity of sushi and sashimi. The green variety will be more assertively flavored and have a cinnamon-like heat. This herb is strongly flavored and tastes much like anise or fennel and mint. Shiso is most often used in Japanese cooking wrapped around sushi or shredded into miso soups. Avoid leaves with an off color or wilted texture.

Pack Size: 100 leaves in a 2-oz pack
Shelf Life: 3 to 4 days
Storage Conditions: 40°F/4°C
Season: Available year-round

TARRAGON

Tarragon has long, thin, dark green leaves and a beautiful rich scent. The flavor is subtly anise-like and elegant and matches well with classic French dishes. Be aware that although it seems smooth and elegant, the flavor is assertive and can dominate a dish if not used carefully. Tarragon is the key seasoning in the famous béarnaise sauce, is wonderful for infusing vinegar, and works well with seafood such as scallops and shrimp, and sautéed or stuffed mushrooms. Tarragon is also one of the key components in fines herbes.

Like with many other herbs, tarragon is a fragile herb and should be chosen well and used quickly. Look for a vibrant, well-perfumed leaf with no signs of withering or decay. As the flavor is assertive and can become bitter, it is wise to taste a leaf before adding to your dish.

Pack Size: By the ounce, pound, or kilogram
Shelf Life: 2 to 3 days
Storage Conditions: 40°F/4°C
Season: Available year-round but best when purchased from your local farm stand

FIGURE **12.23** Tarragon

THYME

Thyme is an herb that is used abundantly in cooking whether in Mediterranean cuisine (where it originated), classic European cooking, or in the United States. It has a highly agreeable aroma and flavor that combines well with a multitude of other ingredients. Thyme accentuates the positive aspects of other herbs and flavors without becoming too assertive or disruptive. Bouquet garni requires its balance and stocks, sauces, stuffing, soups, chowders, seafood, poultry, pork, and sausage are all enhanced by its addition. Several types of thyme marketed in foodservice are used in the same fashion and combine well with the other flavors in the dish being created. Lemon thyme is somewhat different, adding to thyme's rich flavor a tart citrus undertone that pairs well with poultry and seafood. This herb can also be steeped into a tea if desired.

Thyme has small, pale green leaves that can be profuse on rigid stems or somewhat sparse on delicate pliable stems, depending on age and variety. The leaves are small so check carefully to ensure they have not begun to wither or show signs of mold. The aroma should be assertive and bright and not sour or off.

Pack Size: By the ounce, pound, or kilogram
Shelf Life: 3 to 4 days
Storage Conditions: 40°F/4°C
Season: Available year-round but best when purchased at your local farm stand

Nutritional Information

Serving Size:	3-1/2 oz/100 g
Water:	65.11 g
Calories:	101
Protein:	5.56 g
Fat:	1.68 g
Saturated Fat:	0.467 g
Fiber:	14 g
Sodium:	9 mg
Iron:	17.45 mg
Potassium:	609 mg
Vitamin C:	160.1 mg

13

APPLES AND PEARS

Both the apple and pear are members of the *Rosacea* family and are tree fruit. They are both referred to as "pomes," which means they have a paper-like core surrounded by flesh and covered with a thin skin. The flesh in each is white or pale yellow and crisp and juicy, although the pear is generally juicier and the flesh usually softens when ripe. The flavor of the apple can range from very sweet to quite tart, whereas the pear is generally sweet. The apple varies in size but is always round in shape, whereas the pear can be round but usually has either an elongated or squat teardrop shape. Both fruits have some year-round availability due to improved controlled-atmosphere storage techniques, but apples and pears are truly best in the fall and winter when they first come into season. Look for a designation on the case to ensure the product has been properly stored over the winter.

Avoid fruit that is shriveled, washed out in color, pitted, or that has soft brown bruising. Apples and pears should be heavy for their size to ensure high moisture content. Russeting on the skin is not an indication of poor quality unless the fruit is being used only for presentation.

APPLES

A whole book could be written about apples, given their popularity, their great variety, and the number of countries where they are enjoyed. Apples are the number one tree fruit in the world and have been cultivated as far back as 300 B.C. in Greece. World-wide over 80 percent of all apple varieties are used commercially (cooked into other forms), but in the United States over half of all apples grown are consumed raw. There are literally hundreds of varieties of apples grown worldwide; many are almost exclusively grown in certain regions while others are very widely grown. In this chapter we will focus on the most popular eating and culinary apples appreciated in this country. However, when traveling, stop by local farm stands and try the varieties grown in that orchard, and fresh off the tree.

BRAEBURN

An apple of New Zealand heritage, this is a relatively new species originating in the 1950s. It is a good multipurpose apple that can be used in most any application. It is reddish-orange in color over a yellow background. This is a late fall apple that will last until late spring or summer. The Braeburn has a spicy, sweet flavor and is a very juicy crisp apple.

Pack Size: 20 or 40 lb/9.07 or 18.14 kg box
Shelf Life: 1 to 2 weeks
Storage Conditions: 32° to 34°F/0° to 1°C
Season: Mostly available year-round but best in the fall and early winter

CORTLAND

This is a New York state apple and was developed from McIntosh parentage. It has a sweet flavor profile with only a touch of tartness. This apple is a good choice in fresh salads as it tends to oxidize and brown less than many other varieties. This apple is best from early fall to early spring. Look for crimson over yellow color with darker red stripes and green specks on the skin.

Pack Size: 20 or 40 lb/9.07 or 18.14 kg box
Shelf Life: 1 to 2 weeks
Storage Conditions: 32° to 34°F/0° to 1°C
Season: September to December

FIGURE **13.1** Braeburn

EMPIRE

As its name suggests, this is another New York state apple and it was developed in the mid 1960s. The Empire is a mixture of Red Delicious and McIntosh apples with a sweet tart flavor. Excellent cold in salads and for eating out of hand, this is a popular apple with children. Empires are also very good for baking and making sauce. The coloring is a warm red with green splotches and snow white flesh. Empire apples are available from autumn to late spring and into summer.

Pack Size: 20 or 40 lb/9.07 or 18.14 kg box
Shelf Life: 1 to 2 weeks
Storage Conditions: 32° to 34°F/0° to 1°C
Season: September to June

FUJI

Developed in Japan in the early 1930s, the Fuji didn't appear in many western markets for another 50 years. Since then, its popularity has soared due to a rich sweet flavor and good firm texture. Look for red and yellow striped fruits, usually all year long. Fuji apples have a warm, sweet flavor and are very juicy; they are excellent in salads and eaten out of hand. Also, try Fuji apples in applesauce, as little additional sugar is needed, or in an apple tatin. This apple is available all year, except in mid-summer.

Pack Size: 20 or 40 lb/9.07 or 18.14 kg box
Shelf Life: 1 to 2 weeks
Storage Conditions: 32° to 34°F/0° to 1°C
Season: Available year-round, except in mid-summer

GALA

The Gala is another New Zealand apple whose popularity has increased dramatically in recent years. Galas are primarily a snack apple with a juicy soft texture and very high sweetness. This apple can be pale red with a cream to soft green background to red and yellow striped, with a pale yellow flesh. Galas have an Orange Pippin and Red Delicious heritage and come into season in mid-summer, but are generally available year-round. Orange Pippin is a variety of apple that is no longer commercially grown, but was used as breeding stock for several varieties of apples available now.

Pack Size: 20 or 40 lb/9.07or 18.14 kg box
Shelf Life: 1 to 2 weeks
Storage Conditions: 32° to 34°F/0° to 1°C
Season: Available year-round

FIGURE **13.2** Empire

FIGURE **13.3** Fuji

FIGURE **13.4** Gala

GINGER GOLD

A Virginia farmer reportedly discovered this apple sprouting in his family orchard after a hurricane had wreaked havoc there in the 1960s. Its origins and lineage are uncertain but it is believed to be part Pippin. This apple is greenish-gold in color, with crisp white flesh, and has an interesting and delicious sweet tart flavor. Best eaten raw, this is a good choice for salads as it is slow to oxidize. This is still considered a small crop apple, but the popularity is growing. The season for Ginger Gold apples will open in late summer to early fall, but end before winter.

Pack Size: 20 or 40 lb/9.07 or 18.14 kg box
Shelf Life: 1 to 2 weeks
Storage Conditions: 32° to 34°F/0° to 1°C
Season: September to December

FIGURE **13.5** Golden Delicious

GOLDEN DELICIOUS

The Golden Delicious is an old standard and hugely popular in America. It is pale yellow in color and often with a soft red blush, with a crisp pale yellow flesh; this is a very popular apple for eating out of hand. Its resistance to oxidation also makes it a good choice in salads. The Delicious apples have a more erect, or bell pepper shape, than other rounder varieties and can be identified by the distinctive bumps along their base. When used in baking, adjust the recipe's sugar content due to this apple's great sweetness. The season for Golden Delicious opens in early fall, but it is available year-round.

Pack Size: 20 or 40 lb/9.07 or 18.14 kg box
Shelf Life: 1 to 2 weeks
Storage Conditions: 32° to 34°F/0° to 1°C
Season: Available year-round

GRANNY SMITH

The Granny Smith apple has a pale green skin with an occasional pale red blush. The flesh is white, very crisp, juicy, and tart, making it good to eat out of hand and an extremely popular baking and cooking apple. The Granny Smith is another slow-to-oxidize apple, making it an excellent choice for salads. This apple has an Australian background, but is now grown heavily in the Pacific Northwest. In the United States, harvest begins in late summer, but this is a year-round apple.

FIGURE **13.6** Granny Smith

Pack Size: 20 or 40 lb/9.07 or 18.14 kg box
Shelf Life: 1 to 2 weeks
Storage Conditions: 32° to 34°F/0° to 1°C
Season: Available year-round

HONEYCRISP

The Honeycrisp apple is relatively new to the market, but very highly prized. The flesh is cream- to honey-colored with a coarse texture and a powerful crispness to accompany its mild sweet flavor. The apple is a Macoun and Honeygold cross with mottled red stripes/splotches over yellow skin. Honeycrisp apples are excellent in salads, for eating out of hand, baked whole, and in applesauce. The season begins in early autumn, but runs out quickly as demand is now greater than production. The production levels should be increasing with time due to the demand as farmers adapt to this growth in the market. The Honeycrisp apple is thin skinned so producers and consumers alike need to treat this special apple gently to avoid damage to the crisp sweet flesh.

FIGURE **13.7** Honeycrisp

Pack Size: 20 or 40 lb/9.07 or 18.14 kg box
Shelf Life: 1 to 2 weeks
Storage Conditions: 32° to 34°F/0° to 1°C
Season: September to December

IDA RED

The Ida Red is a very large, bright-red–colored apple that was developed back in the 1940s in Idaho. This is a good choice for eating out of hand but is usually preferred for pies or baking whole as it has a bright tangy flavor. The Ida Red was bred from a Wagener and Jonathan apple and this is where it gets its bright flavor. Try using this apple for applesauce and leave the skin on to deliver a beautiful pink applesauce once strained. The Ida Red is available from early autumn to late spring.

Pack Size: 20 or 40 lb/9.07 or 18.14 kg box
Shelf Life: 1 to 2 weeks
Storage Conditions: 32° to 34°F/0° to 1°C
Season: September to May

JONAGOLD

The Jonagold has crisp, yellow-colored flesh that complements its unusual honey-like flavor with tart undertones. This apple is a cross between a Golden Delicious and Jonathan apple (hence the name) and has a pink blush over its yellow to green-hued skin. The blend of tart and sweet flavors makes this a good all-around apple suited for eating raw and for cooking and baking. This apple becomes available in mid to late fall and can be found in the market until early summer. However, this apple softens in storage, so enjoy it in the fall and winter.

Pack Size: 20 or 40 lb/9.07 or 18.14 kg box
Shelf Life: 1 to 2 weeks
Storage Conditions: 32° to 34°F/0° to 1°C
Season: September to June

JONATHAN

The Jonathan apple is another native of New York state and is an all-purpose apple good for eating out of hand. Its high acidity gives this apple a unique spiciness which makes it a good choice for cider, pie, and sauce and it works very well in these applications when mixed with other apples with a lower acid content. This red apple has some pale green to yellow streaking and a dense firm flesh. The Jonathan apple is available from autumn into spring.

Pack Size: 20 or 40 lb/9.07 or 18.14 kg box
Shelf Life: 1 to 2 weeks
Storage Conditions: 32° to 34°F/0° to 1°C
Season: September to June

FIGURE **13.8** Jonagold

LADY

The Lady apple is one of the oldest heirloom varieties still on the market. It is slightly flattened, round red and green to yellowish apple that is used in canning, for sauce, and snacking out of hand. It is a tiny apple about 1-1/2 inches/3.75 centimeters across, roughly the size of a silver dollar, making it very useful for decorative purposes. It has a late fall harvest and is sometimes referred to as a Christmas Apple. The flesh of this apple is white, crisp, juicy, and very bright in flavor; much of the flavor comes from the skin so don't peel it when eating or cooking. Despite its name, this apple is not related to the Pink Lady which is a relatively new hybrid species. Due to its late harvest, this apple should be available into March.

FIGURE **13.9** Lady

Pack Size: 10 lb/4.54 kg box
Shelf Life: 5 to 7 days
Storage Conditions: 32° to 34°F/0° to 1°C
Season: Late October into March

McINTOSH

The McIntosh is an old favorite, and best used for either eating out of hand or in making applesauce. The flesh breaks down too much to be the best choice in pies. This red and green apple has white flesh and a bright sweet to tart flavor. The McIntosh is available from fall into spring and is a perennial favorite in the Northeast. It is a great choice for a child's snack.

Pack Size: 20 or 40 lb/9.07 or 18.14 kg box
Shelf Life: 1 to 2 weeks
Storage Conditions: 32° to 34°F/0° to 1°C
Season: Available year-round

MUTSU, CRISPIN

The Mutsu is a large yellowish-green skinned apple, often with a blush of red. This apple, also known as the Crispin, has moderate to strong tartness, moderate sugar, with a crisp, white, juicy flesh. This apple is very good eaten out of hand, but is also excellent in pies and applesauce. The skin tone and shape can be reminiscent of the Golden Delicious, which is in its parentage. It is available from early fall well into the winter months.

Pack Size: 20 or 40 lb/9.07 or 18.14 kg box
Shelf Life: 1 to 2 weeks
Storage Conditions: 32° to 34°F/0° to 1°C
Season: September to March

PAULA RED

The Paula Red is an early harvest apple with a bright, tart flavor. This apple is pale red over yellow skin with a full, round shape. The flesh is pure white, very crisp, and juicy. The Paula Red is good for eating out of hand and makes excellent applesauce, needing little sugar. Look quickly for this apple as its season only runs from August into October.

Pack Size: 20 or 40 lb/9.07 or 18.14 kg box
Shelf Life: 1 to 2 weeks
Storage Conditions: 32° to 34°F/0° to 1°C
Season: Late August into October

PINK LADY

The Pink Lady gets its name from the pink color of its skin wrapped over a pure white flesh. This apple is a cross between a Golden Delicious and a Lady Williams apple and is closest to the Gala in flavor with its blend of sweetness and high acid content. The Pink Lady is best suited for eating raw but it can be baked as well. This is a late autumn pick and is available into late spring.

FIGURE **13.10** McIntosh

FIGURE **13.11** Mutsu/Crispin

FIGURE **13.12** Pink Lady

FIGURE **13.13** Red Delicious

FIGURE **13.14** Rome, Rome Beauty

Pack Size: 20 or 40 lb/9.07 or 18.14 kg box
Shelf Life: 1 to 2 weeks
Storage Conditions: 32° to 34°F/0° to 1°C
Season: October to June

RED DELICIOUS

The Red Delicious is the best-known and most widely consumed apple in the United States. At one point this apple accounted for over 70 percent of the apple production in Washington State. That number has shrunk markedly over the years as new varieties have caught on, but it is still the number one selling apple in the country. This apple has the well-known elongated or bell pepper shape and the small bumps or feet on the base, although in some areas it has a rounder shape. The skin of this apple varies from pale to dark red striations to a full deep dark red. The flesh of the Red Delicious is pale yellow, crisp, sweet, very juicy, and best suited for eating raw. The season starts in September but this apple is available year-round.

Pack Size: 20 or 40 lb/9.07 or 18.14 kg box
Shelf Life: 1 to 2 weeks
Storage Conditions: 32° to 34°F/0° to 1°C
Season: Available year-round

Nutritional Information

Serving Size:	3-1/2 oz/100 g
Water:	85.56 g
Calories:	52
Protein:	0.26 g
Fat:	0.17 g
Saturated Fat:	0.028 g
Fiber:	2.4 g
Sodium:	1 mg
Iron:	0.12 mg
Potassium:	107 mg
Vitamin C:	4.6 mg

ROME BEAUTY, ROME

The Rome or Rome Beauty apple is a full red, round apple that looks better than it eats out of hand. However, it does well in baking as the flavor grows and improves when the white firm flesh is cooked. It has a long storage life and comes into season in early to mid autumn.

Pack Size: 20 or 40 lb/9.07 or 18.14 kg box
Shelf Life: 1 to 2 weeks
Storage Conditions: 32° to 34°F/0° to 1°C
Season: Available year-round

Key: E = excellent
G = good
N = not recommended

	Snacking	Salads	Pies	Souce	Baking	Freezing
Braeburn	E	G	G	G	G	G
Cameo	E	E	E	E	E	G
Cortland	E	E	E	E	E	G
Empire	E	E	G	G	G	G
Fuji	E	E	G	G	G	E
Gala	E	E	G	E	G	E
Ginger Gold	E	E	G	G	G	N
Golden Delicious	E	E	E	E	E	E
Granny Smith	E	E	E	E	E	E
Honeycrisp	E	E	E	E	G	E
Ida Red	G	G	E	E	E	G
Jonagold	E	E	G	E	E	G
Jonathan	G	G	E	G	E	G
McIntosh	E	G	E	E	N	G
Newtown Pippin	G	G	E	E	G	G
Cripps Pink	E	E	E	E	G	G
Red Delicious	E	E	N	N	N	N
Rome Beauty	G	G	E	E	E	G

U.S. Government Apple Usage Chart
Source: United States Apple Association

PEARS

The pear comes from the same genetic family as the apple but is not known to have the great number of varieties as the apple. Sadly, in America, the pear is often not eaten when fully ripened and sweet. We often see them consumed when still quite firm before the sweetness and silkiness of the flesh develops. Try waiting to find pears that look about ready to turn too soft in order to taste the best flavor when eating raw. For poaching or baking you will likely require the fruit to still have some firmness to it.

Pears are usually either an elongated or squat teardrop shape, although some are round like an apple. The skin, depending on variety, can be green to yellow to red to tan in color. When the pears are not fully ripened, they can have grains in the flesh, known as stone cells, which give them an unpleasant sandy grit. Pears are always picked before fully ripe, but continue to ripen on the shelf. Refrigeration inhibits that process. Pears do not have the strong acid balance in the flesh that many apples will have and are generally sweeter and juicier when allowed to ripen fully. When choosing pears, always seek out fruit that is fully matured and aromatic, with no scuffing, pits, bruising, or shriveling in the skin or neck.

ASIAN, NASHI, SAND PEAR

The Asian pear has a light green/gold to brown russet color skin and is round like an apple. The flesh is pale yellow, juicy, and crisp and remains crisp as it ripens unlike the softening that occurs in other pears. The flesh of this fruit is also slightly gritty when young, which lessens when the fruit matures. This grittiness and its high water content make it unsuitable for cooking. The Asian pear is best eaten simply peeled and in its raw state, or shredded into a slaw. Despite its shape and common misnomer "apple pear," this is not a cross between an apple and a pear. This pear comes into season in mid to late summer and runs until late autumn.

The Korean pear is a very large variety of Asian pear that weighs approximately 1 pound 8 ounces/680 grams. These are exceedingly juicy and sweet and delicious eaten out of hand. The pear can also be shredded into fruit and/or vegetable salads to bring added sweetness and crunch. Look for large, heavy and very firm fruit with a warm, russet-colored skin.

Pack Size: 20 to 40 lb/9.07 or 18.14 kg
Shelf Life: Ripen at room temperature then store in refrigeration for up to 1 week
Storage Conditions: 35°F/1.5°C
Season: Many varieties are available year-round but are best in fall and early winter

FIGURE **13.15** Asian/Nashi/Sand Pears

FIGURE **13.16** Korean Pear

Nutritional Information

Serving Size:	3-1/2 oz/100 g
Water:	88.25 g
Calories:	42
Protein:	0.50 g
Fat:	0.23 g
Saturated Fat:	0.012 g
Fiber:	3.6 g
Sodium:	0 mg
Potassium:	121 mg
Vitamin C:	3.8 mg

FIGURE **13.17** Bartlett/Williams Pears

BARTLETT, WILLIAMS PEAR

The Bartlett is one of the most common pears in the United States and exhibits the shape most people think of as "pear shaped," with a thick bulbous base, pronounced shoulders, and a thinner neck. This pear is green skinned when mature and then turns a soft yellow when ripened. Bartletts are not allowed to ripen on the tree as the flesh turns mealy unless picked when mature but not yet ripe. Bartletts also develop a distinct sweet pear aroma as they ripen. Originally called the Williams pear, this pear is often canned commercially, but is delicious when eaten out of hand, poached, or baked. Bartletts come into season in late August or early September and will last into the winter months.

Pack Size: 20 or 40 lb/9.07 or 18.14 kg box

Shelf Life: Up to 1 week

Storage Conditions: Ripen at room temperature then store at 35°F/1.5°C for up to 1 week

Season: Available year-round but best in the fall and early winter months

Nutritional Information

Serving Size:	3-1/2 oz/100 g
Water:	83.71 g
Calories:	58
Protein:	0.38 g
Fat:	0.12 g
Saturated Fat:	0.006 g
Fiber:	3.1 g
Sodium:	1 mg
Iron:	0.17 mg
Potassium:	119 mg
Vitamin C:	4.2 mg

BARTLETT, RED

Except for the beautiful red color of the skin, this is essentially the same pear as the preceding yellow Bartlett. Both have the same conformation and flavor, although the red variety is often a bit smaller in size. The only reason to decide between the two is when aesthetically the color of the skin supplies contrast and/or eye appeal.

FIGURE **13.18** Red Bartlett Pears

FIGURE **13.19** Bosc Pears

FIGURE **13.20** Comice Pears

Pack Size: 20 or 40 lb/9.07or18.14 kg box
Shelf Life: Up to 1 week
Storage Conditions: Ripen at room temperature then store for up to 1 week at 35°F/1.5°C
Season: Available year-round but the peak season is July through November

BOSC

The Bosc pear has distinct characteristics from other pears. First, it has a unique brown russet-colored skin. Secondly, the pear has a longer, more slender line and shape. It still has a thin neck and thicker base, but with a more graceful flowing shape. The white flesh is also crisper, with a firmer crunch to the bite even when ripe. This firmness of texture makes the Bosc an excellent choice to bake and poach. Their assertive and spicy flavor also holds up well with other flavorings when baked or poached. This sweet flavor develops earlier in the ripening process than with other pears, thus allowing them to eat well even when not fully softened. Look for Bosc pears from October through the winter months.

Pack size: 20 or 40 lb/9.07 or 18.14 kg box
Shelf Life: Up to 1 week
Storage Conditions: Ripen at room temperature then store for up to 1 week at 35°F/1.5°C
Season: Available year-round but best when in the fall and winter months

COMICE

The Comice is highly prized for its creamy, soft white, and very sweet, juicy flesh. This pear is often quite large but comes in a range of sizes. It is green skinned, often with a maroon blush, and has a heavy, rounded, bell shape. Comice pears often begin to yellow when they ripen, but a better test for ripeness is that they will have some give in the flesh near the neck. This pear is delicate and has a fine skin, so treat it gently and understand that small skin blemishes and russeting do not necessarily mean the pear has gone bad. Comice pears can be baked and cooked, but are most appreciated in their natural state. This is a winter pear and is at its peak for the holidays.

Pack Size: 20 or 40 lb/9.07 or 18.14 kg box
Shelf Life: Up to 1 week
Storage Conditions: Ripen at room temperature and then refrigerate for up to 1 week at 35°F/1.5°C
Season: September through March

D'ANJOU, ANJOU

The Anjou pear is slightly larger than other pears and it has a thick bulb and short neck. This pear is green skinned, and like the Bartlett, there is a Red D'Anjou variety whose only difference is the skin pigment. There are some varieties of the D'Anjou that will turn yellow when fully ripe, but most are green or red. This pear is more characteristically tart in flavor than other varieties of pear, so it is preferred for cooking rather than eating raw. The flesh is creamy white, aromatic, and juicy, and can feel somewhat gritty on the tongue. The D'Anjou has an excellent shelf life and is therefore popular for sale in supermarket chains where it can be found year-round. The Anjou will have some give in the flesh as it ripens. Like the Bartlett, this pear is better if it ripens off the tree. This pear is available from mid September to early May.

Pack Size: 20 or 40 lb/9.07 or 18.14 kg box
Shelf Life: 1 week
Storage Conditions: Ripen at room temperature and then refrigerate for up to 1 week at 35°F/1.5°C
Season: Mid September to May

FORELLE

The Forelle is another deliciously sweet small pear, just a bit larger than the Seckel. This pear is 2 to 3 inches/5 to 7.5 centimeters and bell-shaped with the body tapering cleanly into the neck. This pear is striking to look at when ripened as it goes

FIGURE **13.21** D'Anjou/Anjou Pear

FIGURE **13.22** Red D'Anjou/Red Anjou Pear

FIGURE **13.23** Forelle Pears

from green to yellow with red freckles (or lenticels) all over the skin. Like the Seckel, the small size and very sweet flavor of the Forelle make it a great snacking pear and well suited for children. In addition to their sweetness, the flesh has a cinnamon-like spiciness and a buttery or silky texture when ripe. Forelles are best eaten while still fairly firm; over-ripening will give them a mushy texture. The flavor of this pear can even be further enhanced by heating them; either in a microwave or by poaching them briefly. The season of this unique fruit is short, starting in early October and ending by mid winter. Look for these when they're available and use them for display to take full advantage of their bright festive appearance.

Pack Size: 10 lb/4.54 kg box
Shelf Life: 1 week
Storage Conditions: Ripen at room temperature and then refrigerate for up to 1 week at 35°F/1.5°C
Season: Late September to February

SECKEL

The Seckel (not Seckle) pear is the smallest of the commercially grown pears and it is also the sweetest. These have a small, 2 inch/5 centimeter, round body and a short neck with a greenish skin; there is often a dark maroon hue that can cover some or all of the green. The size and sweetness of this pear make it an excellent snack fruit, especially for children. They are excellent when canned whole or used as a plate garnish. The Seckel pear is in the market from late summer until early winter.

FIGURE **13.24** Seckel Pears

Pack Size: 10 or 20 lb/4.54 or 9.07 kg box
Shelf Life: 1 week
Storage Conditions: Ripen at room temperature and then refrigerate for 1 week at 35°F/1.5°C
Season: August to February

CITRUS

All members of the citrus family are noted and prized for their acidity, which provides food and beverages with a brightness and balance to other flavors. The rinds come in bright and easily recognizable colors that also add to the visual presentation of the plate. This is only true when the fruit is grown in areas with cold winters however; all citrus fruits grown at tropical temperatures remain green in color. The zest of the rind is the thin outer coating which has the distinctive bright orange, yellow, red, and green color; this zest also contains the oils that energize dishes with their fragrance and bright, sweet, or tart flavor. The white pith that lies between the zest and fruit segments is bitter and should be avoided if possible. The flesh of the fruits is formed in segments circling the fruit's core; these segments will either be seedless or carry several seeds each, depending on the specific fruit.

Nearly every citrus fruit utilized today in foodservice is a hybrid or cultivar of other fruits. The heritage is discussed for each variety as they are covered in this chapter. As noted, these fruits are widely used in foodservice due to their acid content, color, and aroma. It should also be noted that these fruits are very healthy, are rich in vitamins, fiber, flavonoids, and low in calories.

Many of these fruits are equally, or more so, valued for the juice they provide. These juices, when used as a dietary supplement, provide the nutritional content of the fruit in a more easily accessible manner. However, the juice will add less fiber to the diet and has a higher calorie density than the whole fruit. Also, due to their tartness, many of these juices, such as lemon and lime, require a good deal of sweetening to be palatable. The juice in its unsweetened form is utilized in many different recipes to provide the acidic kick desired as well as a bright flavor. Such recipes include Caesar salad, lemon chicken, duckling à l'orange, and many others.

Citrus is grown and appreciated in cuisines all over the world. Here in the United States almost the entire commercial crop comes out of Florida and California, but our total crop yield is not even in the world's top ten due to more optimal growing conditions and the enormous demand for these fruits worldwide. When receiving citrus, look for fruit that is heavy for its size, which indicates that it is not dehydrated; it should also be firm and unblemished with no signs of mold.

ORANGES

The orange is a very popular fruit that, not surprisingly, is bright orange in color. There are three main classifications of oranges in foodservice: the eating orange, juicing orange, and mandarin. Bitter oranges are lesser known and primarily used in cooking, especially in orange marmalade. Most common in the eating orange group is the navel orange and the Cara Cara, which is gaining in popularity. These are known for their lack of seeds and sweet rich flavor. Juicing varieties consist primarily of the Valencia and Hamlin types and provide a balance of acid and sugar that gives great balance to the drinkability. The smaller mandarin variety is characterized by a thin, easy-to-peel skin that makes it easy to eat out of hand. Popular mandarin varieties include clementines, tangelos, tangerines, and Minneola.

EATING ORANGES

CARA CARA

The Cara Cara is a highly prized variety of navel orange from Venezuela. It has a short season, from December to March, but is in high demand during that brief time. This orange has reddish flesh and less acidity than typical navel oranges. This gives them a sweeter flavor that some describe as having berry overtones. Like other navel oranges, a hefty weight for their size is an essential quality check. The thick skin should be tight and the fruit should have a distinctively sweet aroma. They are good for eating raw out of hand but their unique flavor will also lead the creative cook to find culinary applications for this unique fruit. Cara Cara oranges are usually medium sized, averaging three per pound. Look for these when they are in season.

Pack Size: 20 lb/9.07 kg carton
Shelf Life: 1 to 2 weeks
Storage Conditions: 45° to 48°F/7° to 9°C
Season: December to March

NAVEL

Navel oranges were created in a single mutation back in the early 1800s. This mutation caused a second orange to begin to form inside the skin at the end opposite of the stem. This second orange does not fully develop but does create the mark at the bottom of the orange which is often compared to the human navel. This mutation leaves the orange sterile and consequently seedless. Therefore, the Navel orange must be cultivated by grafting cuttings onto existing trees rather than planting. This is a sweet, juicy, well-loved fruit that is eaten raw out of hand and segmented into salads. Look for heavy fruit indicating high juice content, with no soft spots or shriveling in the thick rubbery skin. A green tinge called "greening" is not a negative sign. This indicates that the fruit stayed on the tree longer into chilly temperatures, which actually improves the flavor. Also note that the skin should be shiny and the fruit should exhibit a sweet smell. Navels are available from fall into the late spring but are clearly superior in the middle winter months. Oranges pack by count per case with the lower count indicating a larger orange; an 88 count is common in the industry.

Pack Size: 48, 56, 72, 88, 113, or138 per 40 lb/18.14 kg case
Shelf Life: 1 to 3 months
Storage Conditions: Florida oranges 34°F/1° C. California and Arizona oranges 40°F/4°C.
Season: Available from October to May but will be best December to March

Nutritional Information

Serving Size:	3-1/2 oz/100 g
Water:	85.97 g
Calories:	49
Protein:	0.91 g
Fat:	0.15 g
Saturated Fat:	0.017 g
Fiber:	2.2 g
Sodium:	1 mg
Iron:	0.13 mg
Potassium:	166 mg
Vitamin C:	59.1 mg

JUICING ORANGES

VALENCIA

This orange was developed in California, but today's production comes mostly out of Florida. This orange is generally raised and utilized for juice production, but can be enjoyed eaten out of hand as well. Although not seedless like the navel orange, it has good color and a pleasant flavor. The season runs from March into the summer months, making it the only orange worldwide to be in season during the summer.

FIGURE **14.1** Navel Orange

FIGURE **14.2** Valencia Oranges

Because its primary use is for juicing, choosing oranges that are very heavy for their size is essential. Valencias are generally not very large in size (up to 3 inches/8 centimeters in diameter) and are sold by the count per case. The skin should be thin and finer in texture than navels and a sweet scent should be evident. Again, "greening" on the skin is a good indication of better flavor.

Another, lesser known, variety of juicing orange is the Hamlin. This is a small, round, thin-skinned fruit that, while primarily known as a juicer, is nearly seedless and great for eating. It has an excellent balance of acid to sugar, giving it a splendid flavor. Primarily grown in and consumed around Florida, this delectable fruit is only in season from fall into December.

Pack Size: 40 lb/18.14 kg carton
Shelf Life: 2 to 3 weeks
Storage Conditions: 45° to 48°F/7° to 9°C
Season: Valencia: March to July; Hamlin: September to December

Nutritional Information

Serving Size:	3 1/2 ounces/100 grams
Water:	86.34 g
Calories:	49
Protein:	1.04 g
Fat:	0.30 g
Saturated Fat:	0.035 g
Fiber:	2.5 g
Sodium:	0 mg
Iron:	0.09 mg
Potassium:	179 mg
Vitamin C:	48.5 mg

BLOOD ORANGES

This member of the orange family gets its name from its dark red flesh and juice. The fruit is smaller then most other oranges and the skin can be finely pebbled to smooth. There is often, but not always, a deep red blush on the rind as well. These oranges are very popular, especially in the Mediterranean and more recently in America. There are a variety of blood oranges cultivated, but three types dominate the market: Sanguinello (bull's blood), Moro (more recently developed and similar to the Sanguinello), and Tarocco. The Moro has the deepest color flesh and shows the most red on the rind; it is similar to the Sanguinello but just a bit more bold and assertive. The Tarocco is considered the sweetest and best eating of the three and is the most popular table orange in Italy, but lacks as much vibrant color as the other two varieties.

FIGURE **14.3** Blood Oranges

Blood oranges arrive in the market in December and last well into spring, sometimes into July. Look for heavy, firm fruit with tight, unblemished skin. Remember, the amount of red pigmentation on the rind is not necessarily indicative of the redness of the flesh. If a deep red color is essential, the Moro variety is the best bet. Blood oranges are great eaten raw, in salads, juiced, and made into refreshing sorbets.

Pack Size: 20 lb/9.07 kg carton
Shelf Life: 2 to 3 weeks
Storage Conditions: 45° to 48°F/7° to 9°C
Season: December to June

MANDARIN ORANGES

Mandarin oranges are a group of oranges characterized by being somewhat oblate in shape, smaller in size than the other types of oranges, and having a looser, thin skin. The rind is brightly colored orange, and the term *mandarin* comes from the brightly colored robes worn by ancient Chinese court officials. The rind can usually be slipped off the fruit by hand without much mess. This makes them a good choice for snacking and eating out of hand. Look for oranges that are firm and heavy for their size with a sweet citrus aroma. The skin should peel easily without being baggy and shriveled or show any sign of mold.

Mandarins have long been used for canning, primarily the Satsuma variety, and there are other varieties excellent for eating either as is or in a salad. These varieties include clementines, tangerines, and tangelos. These varieties are sweet/tart in flavor; some are seedless and others are not. As a group they tend to contain more water and less sugar than other oranges.

FIGURE **14.4** Satsuma Mandarin Oranges

CLEMENTINES

Clementines are a small, slightly flattened mandarin with a bright and sweet flavor. Bright orange in color with a smoother, easily peeled rind, this fruit is usually seedless unless they are inadvertently cross-pollinated with other varieties on the tree. The small size, almost-seedless nature, and great sweet flavor have made this fruit the fastest growing mandarin in popularity over the past 12 to 15 years. Generally sold in small wooden crates or mesh bags, the clementine should be consumed quickly as it has a short shelf life. Generally imported from Spain and North Africa, look for a soft but firm texture and well colored orange skin that is still relatively tight to the flesh. As with tangerines, avoid fruit that has begun to dehydrate or show signs of white mold.

Pack Size: Usually 20 count boxes weighing approximately 5 lb/2.27 kg
Shelf Life: Up to 1 week
Storage Conditions: 45° to 48°F/7° to 9°C
Season: October to February

FIGURE **14.5** Clementines

Nutritional Information

Serving Size:	3-1/2 oz/100 g
Water:	86.58 g
Calories:	47
Protein:	0.85 g
Fat:	0.15 g
Saturated Fat:	not listed
Fiber:	1.7 g
Sodium:	1 mg
Iron:	0.14 mg
Potassium:	177 mg
Vitamin C:	48.8 mg

TANGERINES

Tangerines are often referred to as a mandarin, which is somewhat true. All tangerines are mandarins, but all mandarins are not technically tangerines. Although native to China and enjoyed for many centuries, this type of orange was not imported into the West until the nineteenth century. At that time they were shipped west out of Tangiers, which is how the moniker *tangerine* originated. Tangerines come in several varieties including Satsuma, Fairchild, and Sunburst. A Tangor is a cross between a tangerine and orange. Honey, Honey Murcott, and Temple are common varieties. These tend to be larger and sweeter than other tangerines and more similar to an orange in flavor.

Tangerines will be bright orange to reddish in color. Look for fruit with some softness and a mild sweet aroma. The skin will be thin and pebbly and should be relatively tight against the fruit. Avoid scarred or discolored fruit and fruit with loose and puckered skin. This is a sign of dehydration, which indicates water loss, and is not acceptable in a fruit prized for its juice content. Tangerine juice is also available commercially and can complement certain foods such as poultry and seafood. Chocolate also works well with tangerine's bright sweet and tart flavor profile.

Pack Size: 40 lb/18.14 kg carton

Shelf Life: Up to 1 week

Storage Conditions: 45° to 48°F/7° to 9°C

Season: November to April but best from November to January

FIGURE **14.6** Tangerines

Nutritional Information

Serving Size:	3-1/2 oz/100 g
Water:	85.17 g
Calories:	53
Protein:	0.81 g
Fat:	0.31 g
Saturated Fat:	0.039 g
Fiber:	1.8 g
Sodium:	2 mg
Iron:	0.15 mg
Potassium:	166 mg
Vitamin C:	26.7 mg

TANGELO

The Tangelo is a mandarin that has been crossed with a grapefruit or pomelo (pummelo). They are the size of a large orange but peel and taste much like a tangerine. It has a reddish-orange, thicker, pebbly skin and a small neck, or knob, at the stem end. The tangelo is a very juicy fruit and more prized for its juice than the meat of the fruit, but it does have a nice, mild sweet flavor with low acid. Minneola, Honey Bell, and Orlando are all varieties of tangelos, as is the aptly named Ugli fruit. This fruit's name and appearance may account for its lack of popularity in this country. Under that lumpy exterior is the sweet and juicy flesh of a large tangelo. It is much less bitter than the grapefruit it most resembles.

Look for very heavy fruit for the size with an unscarred and firm skin with a sweet smell; except for the Ugli fruit, which has a distinctly baggy appearance.

Pack Size: 40 lb/18.14 kg carton
Shelf Life: 1 to 2 weeks
Storage Conditions: 45° to 48°F/7° to 9°C
Season: November to March

SEVILLE

Bitter, or sour, oranges are raised primarily for the oil in their rind, which is used in perfumes, flavorings, and in marmalade. The Seville orange is widely grown in Europe and has a thick, dimpled skin. The high pectin content in this fruit and the thick flavorful rind make it an ideal choice for use in marmalade, for which it is chiefly known. The very tart juice is prized in some Latin cocktails and cuisines, especially that of Cuba. Look for heavy, bright yellow-tinged oranges with no soft spots or blemishes. The Seville orange has a short season in early to mid winter.

Pack Size: 20 lb/9.07 kg
Shelf Life: 1 to 2 weeks
Storage Conditions: 45° to 48°F/7° to 9°C
Season: December to February

FIGURE **14.7** Tangelos

FIGURE **14.8** Ugli Fruit/Uniq Fruit

FIGURE **14.9** Seville Oranges

FIGURE **14.10** Bergamots

BERGAMOT

The bergamot is a pear-shaped, very sour citrus mostly utilized for its thick peel and the oils within. The peel is most famously known as the characteristic flavoring ingredient in Earl Grey tea. The rind is also utilized in some confection making. In parts of the Mediterranean this fruit is also made into marmalade and jam.

POMELO

The pomelo is a large, green to pale yellow citrus that originated in Southeast Asia and the Pacific and is not a huge part of the commercial market in America. These fruits can range in size from that of a large grapefruit to a soccer ball. These are noted for the poor ratio of flesh to pith and rind and are characterized by a thick, foamy coating around the flesh. The pink flesh is sweet in flavor.

This fruit is most noted for the hybrids resulting from crossbreeding with it. The grapefruit is a hybrid of orange and pomelo origin, and the tangelo is a hybrid from the pomelo and tangerine.

Pack Size: 40 lb/18.14 kg carton
Shelf Life: 1 to 2 weeks
Storage Conditions: 45° to 48°F/7° to 9°C
Season: November to March

GRAPEFRUIT

Grapefruit are large, yellow or yellow with a pink blush, citrus fruits with pink, red, or white/yellow flesh. This fruit has a distinctly bitter quality in the flavor and the level of sweetness varies with the specific type of grapefruit. All citrus fruits have distinct health benefits, but grapefruits are especially well known for their high antioxidant (lycopene) content, their ability to lower cholesterol levels in the blood stream, and their believed ability to aid the body in burning fat.

As with all citrus, grapefruits should be heavy for their size which indicates high moisture content. Grapefruit are either tropically grown or grown in a desert climate. The latter will have thicker skin, fewer blemishes, and be less sweet. The tropical fruit will be sweeter with a thinner skin and subject to more mottling. The quality of the skin is not an indicator of quality; the rind may be scarred, discolored, and mottled in color without affecting the quality of the flesh. A grapefruit with a rind that has started to "re-green" simply indicates it was left on the tree longer and can be a good sign. However, the rind should be tight and shiny. Softness at the base of the fruit, areas that appear soaked through, or shriveled and baggy skins are all indications of poor quality. Like many citrus fruit, grapefruit pack by the count per case.

WHITE GRAPEFRUIT

The meat or pulp of the white grapefruit is actually pale yellow or blond in color. The rind will be from pale to rich yellow in hue. The flesh should have an assertive tangy tart flavor with some underlying bitterness. Best known as a breakfast food eaten cold and raw; the grapefruit is excellent broiled and is used in some Caribbean seafood preparations. The juice is highly nutritious and widely available commercially.

PINK GRAPEFRUIT

The pink grapefruit are similar in size and weight to white grapefruit, but the skin will have a slight rosy blush and the flesh is pink in color. The pink color indicates a higher level of carotene in the fruit, which increases their health benefits. The carotene will increase the antioxidant levels and the vitamin A provided. Most pink grapefruits will be sweeter than whites and have few seeds.

RED GRAPEFRUIT

These are much like the pink grapefruit and were developed from them. As you may expect, they have darker and richer red flesh color. This again means a higher level of carotene and the corresponding health benefits. These should be the sweetest grapefruits available and are in great demand when in season. Due to their higher nutritional benefits and sweeter flavor, both red and pink grapefruits are now in higher demand in the market than the white grapefruit. The Ruby Red grapefruit was patented in the early 1900s and has greatly increased this fruit's popularity. Pink and red grapefruits are popular eaten by the half for breakfast, cooked, often in seafood dishes, and the juice is widely available commercially.

Pack Size: 35 to 40 lb/15.88 to 18.14 kg case
Shelf Life: 2 to 3 weeks
Storage Conditions: 45° to 48°F/7° to 9°C
Season: Best October to June but available year-round

FIGURE **14.11** White Grapefruit

FIGURE **14.12** Pink Grapefruit

FIGURE **14.13** Red Grapefruit

Nutritional Information

Serving Size:	3-1/2 oz/100 g
Water:	90.89 g
Calories:	32
Protein:	0.63 g
Fat:	0.10 g
Saturated Fat:	0.014 g
Fiber:	1.1 g
Sodium:	0 mg
Iron:	0.09 mg
Potassium:	139 mg
Vitamin C:	34.4 mg

LEMONS

The lemon is a brightly flavored, small yellow fruit that can be fully round, but typically comes to a point at either end. Generally the fuller, rounder fruit will have a better yield of juice and pulp. Lemons enjoy huge worldwide popularity due to the refreshing, tart flavor of the juice and the oils in the rind.

The pulp, zest, and juice have wide culinary appeal. They work well with pork, poultry, and seafood, in salads, marmalade, and pastry. The flavor of lemon juice is extremely popular when sweetened for soft drinks and lemonade or can be used unsweetened to marinate seafood, as in ceviche. Lemon juice is also frequently used to prevent the oxidation of the cut surfaces of other fruits and vegetable such as apples or avocados. Oils from the rind are used in both culinary applications and in cosmetics. It is little wonder this is the number one selling citrus fruit in the world.

FIGURE **14.14** Standard Lemons

Lemons should be heavy for their size with a bright shiny rind. Avoid lemons with dry pebbly rinds, puckering of the skin, or browning and soft spots. Fully round fruit with thin skin is optimal if juice is the prime objective.

Pack Size: 40 lb/18.14 kg box
Shelf Life: 2 to 3 weeks
Storage Conditions: 45 to 48°F/7 to 9°C
Season: Available year round

Nutritional Information

Serving Size:	3-1/2 oz/100 g
Water:	88.98 g
Calories:	29
Protein:	1.10 g
Fat:	0.30 g
Saturated Fat:	0.039 g
Fiber:	2.8 mg
Sodium:	2 mg
Iron:	0.60 mg
Potassium:	138 mg
Vitamin C:	53 mg

MEYER LEMON

The Meyer lemon is believed to have originated as cross between a lemon and mandarin. They are smaller and rounder than other lemons, with a thin, shiny, yellow-orange skin and sweeter flesh. They are widely used in pastry work and for preserving, and are great for lemon curd and candied peel. Many prefer them to typical lemons because they get the color and flavor without the bite. When purchasing, look for nice fully round fruit with a bright orange to yellow, smooth, shiny rind with a bright fragrance. Avoid soft, shriveling, scarred fruit.

> **Pack Size:** 10, 20, or 30 lb/4.54, 9.07, or 13.61 kg carton
> **Shelf Life:** 2 weeks
> **Storage Conditions:** 45° to 48°F/7° to 9°C
> **Season:** September to May

FIGURE **14.15** Meyer Lemons

LIMES

A lime is a small dark green or yellow-green citrus fruit with pointed tips. Limes are closely related to lemons, and like lemons are prized for the bright, tart, acidic flavor of the juice and the floral scent from the oils in the rind. The most common lime in the United States is the Persian lime, which is a hybrid of a Key lime and citron. Worldwide, Key limes are the most prevalent. Limes should be heavy for their size and brightly colored; small brown patches on the rind do not affect quality unless the bright green zest is the crucial component desired.

FIGURE **14.16** Standard Limes

Limes are greatly favored in the cuisines of Thailand, South America, Central America, Mexico, and the southwestern United States. The juice is also widely used for marinating fish in ceviche and bottled for a variety of culinary and mixology uses. Like lemons, the acid in the juice can be used to prevent oxidation and add flavor to dishes where the food's cut surfaces would otherwise turn brown, such as in guacamole.

Limes are an excellent source of vitamin C and were heavily favored at one time by British sailors to prevent scurvy in ocean voyages. This is the source of the moniker "limey" once applied to British sailors.

> **Pack Size:** 8 lb/3.63 kg carton
> **Shelf Life:** 2 weeks
> **Storage Conditions:** 45° to 48°F/7° to 9°C
> **Season:** Available year-round

Nutritional Information

Serving Size:	3-1/2 oz/100 g
Water:	88.26 g
Calories:	30
Protein:	0.7 g
Fat:	0.2 g
Saturated Fat:	0.022 g
Fiber:	2.8 g
Sodium:	2 mg
Iron:	0.6 mg
Potassium:	102 mg
Vitamin C:	29.1 mg

KAFFIR LIME, MAGROOD

The Kaffir lime is not a true lime, but a Southeast Asian citrus fruit prized almost exclusively for its leaves. The fruit is a small knobby green citrus with little edible pulp and very little juice. The juice is very pungent and sour. The rind is sometimes grated into some Thai or Laotian dishes, such as curries, to add a lemony fragrance. However, the 2 to 3 inch/5 to 7.5 centimeter long hourglass-shaped leaves are what are truly treasured and used in the cuisines in that part of the world, especially Thailand. Outside of Southeast Asia, only the leaves are found most commonly and they can be sourced from specialty produce houses. When the leaves are finely shredded they release a powerful citrus scent and provide a pronounced fresh lemon flavor to dishes, especially soups and green curries. The leaves may also be used whole or you can bruise them to release the oils and then simmer the leaves in the broth for the dish you are making. Although the aromas and flavors released are all described here as citrus, or lemon-lime in quality, the flavor and aroma of these leaves is special and unique and cannot be duplicated with a substitute when making Thai dishes. Look for dark green, shiny leaves with no black spots or yellowing around the edges.

FIGURE **14.17** Kaffir Lime Leaves

Pack Size: Leaves are sold by the pound
Shelf Life: Up to a week under refrigeration. Up to 3 months frozen
Storage Conditions: 45°F/7°C or frozen
Season: Available year-round

KEY LIMES

The Key lime is also an acidic lime; the Mexican variety is smaller than the Tahitian variety and has a thinner, smoother skin. Key limes are the most commonly used lime worldwide and are available year round.

FIGURE **14.18** Key Limes

These limes are characterized by their small round shape, and their leathery rind with more yellowing. These have a highly potent acid flavor that is prized in many dishes both sweet and savory. Look for firm, well-colored limes with a good weight to indicate high moisture content.

Pack Size: 10 lb/4.54 kg carton
Shelf Life: 1 to 2 weeks
Storage Conditions: 45° to 48°F/7° to 9°C
Season: Available year-round

PERSIAN LIMES

Limes are generally classified as either acidic or sweet. In this country, almost all limes sold are of the acidic variety. The Persian lime is grown extensively and is a larger or Tahitian-type acidic lime and the most prevalent lime sold commercially in the United States. These limes are larger than the sweet limes and are comparable in size to a small lemon. Other lesser utilized lime varieties include the Bearss and Idemore. The Persian is characterized by its larger size, finely grained green to yellow rind, and juiciness. This lime is marketed when immature for its green color; at fully ripe the lime will be yellowish-orange. Prevalent in California, the Bearss is smaller and thinner-skinned with an extremely juicy pulp. This type has a more yellow rind and neither variety have many seeds in the flesh. Look for well-rounded, heavy fruit with a green to yellow rind. Russeting patches do not harm the quality of the flesh, but may be unappealing aesthetically if served as a wedge with the rind attached. Avoid shriveled-looking or very hard fruit. The aroma should be bright and tart.

Pack Size: 10 lb/4.54 kg carton. The size range is 28 to 63 per box
Shelf Life: 2 to 3 weeks
Storage Conditions: 45° to 48°F/7° to 9°C
Season: Available year-round

YUZU

The yuzu is a Japanese citrus fruit. It is generally the size of a large orange or small grapefruit. The skin is rough and uneven, starting as green and turning more yellow as the fruit ripens. This fruit is not often seen in U.S. markets, and when found can be fairly expensive. Therefore, yuzu juice is the form most commonly found in Western markets.

The yuzu's flavor is much like a strong lemon, but with overtones of grapefruit, lime, tangerine, and pine. The flavor is closer to lime and citron when immature and green, with the lemon flavor becoming more prevalent as the fruit ripens. The unique floral combination in scent and flavor is so prized because it is truly unlike anything else, but reminiscent of other citrus varieties. Yuzu juice, or a piece of rind if it can be found, can be used to brighten and add zest to many Southeast Asian dishes, especially those containing seafood.

KUMQUATS

The kumquat is an orange-colored small citrus fruit which, depending on the exact species, are either oblong or round in shape. The rind of this fruit tends to be the sweetest part and the flesh is tart/salty in character. There are several species of kumquat utilized for culinary purposes. The Nagami variety is tart and juicy and the most commonly

cultivated species in the United States. It is oval or oblong in shape and when eaten out of hand it is best to massage the fruit between fingers and thumb to meld the flavors of the rind and flesh together before eating. The Meiwa variety is round and sweeter and considered the best eating variety. However, the Meiwa is mostly grown in China and Japan, and rarely seen in the United States.

Kumquats are small, usually less than 1-1/2 inches/4 centimeters in length. Because of the bright tart flavor and edible rind, this fruit is most often enjoyed eaten out of hand. However, this fruit is also suitable for making jam and marmalade and for pickling. Kumquats come into the market in December and usually last well into spring. The fruit should be firm, brightly colored, and exude a rich tart oil when rubbed between the fingers.

Pack Size: 5 or 10 lb/2.27 or 4.54 kg carton
Shelf Life: 1 to 2 weeks
Storage Conditions: 45° to 48°F/7° to 9°C
Season: October to May

Nutritional Information

Serving Size:	3-1/2 oz/100 g
Water:	80.85 g
Calories:	71
Protein:	1.88 g
Fat:	0.86 g
Saturated Fat:	0.103 g
Fiber:	6.5 g
Sodium:	10 mg
Iron:	0.86 mg
Potassium:	186 mg
Vitamin C:	43.9 mg

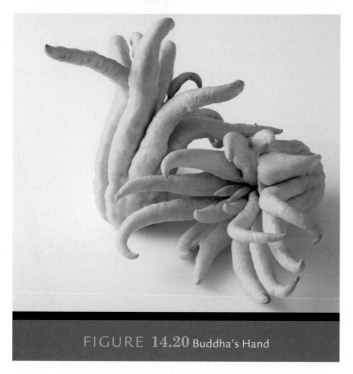

BUDDHA'S HAND

The Buddha's Hand is a very unique citrus fruit; it is a citron with multiple long, finger-like protrusions growing from a small bulb (hence the name). This fruit has a thick rind with little to no pulp. In Western cooking this is most utilized by zesting the thick skin to brighten and enliven other dishes; the skin can also be candied. The zest can also be used in marmalade and to flavor and scent some drinks. The white pith under the rind can be eaten as it lacks the bitterness of other citrus fruits. The fruit should be powerfully scented, which is what it is most prized for, and firm with a bright yellow rind.

Pack Size: 15 lb/6.8 kg case
Shelf Life: 1 to 2 weeks
Storage Conditions: 45 to 48°F/7 to 9°C
Season: January and February

15

GRAPES AND BERRIES

Grapes and berries are not botanically related but both supply small, bite-size packages of delicious fruit that can be utilized in pies, jams, jellies, sauces, salads, or eaten out of hand. They supply color, sweetness, and an acidic bite to many dishes. Berries kick off the U.S. growing season in the spring and come back toward the end of the growing season. Imported product is available year-round but the higher price and diminished flavor can bring their value into question at these times. Grapes, of one type or another, are almost always available, but sample when buying to ensure they are sufficiently sweet to meet your needs.

GRAPES

Grapes are a small, juicy, sweet fruit that grows on woody vines throughout much of the world, virtually everywhere the climate will support any of the many varieties that exist. Europe, in particular Spain, Italy, France, and Germany, is where much of the world's production is concentrated and where cultivation began in earnest many centuries ago. In the United States, grapes are grown in many locations, but the bulk of commercial production is focused in California. In fact, roughly 95 to 98 percent of all table grapes grown in the United States come from California. Grapes are grown for three main purposes: wine making, food production such as jams and juices, and eating out of hand or table grapes. Approximately 70 percent of the world's grape production goes into wine. This chapter will not deal with wine, but with grapes grown and sold for the foodservice industry.

A vast number of grape varieties are grown around the world, far too many to enumerate in this chapter. These many varieties can be separated into two types: white grapes, which are actually pale green, and red grapes, which can vary in shade from a medium red to what is referred to as a black grape. White grapes are of the same family as red grapes, but a genetic mutation blocks their utilization of the chemical components that give red grapes their color. The amount and the combination of the enzymes, anthocyanins, resveratrol, and polyphenols will determine the degree of redness in each type of red grape.

Seedless grapes now account for the overwhelming percentage of world production in table grapes simply because they are easier to prepare and cook and less messy to eat. All of the varieties of seedless grape available today in the United States originated from three sources: the Thompson green grape, the Russian red seedless, and the Black Monukka. These are all native to the western United States. Eastern varieties are bred to be heartier due to the less favorable weather and have a much smaller market; such varieties include the Reliance and Venus varieties.

Grapes do not ripen once they are cut from the vine, so make sure what is purchased is fully ripened; they will not improve sitting in storage. White grapes, when fully ripened, will have a pale yellow or straw-colored cast at the tips. Red grapes should show no tint of green and be a rich, full-bodied color. When purchasing, avoid anything pale or washed out in color, shrunken or shriveled, or showing any signs of mold where the grape met the vine. The vine, or stem, will also be a quality check, it should be green and pliable and hold firmly to the grapes.

Grapes from California will come into season in late May for some red grapes, and June or July for Thompson, and last into early December. Eastern grapes have a shorter season, becoming available in August and then gone by November. Imported grapes are generally available year-round; almost all imported grapes come from Mexico and Chile.

CHAMPAGNE, BLACK CORINTH

The Champagne grape, or Black Corinth, is a very small, crunchy, sweet fruit that is dark purple in color. Surprisingly, given the name associated with them, the principle use of this grape is not in making sparkling wine. They are also referred to as Zante grapes, which are often dried and marketed as Zante currants. Although the grapes are not always widely available, these seedless grapes are in demand when found in the market because of their excellent use as a table grape, with plenty of sweetness and juice. These are excellent paired with cheese and other fruits and adds visual appeal to other plated foods. This combination of flavor and visual appeal makes them highly desired in the foodservice industry. Watch for this grape in its brief season coming in mid to late summer. Look for very firm and brightly colored fruit; reject anything shriveled, showing signs of mold, or not firmly adhering to the stem.

Pack Size: 16 lb/7.26 kg flats
Shelf Life: 3 to 4 days
Storage Conditions: 32°F/0°C
Season: July to October

GREEN, WHITE

The green or white grape will, when fully ripened, always have a pale green hue with a straw-colored tone at the tips. They should be sweet with an acidic finish in the flavor. There are several varieties of white grape in the market, but the Thompson or Sultana grape is by far the most dominant, constituting almost one third of all table grapes grown in this country. This California grape is seedless, somewhat large, elongated in shape, and versatile. Beyond being America's favorite table grape, the Thompson is utilized when making baked goods, juice, wine, and for drying into raisins. This grape has a crisp bite and the flesh is juicy and sweet, but a bit bland in flavor.

Other seedless green grapes in the market appear throughout the growing season and may include the Perlette, which is plump or round in shape and should have a frosted bloom on the grape. The Perlette will have a crisp, juicy bite and be sweet with an acidic balance. The Superior green grape is quite elongated, bright green in color, and sweet in flavor. The Calmeria is a seeded green variety that is oval-shaped, mildly sweet, but a small fraction of what is on the market today. In addition to

FIGURE **15.1** Champagne/Black Corinth Grapes

FIGURE **15.2** Green/White Grapes

eating out of hand, green grapes are delicious in salads, particularly chicken salad, and cooked with cream and fillet of sole. As noted, these green grapes will have an amber or straw-colored cast at the tip when fully ripened. Avoid anything shriveled or showing signs of mold. The individual grapes should adhere tightly to the bunch.

Pack Size: 18 to 20 lb/8.16 to 9.07 kg flats
Shelf Life: 3 to 4 days
Storage Conditions: 32°F/0°C
Season: Available year-round but best when purchased locally and in season

Nutritional Information

Serving Size:	3-1/2 oz/100 g
Water:	80.54 g
Calories:	69
Protein:	0.72 g
Fat:	0.16 g
Saturated Fat:	0.054 g
Fiber:	0.9 g
Sodium:	2 mg
Iron:	0.36 mg
Potassium:	191 mg
Vitamin C:	10.8 mg

FIGURE **15.3** Red Grapes

RED

Red grapes should range from a full, bright, medium red color to a deep, dark claret color. There should be no sign of green color on the skin and they should be full and plump. There is some variance in size amongst the varieties, so size is not an issue, but purchasing grapes that are firm and vibrant is important; avoid anything flabby, soft, or shriveled. As previously noted, the enzymes that give these grapes their beautiful and appetizing color will also provide excellent health benefits.

Flame red grapes are a hybrid of the white Thompson grape and several red varieties, usually the Tokay. The Flame grape is the second most popular seedless table grape sold and their popularity is increasing. This grape is a bright, medium-red color with a good firm crunch to the bite. The flavor is sweet-tart with a good balance of sugar and acid. There are actually two varieties of this grape: Red Flame and Flame. Red Flames tend to be round in shape, redder in color, and medium in size. The Flame is more oblong and a darker red to purple shade.

Ruby red grapes are seedless and elongated with a sweet juicy flesh. The Red Globe and the Tokay Flame are seeded red grapes. The Tokay is quite elongated and bland in flavor despite having good acid and sugar content; the Globe is quite large, round, and fairly sweet but low in acid. Another seeded red grape is the Emperor, which was once very popular but the surge of seedless types in the market has now relegated them to a very small percentage of the total market. The Emperor has low sugar content and a bland, cherry-like flavor.

An eastern red seedless grape variety with great flavor is the Reliance. This is a small grape, pale red to golden in color, which packs a great punch of flavor. They are not widely available but look for this grape in farm stands in the eastern portion of the United States from late summer into fall. Its flavor makes it worth looking for.

The Black Beauty is considered a black seedless grape with a very rich, dark color. The flavor is reminiscent of the Concord grape with a bright, sweet, and spicy nature. This grape is blue/black in color and small with an oblong shape. The domestic season for this grape is short and they are only in the market during early to mid summer. Chilean imports are available year-round and are generally thought to have a more vibrant flavor.

The Venus is an eastern seedless black grape newer to the market; it is similar in color to the Black Beauty but with a larger, rounder fruit. The flavor is well liked even though the skin may have some astringency.

Concord grapes are a seeded, dark blue to purple fruit with a frosty bloom on the skin. Originally developed in Massachusetts, Concord grapes are now grown across the United States' northern tier, especially in the Northwest and New York state. These grapes are used as table fruit, for making juice, candy, and some for wine. They have a pronounced aroma and a sweet-tart, musty flavor. The Concord grape has a short season, coming to market in September and running through October.

FIGURE **15.4** Reliance Grapes

FIGURE **15.5** Black Grapes

FIGURE **15.6** Concord Grapes

With all grapes, look for firm, plump fruit with good color and sweetness. Avoid moldy or shriveled product and grapes that do not adhere to the bunch.

> **Pack Size:** 18 to 20 lb/8.16 to 9.07 kg flats
> **Shelf Life:** 3 to 4 days
> **Storage Conditions:** 32°F/0°C
> **Season:** Available year-round but best when purchased locally and in season

Nutritional Information

Serving Size:	3-1/2 oz/100 g
Water:	81.30 g
Calories:	67
Protein:	0.63 g
Fat:	0.35 g
Saturated Fat:	0.114 g
Fiber:	0.9 g
Sodium:	2 mg
Iron:	0.29 mg
Potassium:	191 mg
Vitamin C:	4 mg

BERRIES

Berry is the name for any of a number of small edible fruits. Botanically, a true berry is different than many of the fruits considered or named as berries in the foodservice. True berries are fruits that have seeds surrounded by pulp and that come from

FIGURE **15.7** Top row, left to right: Strawberry, Raspberry, Blackberry; bottom row, left to right: Gooseberry, Blueberry, Huckleberries

a single ovary. In foodservice, true berries would include the huckleberry and currants. The berries covered in this chapter are not all found in this group. Some are false berries that come from a part of the plant that does not include the ovary; this group would include the blueberry and strawberry. Others are aggregate fruits or those where multiple tiny fruits all spring from a single flower gathered into a single cluster; these include raspberries and blackberries.

BLACKBERRY

The blackberry is similar to a raspberry in its construction but is generally larger and plumper. This berry has a relatively short season from May to July and a very short shelf life once purchased. As with other berries, they can be found imported out of season but the quality does not always match the higher cost.

FIGURE **15.8** Blackberries

Look for plump, well-colored fruit with no shriveling or signs of mold. Wet fruit will mold quickly and shorten the shelf life even further. If they show signs of either red or green, they will be under-ripe, likewise if the hull is still attached. Do not wash these berries until just before utilizing them as the moisture will further their decay.

Blackberries are good for eating out of hand and for baking, and combine well with other fruits. They can be also be made into wine.

Pack Size: Twelve 1/2-pint flats
Shelf Life: 1 to 2 days
Storage Conditions: 34°F/1°C
Season: Available year-round but best when purchased locally and in season

Nutritional Information

Serving Size:	3-1/2 oz/100 g
Water:	88.5 g
Calories:	43
Protein:	1.39 g
Fat:	0.49 g
Saturated Fat:	0.014 g
Fiber:	5.3 g
Sodium:	1 mg
Iron:	0.62 mg
Potassium:	162 mg
Vitamin C:	21 mg

BLUEBERRY

The blueberry is small, about the size of a large pea, and blue-black to violet in color with a frosty blush. They grow either in the high bush variety, which can reach up to 5 feet/1.52 meters in height, or the low bush variety, which are thick bushes about a foot in height and the most prominent variety found wild in the northern parts of the United States and Canada. These berries can be found in the wild, but almost everything seen in the market today is cultivated and found in the late spring into the summer. Most of the world's production comes from several northern states and parts of Canada. Imported blueberries from South America are available at other times of the year for considerably more money and often have much less flavor.

Look for plump berries with a deep, dark purple to blue-black color. Red hues indicate premature picking that may only be good for cooking, and tints of green should be avoided. Taste the berry when inspecting to ensure they have the proper sweetness. Blueberries beginning to shrivel or show sign of mold should be avoided. Wet product may also turn moldy quickly. Spread the berries out upon purchasing and examine them for anything about to turn and remove from the rest. If washing the berries prior to using them be sure to dry on paper towels prior to storing, or the moisture will encourage their mold and decay.

Blueberries are immensely popular and good in muffins, pies and tarts, with hot cereal, in salads, or with fresh peaches and cream. They're very easy to use, just rinse, pat dry, and cook or eat.

Huckleberries are closely related to the blueberry but will only be found in the wild or from your neighborhood forager. These are small, round, seeded berries ranging from red to purple and blue in color. They taste very similar to blueberries, but the many seeds make the eating more work.

Pack Size: Twelve 1-pint flats
Shelf Life: 3 to 4 days
Storage Conditions: 34°F/1°C
Season: Available year-round but best when purchased locally and in season

FIGURE **15.9** Blueberries

FIGURE **15.10** Huckleberries

Nutritional Information

Serving Size:	3-1/2 oz/100 g
Water:	84.21 g
Calories:	57
Protein:	0.74 g
Fat:	0.33 g
Saturated Fat:	0.028 g
Fiber:	2.4 g
Sodium:	1 mg
Iron:	0.28 mg
Potassium:	77 mg
Vitamin C:	9.7 mg

BOYSENBERRY

The boysenberry is a cross between the loganberry, blackberry, and raspberry. This large berry is quite juicy and maroon red in color. It was reputedly developed and marketed on what eventually became Knott's Berry Farm. The tart raspberry flavor works very well in jams and jellies and this is the berry on which the Knott family built their business. Boysenberries are also excellent in preserves and syrups as well as for eating out of hand. If consuming these fresh, be sure to utilize them almost immediately as they have a shelf life of just two to three days from harvest.

Boysenberries come into the market in late spring and are gone by mid to late summer. Avoid anything that appears shriveled, squashed, or flat and check carefully for mold. The fruit should be plump, fragrant, and sweet. Never wash these berries until just before cooking or eating.

Pack Size: Twelve 1-pint flats
Shelf Life: 3 days from harvest
Storage Conditions: 34°F/1°C
Season: June to August

CRANBERRY

The cranberry is an unusual fruit in that grows in wet bogs primarily in the American North. Wisconsin is the heaviest producer, followed by Massachusetts, but cranberries are also grown in New Jersey and the Pacific Northwest. This, along with the blueberry, is one of two berries native to North America. Cranberries are round like large marbles with a deep red color and a bright, very tart flavor. They are harvested throughout the year but are typically associated with the holidays in the colder seasons. They should be plump and bright; avoid berries that are shriveled or pale in color. Most often cranberries are found in the supermarket or from your produce vendor in 12 ounce/340 gram bags. Fresh cranberries can be found around the holidays or they can always be found frozen or canned. Freezing does well in maintaining the quality of the fruit. They have also become very popular in a sweetened and dried form.

FIGURE **15.11** Cranberries

Cranberries are most famous for being cooked with sugar into a sauce to accompany turkey; their tartness makes them inedible when they are served plain. They are also used in puddings, relishes, baked goods, and chutneys. These berries are excellent when combined with other sweeter fruits to balance their tartness. The juice is a very popular and healthy drink for breakfast or in cocktails.

Pack Size: 1 lb/454 g bags
Shelf Life: Up to 1 week
Storage Conditions: 40°F/4°C
Season: September into December but available year-round

Nutritional Information

Serving Size:	3-1/2 oz/100 g
Water:	87.13 g
Calories:	46
Protein:	0.39 g
Fat:	0.13 g
Saturated Fat:	0.011 g
Fiber:	4.6 g
Sodium:	2 mg
Iron:	0.25 mg
Potassium:	85 mg
Vitamin C:	13.3 mg

CURRANTS

The currant is a small, seeded berry related to the gooseberry, found in three distinct colors: red, white, and black. This is not the same fruit as the dried currant; that is the Zante grape in its tiny, wrinkled, raisin-like form that is used primarily in cooking.

Of the three fresh varieties, the black is best served in preserves or fermented into cassis. The brighter colored red and white types are good eaten right out of hand, but the red will be more acidic in flavor. These can also be used for jams, jellies, and the red currant is in the hallmark of Cumberland sauce. The berries should be dry, plump, firm, and well-colored when purchased and exhibit a sweet tart flavor. Look for them at farm stands in the early to mid summer.

Pack Size: Twelve 1/2 pint flats
Shelf Life: 2 to 3 days
Storage Conditions: 34°F/1°C
Season: July through September

Black Currants
Nutritional Information

Serving Size:	3-1/2 oz/100 g
Water:	81.96 g
Calories:	63
Protein:	1.40 g
Fat:	0.41 g
Saturated Fat:	0.034 g
Sodium:	2 mg
Iron:	1.54 mg
Potassium:	322 mg
Vitamin C:	181 mg

Red and White Currants
Nutritional Information

Serving Size:	3-1/2 oz/100 g
Water:	83.95 g
Calories:	56
Protein:	1.4 g
Fat:	0.2 g
Saturated Fat:	0.017 g
Fiber:	4.3 g
Sodium:	1 mg
Iron:	1 mg
Potassium:	275 mg
Vitamin C:	41 mg

GOOSEBERRY

The gooseberry originated in Europe and the European variety differs somewhat from the North American variety even though it was genetically derived from the European. The berry is roughly marble-sized and is most frequently found in shades of very pale green to yellow. They can also be found varying from a pale rose blush all the way to a deep dark red, much like the currant to which they are related. They all have pale yellow stripes running down from the stem. This is a seeded berry, containing a cluster of small seeds inside the flesh. The skin is also found both smooth or with a faint fuzzy coat.

FIGURE **15.12** Gooseberries

Look for full, plump, evenly colored berries with a green stem. They should be slightly tart in flavor, which makes them work well in baked goods and jams or jellies or covered with chocolate. Native American gooseberries are rarely found in the market; most are imported from New Zealand in the summer months.

Pack Size: Twelve 1-pint flats
Shelf Life: 1 week
Storage Conditions: 62° to 68°F/16° to 20°C or refrigerate
Season: July to October

Nutritional Information

Serving Size:	3-1/2 oz/100 g
Water:	87.87 g
Calories:	44
Protein:	0.88 g
Fat:	0.58 g
Saturated fat:	0.038 g
Fiber:	4.3 g
Sodium:	1 mg
Iron:	0.31 mg
Potassium:	198 mg
Vitamin C:	27.7 mg

CAPE GOOSEBERRY

Also known as a ground cherry, the Cape gooseberry has a papery husk much like the tomatillo. When this husk is peeled back, an opaque but slightly golden-hued fruit is revealed. This piquant fruit can be made into preserves, baked into pies, or eaten raw and is a good accompaniment to savory dishes such as roast game. The Cape gooseberry grows wild in some parts of the United States and wild in various tropical regions.

Pack Size: Twelve 1-pint containers per flat
Shelf Life: 2 weeks
Storage Conditions: 34°F/1°C
Season: March through October

FIGURE **15.13** Cape Gooseberries

LOGANBERRY

Developed in California, the loganberry is a large, dark red to purple fruit that is a cross between the blackberry and raspberry. The raw fruit was not originally popular for its flavor, but it is mild and pleasant and has gained some admirers. The loganberry can be eaten raw, but is most prized for the excellent jam that it produces. These berries are also good for making syrup and in wine making.

Loganberries come into the market in the summer months. Look for plump, well-colored fruit with a full, dark red color. Avoid anything soft or moldy and utilize quickly because of their short shelf life. Washing just before using is also recommended as the moisture will promote mold and encourage decay.

RASPBERRY

The raspberry is actually a bunch of tiny drupelets attached to one small aggregate fruit. This berry is usually red in color, but is also found in golden or dark purplish-black varieties, and these all should be quite fragrant with a bigger punch of flavor than other berries. Look for plump, brightly colored berries with a hazy glow and a sweet flavor; the golden variety's flavor may be reminiscent of ripe apricots. Avoid anything that is wet as they will mold quickly, as well as berries that are flattened or shriveled in appearance. If the hull is still attached, the berry was picked prematurely and will lack flavor and sweetness. Raspberries are found seasonally from spring into fall with the best crops coming early and late in the season. Imported product is always available, but the

FIGURE **15.14** Raspberries

value for flavor versus price will often be lacking. Always use this fruit quickly as they have a short shelf life. Avoid washing until just ready for use as this will dramatically curtail the shelf life and cause molding.

Raspberries make excellent jam, combine well with peaches, cream, or champagne, complement duck, and are used in Linzer tortes. Raspberries are also used to flavor vinegars for salad dressing or marinating poultry.

Pack Size: Twelve 1/2-pint flats
Shelf Life: 1 to 2 days
Storage Conditions: 34°F/1°C
Season: Available year-round but best when purchased locally and in season

Nutritional Information

Serving Size:	3-1/2 oz/100 g
Water:	85.75 g
Calories:	52
Protein:	1.20 g
Fat:	0.65 g
Saturated Fat:	0.019 g
Fiber:	6.5 g
Sodium:	1 mg
Iron:	0.69 mg
Potassium:	151 mg
Vitamin C:	26.2 mg

STRAWBERRIES

The strawberry is a red, conical-shaped berry with small yellowish flecks, which are the seeds of the berry. This berry grows wild but today the market primarily consists of cultivated berries. The most common type available is the larger, very firm berry that originated as a hybrid of the once-wild berry and a Chilean variety. This variety can be quite good and sweet or quite bland and watery, so be sure to taste them upon receipt. This berry is very hardy, making it able to withstand the rigors of travel, which improves the shelf life so that it can be marketed well. However, mass-produced berries that are picked, chilled, and packaged to withstand shipping will not match the tender sweetness and bright luscious flavor of those purchased from a local farm stand, which are well-worth purchasing even though they have a shorter shelf life.

There is another strawberry, the fraise des bois, which is grown in France. It is prized as the sweetest and most flavorful variety of all. However, harvesting this tiny berry is labor intensive and since it is highly perishable, it is rarely found in the market. When they are available, these will be very expensive but very delicious.

FIGURE **15.15** Strawberries

Strawberries are available year-round, but their flavor is almost always better during the warm months of spring into early fall. Look for fully ripened and red berries, without white shoulders, that have a rich sweet aroma. Avoid anything still showing signs of green, that are wet, or that have dark or soft spots and signs of mold at the stem. Handle these berries gently and utilize them quickly if farm fresh.

Enjoy strawberries puréed into drinks, in jams and sauces, on or in ice cream, with rhubarb in a pie, simply macerated with sugar, dipped into chocolate, or, best of all with whipped cream and shortcake.

Pack Size: Twelve 1-pint flats or eight 2-lb/907-g clamshells per flat
Shelf Life: 3 to 4 days
Storage Conditions: 34°F/1°C
Season: Available year-round but best when purchased locally and in season

Nutritional Information

Serving Size:	3-1/2 oz/100 g
Water:	90.95 g
Calories:	32
Protein:	0.67 g
Fat:	0.3 g
Saturated Fat:	0.015 g
Fiber:	2 g
Sodium:	1 mg
Iron:	0.41 mg
Potassium:	153 mg
Vitamin C:	58.8 mg

16

STONE FRUIT

This category of fruit is so named due to the large hard pit, or stone, common to each variety. Botanists refer to this category as "drupes," from the Latin *drupa,* wherein the seed of the plant is surrounded by a thick, fleshy wall. Coffee, almonds, olives, avocados, and mangos are part of this grouping. In foodservice, however, the term "stone fruit" generally signifies nectarines, peaches, plums, cherries, and a few hybrid or specialty fruits such as pluots and apriums.

These fruits are usually divided into either "freestone" or "clingstone" varieties. In a freestone fruit, as their name suggests, the seed, or stone, more easily separates itself from the flesh, whereas the clingstone pit more tightly adheres to the flesh of the fruit. Because of their ease of use, freestone varieties are more frequently utilized for cooking purposes that requires the removal of the stone. For many people, this ease of use translates to a higher consumption of raw freestones as well, even though the clingstone variety is considered a juicier and sweeter choice. Consequently, due to this trend, the freestone variety has become nearly the total focus of the marketplace and in retail markets. Clingstone varieties are rarely seen outside of farm markets and stands these days.

Stone fruits are generally only available in the summer months, except for some imports from South America. Most domestic peaches are from California, Georgia, South Carolina, and Michigan. They will soften once picked but not gain any sweetness. Therefore, the fruit generally found in the marketplace will have been picked while still very firm or hard to facilitate shipping without incurring damage to the soft, fully ripened fruit. Color is the best indicator of a fruit that is fully matured before picking; look for full and vibrantly colored fruit with no hint of green. There should also be a full, sweet aroma indicative of the flavor when the fruit is softened.

When allowing stone fruits to soften, it is important to not refrigerate them. Spread the fruit out in single layer to prevent the weight of the fruit from flattening and bruising each other. If the fruit must be refrigerated prior to use, storing the fruit in colder conditions (below 35°F/1.6°C) is much better. Storing stone fruits between 36° and 50°F/2.2° and 10°C can actually hasten their decay.

NECTARINES

Nectarines get their name from "nectar of the gods." They are essentially a cultivar or type of peach without the fuzzy skin, despite being generally treated and considered a wholly different fruit. The smooth shiny skin is simply a recessive gene that differentiates it from the fuzzier peaches. This lack of fuzz also accounts for the brighter red and yellow hues in the skin.

The fruit should be fairly large and heavy for its size. The flesh should feel firm and requires two or three days to soften properly. Avoid anything that is rock hard, fruit that is too small, or that has pitted, wrinkled skin, bruises, or molding. A fragrant sweet smell that increases as the fruit softens at room temperature is preferred.

Like peaches, nectarines have either yellow or white flesh and are available in freestone and clingstone varieties. They are often, but not always, slightly smaller than their peach relations and are often sweeter as well. Nectarines are very fragile and bruise easily, so care in storage and handling is critical. There are over a hundred varieties of nectarines and peaches, but this chapter will just focus on white- and yellow-fleshed varieties.

The white nectarine represents only a relatively small percentage of the market but it has seen increasing popularity lately. Besides color, the fundamental difference between white and yellow nectarines is the balance of acid to sugar. The white varieties have a much lower acid level and increased amounts of sugar making them, naturally, much sweeter. They will develop their sweetness quicker, have a softer texture in the flesh, and a shorter shelf life than their yellow counterparts. White nectarines are typically 2 to 3 inches/5 to 8 centimeters in diameter with blotched skin from creamy white to pink to red without the yellow streaks. The skin will feel almost loose against the flesh. The stem end will be whitish to pale green, but the less green the better. A creamy white background with no tinge of green is the best sign of good fruit.

Avoid a green tint, wrinkled and bruised skin, or a brown streak on the surface; all of these are indicators of improper picking timing or poor storage. Nectarines should be allowed to ripen at room temperature and only refrigerated once ripe. Inside, the flesh will radiate pink to white coming away from the pit. The softer texture and lack of acid makes the white nectarine tricky to cook, so they are most frequently utilized raw. With care, however, they can be utilized in pies and cobblers and will require less time and heat than when cooking by other methods.

Yellow nectarines, it follows, are deeper yellow with just a pink blush in the color of the flesh and a firmer texture. There is a greater balance of acid to sugar in the flesh that gives it a bright, spicy flavor as well as more options in preparation. The skin will have a deep yellow background with vibrant streaks or blotches of red. A deep yellow color with no green is the key to determining quality; the shade and amount of red will vary. The acid and texture will require a bit more ripening time once mature, but will also prolong the shelf life. Because of the balance of acid and sugar in the flesh, the sweetness or tartness of the flavor profile can be determined by adjusting the time the fruit is allowed to soften at room temperature. These nectarines can be used in salads, soups, grilled with poultry, or baked in pies, tarts, and cobblers either alone or teamed with other fruits and nuts.

Pack Size: 1 layer tray pack has 20 to 36 per box

Shelf Life: 3 to 5 days

Storage Conditions: Store at room temperature until ripe then refrigerate for up to 2 days at 38° to 40°F/3° to 4°C

Season: January to September

Nutritional Information

Serving Size:	3-1/2 oz/100 g
Water:	87.59 g
Calories: 44	
Protein:	1.06 g
Fat:	0.32 g
Saturated Fat:	0.025 g
Fiber:	1.7 g
Sodium:	0 mg
Iron:	0.28 mg
Potassium:	201 mg
Vitamin C:	5.4 mg

FIGURE **16.1** Yellow Nectarines

PEACHES

Peaches are the fuzzier cousin of the nectarine. Both are essentially from the same genus and the same tree can even produce both fruits; the fuzzy skin is just the more dominant gene to the smooth shiny skin found on nectarines. Yet despite this closeness in nature, the peach seems to have garnered most of the press and usage in the culinary world. Nevertheless, these two fruits have strong similarities. Peaches also have either white or yellow flesh, are either freestone or clingstone, and both have that succulent, sweet, juicy flesh.

The peach market is now predominantly freestone because they provide the greatest ease of use, especially when cooking. The clingstone market is largely a niche in local farm stands due to local appreciation of their higher sweetness and juice content. Peaches tend to grow a bit larger than nectarines and some varieties are a little less sweet, but the similarities are marked. Like the nectarine, there are too many varieties to list them all. The Flamin' Fury is a relatively new peach to the market and is exceedingly popular due to its large size, balance of sweet to acid, and flavor. There are now over twenty different varieties of this single type of peach, and these are constantly being improved and altered. Other notable names are Loring, RedHaven, and

Madison, but the region grown will dictate what is best locally and which best fits the bill for what you are preparing.

White peaches, as with nectarines, differ from yellow peaches by the ratio of sugar to acid in the flesh and, of course, by color. A white peach has less acid and very good sugar content, making them wonderfully soft and sweet. Even if very firm when purchased, the white peach should soften within a day or two. Varieties such as the delicious White Lady will be large, heavy with juice, and sweet but retain enough acidic balance to make them wonderful to eat.

FIGURE **16.2** Yellow Peach

FIGURE **16.3** White Peach

Look for a creamy white background in the skin with a warm pink blush. There should be no green and they should not be rock hard. Avoid dented, bruised, green, or shriveled fruit when purchasing. There should be a distinct sweet peach smell that gives promise to the flavor within when softened. Do not store in bags or piled in bowls or their weight will bruise and flatten each other as they ripen.

Yellow peaches such as the aforementioned Flamin' Fury will have a warm yellow color under blotches of red and pink. They have stronger balance of acid to sugar and are more complex in flavor. The firmer texture causes them to ripen more slowly but also prolongs their shelf life. The flesh will be a rich yellow color with blushes of red around the stone. They will be firm when picked, but should not be rock hard and should have a distinct peach aroma. Delightful eaten out of hand, in cream, on shortcake, or baked into pies, tarts and cobblers for dessert, these peaches can also be served grilled or in soups. The one real trick is buying properly matured and ripened fruit in season when there is simply nothing better to eat.

Pack size: 1 layer tray pack has 18 to 24 count; 2 layer tray pack has 36 to 48 count
Shelf life: 3 to 5 days
Storage Conditions: Ripen at room temperature and refrigerate for up to 2 days at 38° to 40°F/3° to 4°C
Season: Spring and summer for domestic fruit and winter for South American

Nutritional Information

Serving Size:	3-1/2 oz/100 g
Water:	88.87 g
Calories:	39
Protein:	0.91 g
Fat:	0.25 g
Saturated Fat:	0.019 g
Fiber:	1.5 g
Iron:	0.25 mg
Potassium:	190 mg
Vitamin C:	6.6 mg

FIGURE **16.4** Saturn Peaches

SATURN PEACHES, FLAT PEACHES, DONUT PEACHES

Relatively new in the market is the flat peach, its shape evoking both the donut and Saturn monikers used for marketing purposes. This peach is relatively new to this hemisphere but has been cultivated and enjoyed in China for centuries.

A great peach for eating out of hand, they are small and easily peeled and/or eaten. These are white-fleshed, freestone peaches and therefore very sweet, but they retain enough acid to give them a very bright and delicious flavor. There can be a faint almond flavor in the flesh, and the thin skin has little fuzz, which makes peeling unnecessary. This is an early ripening fruit and will likely be the first variety to appear at the farm stand. As with all white peaches, look for an unblemished skin with a cream-colored base and pink splotches. It should have a pronounced sweet aroma and some give in the flesh. Avoid bruised, pitted, or green-skinned fruit and fruit that is still rock hard with only a faint aroma. The Saturn peach should ripen at room temperature within a day or two. Great eaten raw out of hand, this lovely fruit is also delicious in many cooking applications. This is a great peach and should not be overlooked, no matter the end result.

Pack size: 1 or 2 layer tray pack
Shelf life: 2 to 4 days
Storage Conditions: Ripen at room temperature and then refrigerate for up to 2 days
Season: Domestic: May to August; South America: January and February

PLUMS

Plums are a stone fruit like peaches, but have far greater diversity in shape, size, and color. Their season begins in May with the Japanese varieties and runs well into October with the European varieties. The bulk of the crop in this country, and for much of the world, comes from California. Among those grown in California is the French Agen variety, which is primarily dried into prunes.

Japanese plums (actually believed to have originated in China) are the first varieties to arrive in the market each spring. The flesh of these plums range from golden

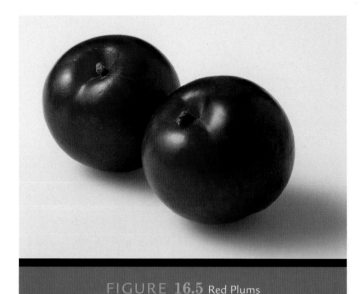

FIGURE **16.5** Red Plums

FIGURE **16.6** Greengage Plums

yellow to reddish and the skin will always be yellow (like a Wickson) or crimson (like a Santa Rosa) to red-black in color, but not blue or purple. These varieties tend to be a bit larger, softer in texture, and more assertive in flavor than the European types. They are very juicy and sweet, and are clingstone fruits. The Japanese plums are the popular choice for eating out of hand in today's market.

European varieties almost always have a blue to purple skin color and yellow flesh. These plums are the freestone variety and range from round to oval or egg shaped. The varieties dried into prunes are always European varieties. Those sold as fresh are often marketed as "prune plums" (such as Italian Prune plums), but can be enjoyed cooked or eaten out of hand. Generally, European varieties are the most sought after for cooking and baking.

There are exceptions to the rules, such as the Greengage plum. This is a European plum but is green to yellow-green in color and developed from a wild variety. This plum's sweetness makes it valued in confectionary applications. The Damson plum is small and yellow in color but very tart, which makes it an excellent choice in making jams and jellies.

Plums will remain firm when ripened and do not soften like a peach or nectarine. However, avoid fruits that are rock hard; there should always be a springy firmness to the flesh. Good rich color and heft are also important factors when selecting plums. These quality checks are valid no matter what variety of plum is purchased.

The plum's long season and great variety in texture, color, flavor, and sweetness make it an excellent test for a cook's imagination and artistic talent. The long season is furthered by the plum's good shelf life, but avoid fruit that appears to be in storage too long, such as those shriveling and/or softening at the ends.

Pack Size: 10 or 20 lb/4.54 or 9.07 kg box
Shelf Life: 3 to 5 days
Storage Conditions: Ripen at room temperature and refrigerate for up to 2 days
Season: Domestic: July and August; South America: February and March

Nutritional Information

Serving Size:	3-1/2 oz/100 g
Water:	87.23 g
Calories:	46
Protein:	0.7 g
Fat:	0.28 g
Saturated Fat:	0.017 g
Fiber:	1.4 g
Sodium:	0 g
Iron:	0.17 mg
Potassium:	157 mg
Vitamin C:	9.5 mg

APRICOT

The apricot is the earliest ripening of the stone fruits and is related to the peach. This fruit is small and round with an orange/yellow flesh when fully ripe. The fruit is freestone with a firm, dry flesh and a silky skin. Outside the United States, apricots can be found that are pink, white, gray, and black, but orange is the color to look for here.

FIGURE **16.7** Apricots

Avoid fruit that is pale yellow, shriveling, and very hard. Apricots should be plump, sweet smelling, and have some give or softness to the flesh. The best eating fruit will be very soft, but these will have virtually no shelf life because of their great delicacy. Small blemishes in the flesh should not negatively affect the flavor.

Apricots taste much different fresh than dried. They have a slightly tart and musky flavor and are still fairly sweet. These are good eaten out of hand, dried, stewed, on a green salad, baked in pastry, or brewed into brandy or wine.

There are hundreds of varieties of apricot and more are constantly evolving. Almost all are essentially similar but there are subtle differences in size, the amount of blush on the skin, sweetness, tartness, and the firmness of the flesh.

Pack Size: 1 or 2 layer tray pack
Shelf Life: 3 to 4 days
Storage Conditions: Ripen at room temperature and refrigerate for up to 2 days
Season: Domestic: June through August; South America: February and March

Nutritional Information

Serving Size:	3-1/2 oz/100 g
Water:	86.35 g
Calories:	48
Protein:	1.4 g
Fat:	0.39 g
Saturated Fat:	0.027 g
Fiber:	2 g
Sodium:	1 mg
Iron:	0.39 mg
Potassium:	259 mg
Vitamin C:	10 mg

CHERRIES

Cherries are either of the sweet or sour type and have been cultivated for two thousand years. The United States is the leading producer in the world but they are grown wherever the climate is temperate enough to allow it, meaning cold but not severe winters and warm but not blazing hot summers. In addition to the sweet and sour types, there is a third, lesser known type, not surprisingly classified as sweet/sour and marketed as Royale and Duke.

Bing is by far the largest produced and most popular sweet cherry in the United States. There are also several heart-shaped varieties called Ox Hearts; and the delicious red and yellow Rainier cherry, which, despite its obvious color, can also be known as a white cherry. Other varieties of sweet cherries do exist, but are similar in nature. Look for plump, firm, richly colored fruit. Avoid shriveling, mold at the stems, brown or slimy stems, and rock hard fruit. The season and shelf life of sweet cherries is relatively short, so enjoy and serve them when the summer season allows them in the market.

Sour cherries, chiefly Morello, Montmorency, and Amarelle, are darker in color and firmer than the sweet varieties. They have a much higher acid content and are therefore much more suitable for baking, saucing, and jams. In the United States, most sour cherries are grown in Michigan and New York, whereas the sweet varieties do better in the Northwest.

Pack Size: 10 or 20 lb/4.54 or 9.07 kg box
Shelf Life: 1 to 3 days
Storage Conditions: Refrigerate immediately at 32° to 35°F/0 to 1.5°C
Season: May to August

Sweet Cherries
Nutritional Information

Serving Size:	3-1/2 oz/100 g
Water:	82.25 g
Calories:	63
Protein:	1.06 g
Fat:	0.2 g
Saturated Fat:	0.038 g
Fiber:	2.1 g
Iron:	0.36 mg
Potassium:	222 mg
Vitamin C:	7 mg

FIGURE **16.8** Sweet Cherries

Sour Cherries
Nutritional Information

Serving Size:	3-1/2 oz/100 g
Water:	86.13 g
Calories:	50
Protein:	1 g
Fat:	0.3 g
Saturated Fat:	0.068 g
Fiber:	1.6 g
Sodium:	3 mg
Iron:	0.32 mg
Potassium:	173 mg
Vitamin C:	10 mg

FIGURE **16.9** Sour Cherries

PLUOTS

This relatively newly developed hybrid is a cross between a plum and an apricot, but is much more plum-like in appearance and flavor. This fruit is delicious and juicy and has very high sugar content.

There is also the plucot, which is very similar; it can be closer to the apricot in appearance while the flesh still eats more like a plum. The plucot is also very delicious, juicy, and sweet.

This, naturally, is followed by the hybrid know as the aprium, another hybrid from the apricot and plum. This fruit takes most of its appearance and flavor from the apricot side of the family, but is still firm and juicy like the plum.

These fruits can be eaten out of hand and utilized in cooking much as you would with the plum or apricot. Avoid rock hard or shriveled fruit, or that which is scarred or too soft at the stem end.

FIGURE **16.10** Pluots

Pack Size: 10 or 20 lb/4.54 or 9.07 kg box
Shelf Life: 3 to 5 days
Storage Conditions: Ripen at room temperature and refrigerate for up to 2 days
Season: Domestic: July and August; South America: February and March

MELONS

Melons are divided into two main categories, those of muskmelon and watermelon. Under these two headings, a surprisingly varied array of types, colors, flavors, and levels of sweetness can be found. This gives way to a wonderful array of options for service; serving a wedge for breakfast or putting diced melon into a fruit salad is no longer sufficiently using this wonderful sweet fruit. Melons can be used in salads married with savory and acidic ingredients, puréed into a refreshing cold soup, served in unusually delightful cocktails, paired with cheese, spiced with pepper, or chilled into a sorbet.

Muskmelons can have netted veins covering their rind as found on the cantaloupe, or smooth waxy rinds like the honeydew. Muskmelon varieties can have orange, green, golden or pale yellow to white flesh with all their seeds held in a stringy wet mass located in the center of each melon. Watermelons come in a variety of sizes with the typical red or bright yellow flesh and with or without seeds.

Most melons are best in the summer months when they are grown domestically and are at their sweetest; warm days and nights are required for maximum sweetness. Melons grown in South America definitely extend availability well into or through the winter, but take care when selecting them in order to find any with good sweetness. Two muskmelon varieties, the Christmas and Santa Claus melons, are available from early fall into December.

Choosing and receiving a good melon requires experience and a good sense of smell. In foodservice, try to actually cut and taste melons when receiving. Often this can't happen at your local market or farm stand although many farmers will gladly let you sample their product. In general, look for melons with the appropriate color, that are heavy for their size, and that have a "full slip" at the stem end. The latter indicates that the melon was fully ripe and fell easily from its stem. Melons with a jagged piece of stem still attached or a flat cut at the stem should be avoided as they were prematurely harvested. Some muskmelons will have a slight give at the blossom end and give off a sweet aroma indicating good sugar content. Another ripeness test is to listen for the sounds of seeds rattling inside when the melon is shook, but this often does not work. When ripe, watermelons should sound hollow if lightly thumped. Watermelons may have a pale area on one side where they lay on the ground; look for those with a yellow cast in that area over a pale or dull white shade.

Selection is not always simple and requires some practice, and there are other indications specific to certain melons that will be mentioned when discussing those varieties. Learning how to select a ripe melon is important because melons will not ripen further once picked. They will soften further as if ripening, but the sugar content and flavor will not improve.

Melons also have better flavor if used when cold. If you prefer your melon this way, chill it only for a few hours just before eating or serving. As with most fruits and vegetables, melons are best enjoyed in season and grown locally whenever possible. Some varieties will stretch that season and your choice in selection should reflect that. This fruit is one of the best eating, most versatile, and refreshing items in the market, just be willing to experiment and reap the full benefit of the menu options they represent.

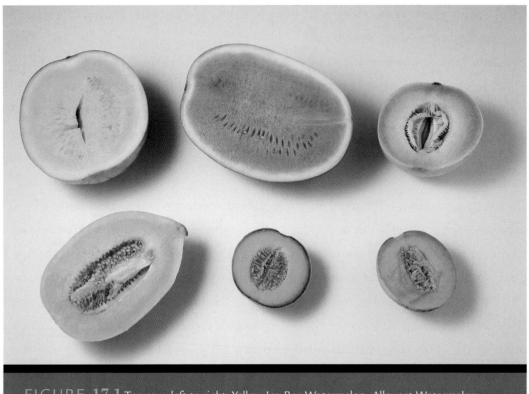

FIGURE **17.1** Top row, left to right: Yellow Ice-Box Watermelon, Allsweet Watermelon, Honeydew; Bottom row: Crenshaw, Cantaloupe, Charentais

MUSKMELON VARIETIES

As previously discussed, all the melons in this section are a cultivar of the muskmelon, and in the United States what is commonly called a cantaloupe is in reality the muskmelon. As noted they mostly have netted rinds, but many do not, and they may be ribbed, but not necessarily. Most are orange fleshed, but others are green to white. For all their differences, they are delicious, refreshing, and healthy. Buy them in season and taste as many as you can find; they are worth the search.

CANARY MELON, JUAN CANARY

This melon is a bit unusual in that its rind is bright yellow when ripe, giving it its canary moniker. Beyond a fully yellow rind with no greening, make sure that there are no soft or bruised areas. There should be some give and they may have a faint sweet smell at the stem end. As with most other musk varieties, make certain that there is a full slip and no stem remnants at that end. Canary melons should be heavy, oblong, and slightly larger than most other muskmelon varieties. The flesh will run from pale green like a honeydew to almost white in color. Although the flesh is similar to the honeydew in appearance, the flavor will more closely mimic the cantaloupe but with a bit more tartness. This variation in flavor makes it a good choice when pairing with other melons and fruits.

> **Pack Size:** 4 to 8 count per case
> **Shelf Life:** 1 week under refrigeration
> **Storage Conditions:** 45°F/7°C
> **Season:** Begins in early summer and through the fall, best in July and August

CANTALOUPE

The two main varieties of this melon are the European and the North American. The melons found in Europe bear little resemblance to the North American variety as they have less netting and a pale green color. They are generally smaller in size and are often thought to be superior in sweetness and flavor. These melons, unlike the American variety, do not slip the vine, so expect to find the stem end attached. Charentais is the most notable variety imported here and is discussed separately.

Several varieties of muskmelon native to America are referred to as cantaloupes. These are known for their mottled netting and often have a ribbed appearance. The Persian melon is a common variety but is best eaten only in season in the warm summer months. Most will fall from their vines

FIGURE **17.2** Cantaloupe

when ripe, so the full slip is a quality check, but just one of many to look for. Cantaloupes should have tan to golden color below the netting; green is indicative of early picking. There should also be a defined musky, sweet aroma that is very appetizing and some yield at the stem end.

Despite the misnomer of its best known name, this is an exceedingly popular melon in the United States and for good reason. Muskmelons are very sweet, rich in color and flavor, and are nutritious and low in calories. A heavy melon has good water content and is desired; however, one that sloshes when shaken has watery flesh and is less desirable.

Cantaloupes and muskmelons are great eaten plain, with Serrano and prosciutto hams, or made into cool soup and spicy salsas.

Pack Size: 12 to 24 count per case
Shelf Life: 1 to 2 weeks
Storage Conditions: 50°F/10°C
Season: Best in warm summer months, but year-round availability exists

Nutritional Information

Serving Size:	3-1/2 oz/100 g
Water:	90.15 g
Calories:	34
Protein:	0.84 g
Fat:	0.19 g
Saturated Fat:	0.051 g
Fiber:	0.9 g
Sodium:	16 mg
Iron:	0.21 mg
Potassium:	267 mg
Vitamin C:	36.7 mg

CASABA MELON

This is a large-sized member of the honeydew group most noted for its long shelf life into the late fall. Casabas are not widely grown so may be more expensive than more heavily cultivated species. Quality is sometimes difficult to assess because they have little to no odor. Casabas range from pale white to yellow in color, and most find that the yellow rind has the better flavor. The Santa Claus and Christmas melons are members of the Casaba family and have plainly wrinkled, rough, bark-like rinds with green mottling mixed with yellow. Of this group, the Santa Claus winter variety is usually the most delicious option. All melons in this group improve the longer they stay on the vine, so late in the harvest is preferred. In the heart of the summer you will likely find sweeter and tastier cantaloupe and honeydew melons, but casabas are good choices later in the fall. These melons are generally eaten simply cut up or tossed into a fruit salad; they can benefit from a touch of lemon or lime juice to brighten their flavor.

Pack Size: 5 to 6 count per case
Shelf Life: 1 to 2 weeks
Storage Conditions: 50°F/10°C
Season: Late summer well into the fall

Nutritional Information

Serving Size:	3-1/2 oz/100 g
Water:	91.85 g
Calories:	28
Protein:	1.11 g
Fat:	0.1 g
Saturated Fat:	0.025 g
Fiber:	0.9 g
Sodium:	9 mg
Iron:	0.34 mg
Potassium:	182 mg
Vitamin C:	21.8 mg

CRENSHAW, CRANSHAW

This selection is a hybrid, bred from the muskmelon and casaba varieties. The Crenshaw was originally known as the Crane melon after the farmer who first grew them. The fine netting on the rind indicates its Persian muskmelon heritage and its shape is reminiscent of the casaba. Its flavor is reputed to be the best parts from each breed, sweet and perfumed; this quality can demand a premium price. Crenshaw melons have a yellow rind with an orange/salmon colored flesh and are large in size. Once purchased, these melons should be utilized quickly as they have a very limited shelf life. Look for heavy, firm melons with some give at the stem and that have an appetizingly spicy, sweet scent.

Pack Size: 5 to 6 count per case
Shelf Life: Several days
Storage Conditions: 62°F/16°C or refrigerate
Season: Mid summer into October

CHARENTAIS, CAVAILLON MELON

This is a true variety of cantaloupe that originated in France but has recently been grown in the United States. This melon is one of the best you will find, with a wonderful aroma and clean, highly sweet, tropical flavor. The skin on this cantaloupe is smooth, or lightly netted, and the shape is ribbed with green. The rind has a golden hue with a greenish tinge and the melon is smaller than a typical cantaloupe, perfect for two servings. The melon's reputation and newness to our markets come at a premium price or about the same price as a melon twice its size. However, when they are good, they are well worth the expense. This should be served simply or with a quality ham to showcase their fresh sweetness and flavor.

FIGURE **17.3** Crenshaw/Cranshaw Melon

Pack Size: 6 to12 count per case
Shelf Life: 1 to 2 weeks
Storage Conditions: 50°F/10°C
Season: Imported in winter, domestically grown in the summer

GALIA

Developed in Israel but now grown in Spain, Brazil, Costa Rica, Panama, and the United States as well, this may be the optimal choice for melons in the cooler months when it is available and smelling sweet. The Galia is a muskmelon and honeydew hybrid, with netting over a greenish to yellow rind. Essentially it looks like a large cantaloupe with attractive dark green flesh. The yield at the stem end will not give you a clear idea of its quality. With this melon it's all about the yellow/green color (more yellow is better) and a sweet aroma. If it smells nice and sweet it will probably eat that way.

Galias tend to be pricey, but their size runs large and their availability when most melons are not in season makes for a better value. They are definitely worth looking into when lower priced melons are no longer available in the quality you desire.

Pack Size: 5 to 6 per case
Shelf Life: 1 week
Storage Conditions: 50°F/10°C
Season: Year-round

HONEYDEW

The honeydew is the most common of the non-netted, inodorous melons. They are larger than most muskmelons and have smooth, waxy, almost silken rind, ranging from pale yellow to almost white in color. The flesh of these melons is normally green, but the orange flesh variety (known as the Temptation) is sweeter and richer in flavor. The mild flavor and intense sweetness of properly grown honeydews make them the most popular melon in America today. Honeydews are enjoyed as is, mixed with other fruit, in combinations with a salty ham, or simply grilled to caramelize the sweet flesh. The size helps in identifying quality because it has almost no odor; the larger and heavier melons tend to taste best and there should be some yield to pressure at the stem end without it actually going soft. The rind will initially be green and ripen into a yellow to silvery white color, which makes the color another indication of its ripeness.

Pack Size: 4 to 6 count per case
Shelf Life: 1 to 2 weeks
Storage Conditions: 40°F/4°C
Season: Best in late summer, but available year-round

Nutritional Information

Serving Size:	3-1/2 oz/100 g
Water:	89.82 g
Calories:	36
Protein:	0.54 g
Fat:	0.14 g
Saturated Fat:	0.038 g
Fiber:	0.8 g
Sodium:	18 mg
Iron:	0.17 mg
Potassium:	228 mg
Vitamin C:	18 mg

FIGURE **17.5** Honeydew Melon

KIWANO, HORNED MELON

A rare find is this oddly shaped and hard to eat, yet delicious tropical melon which originated in Africa but is now grown in Southern California and New Zealand. The kiwano is small in size, yielding only one serving per melon, and is fairly expensive. The outside shell is studded with horn-like protrusions and is orange in color. The inner flesh is a beautiful gelatinous green with a seed in each pocket of flesh. They definitely are decorative and the flesh is cool, very refreshing, and reminiscent of banana, papaya, and cucumber. The trick is in the eating. This is done by sucking the flesh from each cell and trying to catch the seed in your teeth. They are best used as a novelty when you can find them and the price seems reasonable. Look for a well-colored rind with no cracks or bruised soft spots when receiving this melon.

Pack size: 10 lb/4.54 kg box
Shelf life: 1 week
Storage Conditions: 50°F/10°C
Season: March through August

PEPINO MELON

The pepino is not a true melon as it grows on an evergreen bush and not a vine. It is oftentimes referred to as a pepino melon, pear melon, or bush melon. This fruit is so named because the flavor, when ripe, is reminiscent of a combination of cucumber, cantaloupe, and honeydew melon. Originally from Peru, the pepino is now cultivated in California and New Zealand. This fruit is small and makes one serving each. Its rind is yellow with streaks of dark purple, and a greenish cast to the skin indicates that it needs more ripening. When ripe they will be fragrant and yield firmly like a ripe plum. They are good eaten plain or in salads.

Pack Size: 12 count per case
Shelf Life: 1 week
Storage Conditions: 40°F/4°C
Season: Fall into spring

A relative newcomer and gaining in popularity, the Sharlyn is a delicious melon. The Sharlyn is webbed similar to a cantaloupe, more elongated, and it can be fairly large in size. Similar in flavor as well as shelf life to the Crenshaw, look for ripe melons and utilize them quickly. The rind should be golden to brown when ripe; avoid those that are green. The flesh of the Sharlyn will be pale green to white in color and give off a sweet fragrance. As in other similar melons, these should be very heavy for their size, indicating juicy flesh. The flavor has similarities to both honeydew and cantaloupe melons; it is great eaten plain with other aromatic fruits or in a cocktail. This is a versatile melon and delicious in a variety of presentations, but choose carefully as this an uncommon and pricey choice.

> **Pack Size:** 5 to 9 count per case
> **Shelf Life:** Several days to one week
> **Storage Conditions:** 62° to 68°F/16° to 20°C or refrigerated if very warm
> **Season:** May to August

WATERMELONS

The other side of the melon family consists of watermelons. These don't seem to get the respect that the muskmelon varieties do, but their popularity appears to be on the upswing. It is also clear that there are few foods that offer the refreshment of a slice of cool watermelon on a hot summer's day. Surprisingly, there are well over 50 varieties of watermelon, but most of their differences would only be of interest to the farmer. For the consumer there are really four main classifications of watermelon that will be described next.

Quality checks for all watermelon varieties are basically the same. The skin should have a healthy sheen and not look dull or flat nor bright and shiny. The pale area should be a creamy yellow, not dull grayish white and they should smell mildly sweet. The stem should be dry and firm. Avoid any melon with soft spots, cracks, and bruises visible on the rind. The old test of thumping it can be somewhat useful, but it's not definitive. When thumped, the melon should give a hollow ring. There should be some give in the rind, it should not be rock hard, and the melon should be a good weight for its size.

Most watermelons sold are elongated in shape with classic dark and pale green stripes, and some can run over 30 pounds/13.61 kilograms. Other varieties are rounder and smaller in size. Some enterprising growers in Japan have found a way to cultivate rectangular melons that are commanding very high prices and yet still taste the same.

There is, of course, the classic red-fleshed watermelon with numerous black seeds, but they can also be found with yellow, orange, or almost white flesh, and with no seeds. Those seeds are not commonly eaten here, but are a treat in much of Asia when roasted. The rind can also be eaten, usually when pickled; only the thin green skin is not edible.

Besides the refreshing tried and true cool slice of watermelon, they can be used in salads or cocktails, juiced, frozen, spiked, and even grilled. In addition to pickling, the rinds can be stir-fried with spicy aromatics for a whole new side dish. From a back-yard picnic to a sublime sit-down dinner to a refreshing summery cocktail party, the watermelon makes a wonderful addition to your meal.

ALLSWEET

The Allsweet is the classic oblong, heavy watermelon with a dark green, usually striped rind. These are large melons typically running well in excess of 20 pounds/9.07 kilograms. This, as the name would indicate, is a good sweet melon with dark red flesh and small brown seeds. The Allsweet is in many aspects like the typical watermelon you remember growing up.

Pack Size: Sold by the each
Shelf Life: 1 week under refrigeration
Storage Conditions: 45°F°C
Season: Available year-round but best when in season locally

Nutritional Information

Serving Size:	3-1/2 oz/100 g
Water:	91.45 g
Calories:	30
Protein:	0.61 g
Fat:	0.15 g
Saturated Fat:	0.016 g
Fiber:	0.4 g
Sodium:	1 mg
Iron:	0.24 mg
Potassium:	112 mg
Vitamin C:	8.1 mg

FIGURE **17.6** Allsweet Watermelon

ICE-BOX

These are typically smaller and rounder than the Allsweet variety, and run from 5 to 15 pounds/2.27 to 6.8 kilograms each. The rind can be pale to dark green in color with less definitive striping. The flesh of these melons is usually either red or yellow in color, but there is also a much rarer variety with almost transparent white flesh. The white flesh has a more unusual and highly sweet flavor.

The most common ice-box melon in markets today is the Sugar Baby. These are small and round and have become very popular because of their extremely high level of sweetness. The Sugar Baby was a dark green skin over a thin rind and the flesh is smoothly textured.

FIGURE **17.7** Ice-Box Watermelon

Pack Size: Sold by the each
Shelf Life: 1 week under refrigeration
Storage Conditions: 45°F/7°C
Season: Available year-round but best when in season locally

SEEDLESS

These melons can vary greatly in size and shape from small and round to large and oblong. The flesh can be a rich, dark red or a bright yellow in color. Despite the name, some will have a few soft but not fully developed white seeds. The seedless nature of these melons makes them extremely popular with cooks and mixologists for their ease of use in dishes and drinks. People will differ in their opinions; many believe watermelons must have seeds, but it's hard to argue with the ease of use with this type.

Pack Size: Sold by the each
Shelf Life: 1 week under refrigeration
Storage Conditions: 45°F/7°C
Season: Available year-round but best when in season locally

FIGURE **17.8** Sugar Baby Watermelon

YELLOW- AND ORANGE-FLESHED

These are typically large, oblong melons with striped dark to light green rinds. They are useful for adding contrast to kebabs and salads against the red flesh varieties. They tend to have finely grained flesh which can be very sweet in flavor and described as having a honey-like finish. There can be a marked difference in the quality of flavor in some of the varieties however. Sadly, the OrangeGlo, which is touted as the finest eating melon of this type, is too fragile to market on a wide scale and is only rarely found at farm stands. However, the multiple varieties of yellow- and orange-fleshed melons on the market are all very good and just have subtle differences in durability and flavor.

Pack Size: 4 to 8 count per case
Shelf Life: Up to a week under refrigeration
Storage Conditions: 45°F/7°C
Season: Usually available year-round but best when in season locally

18

Florida avocados are larger and more oval in shape. They have a dark green skin but it is smoother and thinner than the Hass skin. The flesh of these avocados is darker green in color but contains less fat and therefore lacks the richness found in the Hass variety. This type is often used if the Hass is unavailable during the summer months.

Avocados should be unblemished and heavy for their size. Look for uniformity in texture; avoid soft spots in otherwise firm flesh. These will generally need several days to ripen at room temperature so plan accordingly unless you have a vendor that can supply you fully ripened product to your specification. As discussed, never accept refrigerated avocados or store them under refrigeration.

FIGURE **18.3** Florida Avocados

Once cut, the flesh of the avocado should be coated with an acid to prevent oxidation and discoloring; lemon or lime juice are the most common choices for this. Avocados are the foundation ingredient in guacamole and are often used in sushi, such as in California rolls. The flesh can be used in some sandwiches and dishes as a meat substitute because of its thick oily texture, and that texture and flavor combines wonderfully with burgers and scrambled eggs. Sliced avocado often accompanies chicken, rice, and meat in Mexican dishes, and some Caribbean cultures whip the avocado into a thick milk shake–like drink.

> **Pack Size:** Hass: 28 to 84 each in a box that weighs around 20 lb/9.07 kg; Florida: Usually 9 per flat that weighs around 5 lb/2.27 kg
> **Shelf Life:** 4 to 5 days depending on degree of ripeness upon receipt
> **Storage Conditions:** 45° to 55°F/7° to 13°C
> **Season:** Hass: Available year-round; Florida: May to January

Florida Avocado
Nutritional Information

Serving Size:	3-1/2 oz/100 g
Water:	78.81 g
Calories:	120
Protein:	2.23 g
Fat:	10.06 g
Saturated Fat:	1.960 g
Fiber:	5.6 g
Sodium:	2 mg
Iron:	0.17 mg
Potassium:	351 mg
Vitamin C:	17.4 mg

BANANA

The banana is one of the world's largest fruit crops. The sweet yellow banana commonly found in Western markets, while a huge commercial crop, actually makes up only about 15 percent of the bananas grown worldwide. Bananas are found less frequently in red

FIGURE **18.4** Standard Bananas

FIGURE **18.5** Baby Bananas

and purple; these types may be a bit sweeter but are similar in flavor and can also be eaten raw or cooked. Other green varieties are less sweet and utilized in cooking or drying into meal. These are a major nutrition source for many tropical countries. All told, the banana is the world's fourth largest staple crop.

The banana originated in Malaysia thousands of years ago and slowly spread across the globe because of traders and explorers. This fruit was originally small, the size of a man's finger, and came in different colors. The large yellow variety that now dominates the market is the result of centuries of crossbreeding and mutation. Bananas did not arrive in the United States until the late 1800s and have rapidly grown in popularity since that time. The reason for this is simple; the banana comes in its own carrying case, can be easily opened and consumed, and is sweet and delicious. The fruit is also very nutritious, high in vitamins and minerals, and loaded with potassium.

The banana most commonly found in foodservice is the Cavendish variety. This banana is picked green to withstand shipping, placed in "ripening rooms" with ethylene gas, and then shipped out to wholesalers and retail markets. It is the Cavendish's ability to maintain its quality during transport, more than its flavor and sweetness, which has made it so popular. Some bananas are shipped as nongassed and develop a sweeter flavor. These are rare in the market and do not develop the bright yellow color a gassed banana has; their color is yellowish-tan and they also have a shorter shelf life once ripened.

Look for brightly colored fruit with no crushing at the tips. The color you purchase should depend on how quickly you need to utilize them. Some green at the ends is desirable if they have a day or two to ripen. Bananas needed for immediate consumption should be fully yellow with pale brown speckles. Black spots can indicate bruising and a pale gray tinge to the skin means the fruit was chilled to a point that has damaged the ripening process and flavor. Never buy or store bananas under refrigeration.

Bananas are most frequently eaten raw out of hand. They are also good raw in cream, on cereal, in a banana split, cooked into fritters or breads, flambéed in Bananas Foster and served with ice cream, or dried into chips.

Small or baby bananas are also found in the marketplace. These are marketed as Oritos, Manzanos, or Lady Fingers as they resemble short pudgy fingers roughly

3 inches/7.5 centimeters in length. Baby bananas are grown at higher altitudes and the skin will have a yellow/pink hue.

The flesh of these bananas is dense, creamy, and sweet with a hint of apple flavor. To ensure maximum sweetness, it is best to enjoy this fruit when the skin becomes freckled with light brown spots. The baby banana is considered a great treat for children because of the portion size and sweetness. In addition to eating out of hand, these bananas can be utilized in all the same ways as other sweet bananas can.

Pack Size: 40 lb/18.41 kg box
Shelf Life: 2 to 3 days at room temperature
Storage Conditions: 58° to 60°F/14° to 15°C
Season: Available year-round

Nutritional Information

Serving Size:	3-1/2 oz/100 g
Water:	74.91 g
Calories:	89
Protein:	1.09 g
Fat:	0.33 g
Saturated Fat:	0.112 g
Fiber:	2.6 g
Sodium:	1 mg
Iron:	0.26 mg
Potassium:	358 mg
Vitamin C:	8.7 mg

PLANTAINS, PLATANOS

The plantain is a green banana that is usually cooked and not eaten raw. It is a staple in many countries, especially in the Caribbean. Botanically the plantain is identical to a sweet banana but they differ greatly from a culinary standpoint. The plantain is larger with a much less sweet flavor and a starchy, very firm texture that requires cooking to make it more palatable. Like potatoes in some temperate climates, the plantain is the starchy dietary staple in many tropical cultures. Nutritionally, they supply a similar amount of vitamins and minerals to the diet as the sweet banana.

Plantains are utilized in both the green, under-ripe state and when fully ripened and blackened in color. Under-ripe, the plantain is neutral, almost potato-like in flavor, and can be served boiled plain, simmered in soup, or fried. Each culture has differences in how they fry and serve this fruit; they can be sliced into thin chips or lengthwise into strips and fried until crispy. Plantains are also fried into tostones when the fruit is cut

FIGURE **18.6** Plantains

into thick chunks, parboiled in oil, and then smashed into a flattened cake and refried until crispy on the outside with a chewy center. Green plantains are also dried and ground into flour.

The flesh of the fully ripe plantain is a richer yellow, softer texture with a sweet yet still starchy flavor. Fully ripened, these can be eaten raw, but are often mashed and served with salt or sweetener. The ripe plantain can also be sliced thick, fried, and served with crema.

Plantains should be large, heavy, and very firm with no shriveled or soft spots. Specify the stage of ripeness desired when ordering to ensure the texture and flavor will work with the desired end use.

Pack Size: 50 lb/22.68 kg case
Shelf Life: 3 to 4 days
Storage Conditions: 58° to 60°F/14° to 15°C
Season: Available year-round

Nutritional Information

Serving Size:	3-1/2 oz/100 g
Water:	65.28 g
Calories:	122
Protein:	1.3 g
Fat:	0.37 g
Saturated Fat:	0.143 g
Fiber:	2.3 g
Sodium:	4 mg
Iron:	0.6 mg
Potassium:	499 mg
Vitamin C:	18.4 mg

DRAGONFRUIT

The dragonfruit is cultivated in Central and South America and in tropical regions of Asia. This beautiful, round, bright red or yellow fruit has large spines or scales protruding from its leathery rind. The pulp of the sweet variety is creamy in color and texture and the flavor is sweet; there is also a variety with a rich, red flesh. The flesh is ridden with many seeds that resemble black sesame seeds and are typically eaten along with the flesh. These supply a nutty crunch that accompanies the mildly sweet pulp. Sour varieties are prized for their pungent, powerfully flavored juice.

Pack Size: 9 to 12 pieces per flat
Shelf Life: 1 week
Storage Conditions: 45 to 48°F/1.5 to 2°C
Season: Available year round

FIGS

The fig is considered to be the sweetest of all fruits, with exceptional sugar content, and the earliest known fruit to be cultivated. Figs originated in the western regions of Asia and are now grown across the world, wherever a similar climate exists, such as in South Africa, Australia, Mexico, Chile, and western parts of the United States.

Figs will not ripen once picked so be careful when choosing and purchasing them; they will not improve in quality while sitting in your kitchen. In fact, because of their high sugar content and thin, fragile skin, they will spoil quickly. Purchase only what you can use right away or refrigerate until needed.

Look for soft, fresh fruit with a clearly sweet aroma and stems that are intact. Avoid any fruit that appears dry, bruised, or is green from being picked when it was under-ripe. Figs may exude a small amount of sticky syrup from the blossom end; this is not a sign the fruit has begun to decay.

Figs were one of the first fruits to be made into a cookie and the sweetness and moist, rich flesh have made them a best seller even today. Most figs are typically either eaten fresh or dried to preserve their quality. Figs can also be used to make jam.

The Smyrna fig came from Turkey centuries ago and was eventually brought into Mexico. Franciscan monks then brought this dark-skinned fig into what is now California and planted them around their missions. This fig eventually evolved into what is now the dark purple Mission fig. This dark-skinned fig has a pale red flesh and small seeds. The flesh has a good sweet flavor and dries well. The Mission fig has a long season running from May into November.

Calimyrna figs are not often seen in their fresh form, but are thought to be best eaten fresh. This California-grown fig has a short growing season in mid summer and a short shelf life. Calimyrna figs are pale yellow with a pink flesh that is sweet and nutty in flavor. These figs are most commonly found dried.

FIGURE **18.7** Black Mission Figs

FIGURE **18.8** Brown Turkey Figs

Kadota figs are the least sweet of the commonly available varieties. This fig is green in color with an amber flesh that has a full rich flavor and is best used for canning or drying. The Kadota fig comes into the market in May and should last into October.

The brown Turkey fig is a coppery-brown color with whitish-pink hued flesh. The brown Turkey is much better eaten fresh than in its dried form. Fortunately this fruit also has a long growing season from late May all the way into December.

Pack Size: Twelve 1-pint flats or a tray pack weighing 2-1/2 to 3 lb/1.134 to 1.36 kg
Shelf Life: 2 to 3 days
Storage Conditions: 34°F/1°C
Season: May to December

Nutritional Information

Serving Size:	3-1/2 oz/100 g
Water:	79.11 g
Calories:	74
Protein:	0.75 g
Fat:	0.30 g
Saturated Fat:	0.06 g
Fiber:	2.9 g
Sodium:	1 mg
Iron:	0.37 mg
Potassium:	232 mg
Vitamin C:	2 mg

GUAVA

The guava is a tropical fruit native to the Caribbean that is now grown in several other areas with tropical climates. This fruit is able to withstand cooler temperatures a bit better than other tropical fruits, but those grown in warmer temperatures are thought to have a sweeter flavor.

The size, shape, and flavor in this fruit varies widely. Guavas can be round, oval, or pear-shaped. The skin can range from thick and bitter to sweet and thin and the colors can fluctuate from those beginning with green and turning yellow to orange or from pale to dark red. The flavor of the flesh is generally sweet but can be quite tart and range from white to pale pink in hue. Some types of guava can have hard, inedible seeds but most are small and edible. The varieties are often named for other fruits that they mimic in color such as the apple or strawberry guava. Guava should have a mild lemony fragrance.

Guavas are very nutritious and the red and orange types have very high anti-oxidant levels. These are so healthy as to be characterized as a "perfect food" due to their life-sustaining high vitamin and nutrient content.

Guavas are best eaten when fully ripened and not dark green. The flesh should be firm but have some give to pressure when held in the hand. Avoid those with shriveled or bruised areas in the flesh. Guavas are not often found in Northern markets but should be best when found in both mid-winter and mid-summer. Guavas may be refrigerated once fully ripened.

Guava pairs well with other fruits such as bananas, coconut, and lime, and can be puréed into drinks and marinades. When not found fresh, guava can be found in concentrate, preserves, and juice.

Pack Size: 10 lb/4.54 kg box
Shelf Life: 4 to 5 days
Storage Conditions: 35°F/1.5°C
Season: June to August and November to March

Nutritional Information

Serving Size:	3-1/2 oz/100 g
Water:	80.80 g
Calories:	68
Protein:	2.55 g
Fat:	0.95 g
Saturated Fat:	0.272 g
Fiber:	5.4 g
Sodium:	2 mg
Iron:	0.26 mg
Potassium:	417 mg
Vitamin C:	228.3 mg

KIWI FRUIT

Kiwis are small, roughly 2 to 3 inches/5 to 7.5 centimeters in length, oblong or egg-shaped, fuzzy fruits that originated in China and then moved to New Zealand. They are now grown in Chile and California. This fruit is sometimes referred to as the Chinese gooseberry. Generally, the fuzzy textured skin of the kiwi is a dusty brown to khaki green color with bright green flesh, a white center, and black seeds. The gold kiwi is similar but has a smooth pale brown exterior and bright golden flesh and less commonly found in the market. The flavor of the kiwi is unique and hard to describe; it is reminiscent of strawberry, melon, and pineapple but clearly has its own taste. The flesh is very sweet and succulent. The green kiwi's flavor will be more pronounced than the milder gold variety.

Kiwis are hardy and generally in the market from one growing region or another year-round. Look for yielding but firm, not rock hard, fruit without any shriveled or moldy areas or bruising. They can be refrigerated once ripened.

Kiwis can be skinned and served as is, combined with other fruit in a salad, blended into a smoothie, or combined with cilantro, lime, and chiles to make a unique salsa. Kiwis have an extremely high concentration of vitamin C, much higher than the orange.

Pack Size: 25 to 45 per flat weighing 6 to 7 lb/2.72 to 3.18 kg

Shelf Life: Up to 2 weeks

Storage Conditions: 32°F/0°C

Season: Available year-round

Nutritional Information

Serving Size:	3-1/2 oz/100 g
Water:	83.07 g
Calories:	61
Protein:	1.14 g
Fat:	0.52 g
Saturated Fat:	0.029 g
Fiber:	3 g
Sodium:	3 mg
Iron:	0.31 mg
Potassium:	312 mg
Vitamin C:	92.7 mg

FIGURE **18.9** Green Kiwis

MANGOES

Mangoes are a large, heavy tropical fruit that originated in India and moved through Southeast Asia. They are now grown in any part of the world supporting a tropical climate such as parts of the Americas, the Caribbean. Australia, the Pacific Rim, and Africa. This is one of the most popular tropical fruits enjoyed in the world. The mango can vary in size and in color from green to yellow, red, and orange; the flesh will be orange to yellow in hue with a large flat seed in the center. When ripened, the mango will be plump and rounded near the stem and give off a decidedly sweet aroma. Mangoes are not shipped when fully ripened in order to prevent damage to the softened fruit, so expect that the fruit will need several days to fully ripen when purchased. Do not refrigerate this fruit unless fully ripe. The flesh of the mango will always be sweet but can vary in texture from pulpy soft to firm like a melon and some can be quite stringy. The better mangoes have firm but yielding sweet flesh that is rich and dense and has not gotten too stringy.

FIGURE **18.10** Standard Mangoes

The Ataulfo mango, also called the honey or Manila mango, is considered by some to be the finest example of what a mango should be. These are small crook-shaped fruit with a dense, sweet, bright yellow or orange flesh and virtually no stringiness. Even though they are small, these mangoes will have a better ratio of flesh to skin and pit than the larger, stringier common varieties and therefore will have a higher yield. Look for yellow to orange skin with no green and a mango that yields to some pressure. Find the Ataulfo mango when in season each spring and again in the fall. These are also marketed as a champagne mango.

The Tommy Atkins mango is the standard mango found in Western markets. This mango is large, heavy, and uniformly shaped. It has become the most dominant variety due to its ability to withstand the rigors of shipping, its long shelf life, and because it is resistant to disease. The quality of the flavor is mild and the pulp can be somewhat stringy, but this mango is still sweet, juicy, and quite popular. The Tommy Atkins has a yellowish-green to red skin and yellow-hued flesh. Other varieties found in the market are the Kent, Hayden, Keitt, and Alphonso; these have rich flavor and are not so fibrous, but do not hold up quite as well in shipping. Haitian mangoes are smaller and run from pale green

FIGURE **18.11** Green Mangoes

to yellow in color with a fairly fibrous flesh. The flesh is prized by some for its full rich flavor. Mangoes can usually be found in the market year-round, but are not at their best toward the end of the year. They should be heavy for their size with no shriveling and have a good color. A clean, sweet smell is important as the sugar content can cause the flesh to sour or ferment, which will give off a characteristic sour smell. Mangoes are often eaten as is, with salt and chiles, or tossed with coconut milk. They are also popular for salsas and chutneys, in desserts, or puréed into smoothies and juice drinks.

Green cooking mangoes are large, round, unripened mangoes that are most often used in Southeast Asian cuisine. Most typically these tart, brightly flavored mangoes are grated into thin strips and combined with acid and hot chiles to accompany fish or meat dishes. These should still be unripe and crisp with no sign of turning plump and ripe.

Pack Size: 6 to 24 count per box for mango; 50 lb/22.7 kg box for green mango
Shelf Life: 4 to 5 days
Storage Conditions: 55°F/13°C
Season: Available year-round

Nutritional Information

Serving Size:	3-1/2 oz/100 g
Water:	81.71 g
Calories:	65
Protein:	0.51 g
Fat:	0.27 g
Saturated Fat:	0.066 g
Fiber:	1.8 g
Sodium:	2 mg
Iron:	0.13 mg
Potassium:	156 mg
Vitamin C:	27.7 mg

PAPAYA

The papaya is a fast-growing, large fruit that thrives in the semi-tropical climates of the world. In the United States that would include Hawaii and Florida, where the Solo variety is the dominant crop. This papaya grows to roughly 6 inches/15.25 centimeters in length and weighs between 1 and 2 pounds/454 and 907 grams. When the papaya has ripened, it will have a beautiful, glowing yellow to golden skin with a flesh color to match. The flesh should have a fatty texture to it, like an avocado, and be juicy and smooth with no stringiness. In the center of the flesh will be a pocket of dark gray seeds. These seeds are edible with a bright peppery flavor and work nicely as a garnish or in a salad dressing. Sadly, most people simply discard them.

FIGURE **18.12** Standard Papayas

FIGURE **18.13** Green Papaya

When selecting papaya, always look for a warm yellow color in the skin, although a green tinge around the neck does not indicate the fruit is unripe. There should be a firm yield to pressure when gently squeezed. Avoid hard or shriveled fruit and beware of a fermented smell. A ripe papaya will have very little odor. Do not refrigerate this fruit unless fully ripe and then be sure to use it within a day or two. A gray tinge to the flesh will indicate it was chilled before it was fully ripe.

Papaya is most often eaten raw but can be cooked; try chunks on a kebab with shrimp or chicken. In fact, papaya can be used in any part of a meal by an inventive cook. Try stuffing the cavity of a ripe papaya with soft cheese or salad and garnishing it with some of the seeds for a luncheon treat. Papaya can also be whipped into smoothies and milk shakes or it also combines nicely on a plate with other fruits and sliced ham.

The green or Mexican papaya is large and dark green with a salmon-colored flesh. If the flesh is pale and not a vibrant pink, this fruit is unripe. Green unripe papaya can be used like a vegetable and cooked. Green papaya matches well with spicy aromatics and works well in spicy Latin and Asian cuisines. Papayas have year-round availability in the market.

Pack Size: 6 to 14 count box for papaya; 50 lb/22.7 kg box for green papaya
Shelf Life: 2 to 3 days
Storage Conditions: 55°F/13°C
Season: Available year-round

Nutritional Information

Serving Size:	3-1/2 oz/100 g
Water:	88.83 g
Calories:	39
Protein:	0.61 g
Fat:	0.14 g
Saturated Fat:	0.043 g
Fiber:	1.8 g
Sodium:	3 mg
Iron:	0.10 mg
Potassium:	257 mg
Vitamin C:	61.8 mg

PASSION FRUIT

The passion fruit originated in Brazil but has grown in popularity, especially in other Latin American countries; it is now grown in Australia, New Zealand, California, Hawaii, and Florida. Most commonly this sweet fruit is about 3 inches/7.5 centimeters in diameter and roughly egg-shaped. When fully ripened, this fruit will be crimson to purple in color with a luscious or jelly-like golden flesh full of small dark edible seeds. The outside skin or shell is tough in texture and will be dimpled when ripe. The flavor is sweet-tart and the aroma should be fully fragrant and perfumed. Look for fruit that is heavy for its size and deeply colored. A yellow-colored passion fruit from Hawaii is sometimes found in the market and is a bit milder in flavor. Passion fruit combines well with other tropical fruits or cream, and works well in desserts. Simply scoop out the seeds and use them as a garnish when they are fully ripe. This fruit will be available in the market during the early winter months. Do not refrigerate this fruit until fully ripened.

FIGURE **18.14** Passion Fruit

Pack Size: 22 to 36 per flats
Shelf Life: Up to 2 weeks
Storage Conditions: 50°F/10°C
Season: March to September

Nutritional Information

Serving Size:	3-1/2 oz/100 g
Water:	72.93 g
Calories:	97
Protein:	2.2 g
Fat:	0.7 g
Saturated fat:	0.059 g
Fiber:	10.4 g
Sodium:	28 mg
Iron:	1.6 mg
Potassium:	348 mg
Vitamin C:	30 mg

PERSIMMONS

The persimmon is a tropical fruit most heavily grown in Asia, but is also grown in California and Israel. There is a small persimmon native to the eastern United States, but the popularity of the Japanese varieties has pretty much eliminated this from the marketplace. The two persimmons most widely seen in western markets are both of Japanese heritage and are the Hachiya and Fuyu. These vary greatly from each other in shape, texture, and astringency of the flesh. However, both have bright orange-red skin and flesh color.

The Hachiya is the most dominant persimmon in the marketplace. It is the larger variety of the two, reaching 3 inches/7.5 centi-meters in diameter, and has an elongated and pointed base. This fruit is highly astringent and unpleasant in flavor unless it is allowed to fully ripen. When ripe, it will feel squishy like a water balloon and the

FIGURE **18.15** Hachiya Persimmons

FIGURE **18.16** Fuyu Persimmons

flesh will be a soft, creamy, ripe apricot-like texture. There may still be a touch of astringency but the flavor should have an inviting tangy sweetness. These can be eaten skin and all, but some prefer to halve this persimmon and spoon the flesh out of the skin. Astringent persimmons may be frozen to lessen the astringency without any real negative effect on the flavor.

The Fuyu persimmon is the next most common persimmon in the market and has a small tomato-like shape, roughly 2 to 3 inches/5 to 7.5 centimeters in diameter. This fruit will have a much firmer texture and will contain no astringency even if it is a bit under-ripe. The Fuyu will retain its firmness until it is well ripened and its spicy-sweet flavor can be enjoyed eaten out of hand. The Fuyu will eventually soften somewhat if allowed to ripen until it is almost ready to turn bad. The fruit's sweetness will be at its peak, but the shelf life will be almost nonexistent.

Sharon persimmons are an old hybrid, but relatively new to Western markets. This fruit is largely grown in Israel, is small in size with a paler, tan-orange color to the skin and flesh, and a squarer shape. Small light brown spots in the skin and flesh are an indication of ripeness and is where the sugar is concentrated in clusters. The flesh of this persimmon is seedless. Like the Fuyu, the Sharon will have a firm texture and spicy-sweet flavor.

When buying persimmons be sure to look for a smooth shiny skin with a full bright color. The texture for the Hachiya should be soft, almost squishy, and the Fuyus should be firm but not rock hard. Avoid pale yellow patches as this is an indicator that the fruit was picked when it was immature. Fully ripened persimmons will hold several days under refrigeration. Also avoid any fruit that is cracked, bruised, or deeply scarred. The Hachiya and Fuyu persimmons come onto the market in October and last through December. The Sharon variety arrives on the market in November and can last into February.

Persimmons can be eaten raw out of hand and made into jams as well. The pulp can be used in quick breads, smoothies, or diced and served in salads. Persimmons can also be used in a spicy-sweet chutney. Their flavor works well with cheese, nuts, yogurt, and ice cream.

Pack Size: 10 lb/4.54 kg flat
Shelf Life: 2 to 3 days
Storage Conditions: 38°F/3°C
Season: October to February

Nutritional Information

Serving Size:	3-1/2 oz/100 g
Water:	80.32 g
Calories:	70
Protein:	0.58 g
Fat:	0.19 g
Saturated fat:	0.02 g
Fiber:	3.6 g
Sodium:	1 mg
Iron:	0.15 mg
Potassium:	161 mg
Vitamin C:	7.5 mg

PINEAPPLE

The pineapple is the very familiar, large, cylindrical tropical fruit with a crown of green spiky leaves and a coarse waxy rind. They may be dark green to golden yellow and reddish in color with flesh that can range from white to pale yellow in hue. This fruit originated in South and Central America and was spread across the oceans by Spanish explorers. This is believed to be how the pineapple was brought to the islands of Hawaii in the 1700s. When horticulturist James Dole arrived there in the late nineteenth century, he quickly made Hawaii the world's largest producer of this fruit, which it remains to this day.

FIGURE **18.17** Pineapple

There are several varieties of pineapple grown in the world, but two are most common to Western markets. The Smooth Cayenne or Sweet Spineless is the most dominant variety in the Hawaiian market. This fruit will ripen to an orange-golden yellow rind and has a rich, mildly acidic, sweet flavor. The Red Spanish variety is the most popular type grown in the Caribbean and Central America. This variety has red-orange skin and a yellow flesh with a rich flavor. The Del Monte hybrid was developed by that company to have twice the sugar level of other pineapples. A variety known as Sugar Loaf is a small species with a very high sugar content; however, it is highly perishable and is usually not brought into the United States.

Pineapples are available year-round, but are usually at their peak in the spring. Look for plump heavy fruit with some yield to pressure at the stem end. A sweet aroma is desired, but not always detectable if the fruit has been well chilled. Fresh green leaves and a bold coloration are the best signs of well-ripened fruit. Avoid fruit with dull or browning leaves or that is dull in color and has soft spots. These can be refrigerated for a few days once fully ripened.

Pineapple is excellent eaten raw, baked into cakes such as Pineapple Upside-Down Cake, broiled in rings or in chunks on skewers, with rum, and as an accompaniment to poultry, ham, or pork.

Pack Size: 4 to 10 count per box weighing about 25 lb/11.34 kg
Shelf Life: 4 to 5 days
Storage Conditions: 45° to 50°F/7° to 10°C
Season: Available year-round

Nutritional Information

Serving Size:	3-1/2 oz/100 g
Water:	86 g
Calories:	50
Protein:	0.54 g
Fat:	0.12 g
Fiber:	1.4 g
Sodium:	1 mg
Iron:	0.29 mg
Potassium:	109 mg
Vitamin C:	47.8 mg

POMEGRANATE

The pomegranate is a hard-shelled, red tropical fruit prized for its flavor despite it being very labor intensive to extract the seeds. This fruit originated in Persia and was brought into Europe by the Moors. The Spanish spread carried the fruit to the Americas where it is grown commercially, as well as in Malaysia, the Middle East, Africa, and India.

Inside the inedible shell lies pockets of delicious translucent red seeds encased in a deep red and sweet jelly. These pockets are held in place by white pith that is not eaten. This fruit is valued for both the seeds and the juice, which is extracted from the seeds and the jelly. In order to the extract the seeds, you must cut off the crown, scoop out the white core, score the shell to pull it apart, and pop out the cells of seeds. Any white pith that adheres to the seeds should be washed off under water. The fruit can also be halved and pressed to extract the juice. This fruit is

FIGURE **18.18** Pomegranate

nutritious, being high in vitamin C and potassium and supplying a moderate amount of antioxidants.

Pomegranates are round and about 2 to 3 inches/5 to 7.5 centimeters in diameter with a red color. The Wonderful variety is the main type found in the United States. This species is large and has a shiny skin that will be dark red to purple in color. Hearing a metallic click when tapping the fruit with your finger is a good indicator of the pomegranate's ripeness. This fruit has a long shelf life and can improve in flavor over time. The pomegranate will hold up under refrigeration for several weeks or more. Avoid fruit that is rock hard, dull in color, shriveled, or cracked.

The seeds of this fruit give a flavorful, sweet, crunchy garnish to dishes. The juice is used in marinades or combined with apple juice or lemonade. The flavor of the pomegranate also complements poultry and pork dishes.

Pack Size: 8 to 16 per flats weighing 10 to 11 lb/4.54 to 4.99 kg
Shelf Life: 5 days at room temperature and up to 2 months under refrigeration
Storage Conditions: 35°F/1.5°C
Season: May to December

Nutritional Information

Serving Size:	3-1/2 oz/100 g
Water:	77.93 g
Calories:	83
Protein:	1.67 g
Fat:	1.17 g
Saturated Fat:	0.12 g
Fiber:	4 g
Sodium:	3 mg
Iron:	0.3 mg
Potassium:	236 mg
Vitamin C:	10.2 mg

STAR FRUIT, CARAMBOLA

The Carambola originated around Ceylon and is now grown over much of Southeast Asia and parts of China and India as well as Hawaii. The star fruit gets its moniker from the shape the fruit has when sliced crosswise. This ribbed tropical fruit starts pale green and ripens into a golden yellow hue and runs from 3 to 5 inches/7.5 to 12.75 centimeters in length. Inside this unusually beautiful, ribbed fruit, the flesh is also a pretty translucent yellow golden hue with dark-colored seeds.

The flesh is juicy and ranges from sweet to quite tart in flavor. Look for the wider fruit

FIGURE **18.19** Star Fruit/Carambola

to be sweeter. The tart variety may have a lemony flavor and, since it lacks sweetness, it is often used in cooking. Look for this fruit in the market from summer into early winter; the tarter variety will come into the market later and not last as long into winter as the sweet variety. If the skin is still tinged with green, allow it to ripen to a full yellow at room temperature; once ripened this fruit can be held under refrigeration for several days. This fruit should be firm and plump with good color; avoid anything that has begun to shrivel or is showing brown spots. However, the ridges of the ribs may show a brown tinge which is not indicative of poor quality. Enjoy this fruit, waxy skin and all, eaten out of hand, in salads, or as an attractive garnish when sweet. The tart variety is good grilled and served with poultry or seafood.

Pack Size: 10 to 24 count box weighing from 3 to 5 lb/1.36 to 2.27 kg
Shelf Life: 2 to 3 days at room temperature
Storage Conditions: 62° to 68°F/16° to 20°C
Season: August to March

Nutritional Information

Serving Size:	3-1/2 oz/100 g
Water:	91.38 g
Calories:	31
Protein:	1.04 g
Fat:	0.33 g
Saturated Fat:	0.019 g
Fiber:	2.8 g
Sodium:	2 mg
Iron:	0.08 mg
Potassium:	133 mg
Vitamin C:	34.4 mg

19

PREPARING PRODUCE

One of the hallmarks of an experienced chef is the way he or she approaches the task of cutting produce. The goal is consistency and speed and it is impossible to achieve either without practice. The ability to quickly and properly prepare produce will also improve the yield from these products and enhance the appearance of the end product.

Begin by determining the proper timing of the work to be done. Make a list and prioritize tasks so that fruits and vegetables that can be prepared well in advance are done first, while those that lose flavor or color when cut too early are done as close to service or cooking time as possible.

Wash fruits, vegetables, and herbs before initially trimming the produce to remove any traces of pesticides or dirt and to avoid getting the work surface unnecessarily dirty. Spin dry leafy greens and herbs before cutting and thoroughly drain or pat dry other vegetables before cutting. Keep both the tools and the work surface clean and free from debris. Remove trim as it accumulates, before it has a chance to fall on the floor. Wipe down knife blades and cutting boards between phases of work, making sure to follow sanitary practices at all times. Sanitize all cutting and work surfaces when switching from one food item to another. Wash your hands, too, and remember to use gloves if the vegetables will not be cooked before serving.

From trimming and peeling to slicing and dicing, many vegetables and herbs need advance preparation before they are ready to serve or use as an ingredient in a cooked dish. Knowledge of various knife cuts is necessary to fully utilize vegetables and herbs. A thorough mastery of knife skills includes the ability to prepare vegetables and herbs properly for cutting, to use a variety of cutting tools, and to make uniform and precise cuts. Making sure all vegetable cuts are uniform in shape and size means that they will cook evenly and present a neat, attractive appearance.

The best dishes begin with the best quality produce. Handle fresh produce carefully to maintain its flavor, color, texture, and nutritional value throughout all stages of preparation and cooking. One key to preserving quality in produce is to perform all cutting tasks as close as possible to cooking time. Another important factor is the ability to select the right tool for the job, and to keep that tool in proper working condition. A steel should be on hand whenever you are cutting any food to periodically hone your knife blade as you work.

The basic knife cuts include:

- Chopping
- Mincing
- Chiffonade (shredding)
- Julienne and batonnet
- Dicing
- Paysanne (fermière)
- Diamond (lozenge)
- Rondelle, bias, oblique, or roll cuts

Your aim should always be to cut the food into pieces of uniform shape and size. Unevenly cut items give an impression of carelessness that can spoil the dish's look. An even more important consideration is that foods of different sizes and shapes won't cook evenly. All of this is crucial in achieving your customers' total satisfaction with each dish.

PEELING VEGETABLES

All fresh produce, even if it will be peeled before cutting, should be properly washed. Washing removes surface dirt and bacteria and other contaminants that might otherwise come in contact with cut surfaces by way of the knife or peeler and your cutting surface. For the best shelf life, wash vegetables as close to preparation time as possible.

FIGURE **19.1a** Use a chef's knife to peel thick-skinned vegetables, such as winter squash

FIGURE **19.1b** Use a swivel-bladed peeler to peel thin-skinned vegetables, such as asparagus

Not all vegetables require peeling before cooking, but when it is necessary, use a tool that will evenly and neatly remove the skin without taking off too much of the edible flesh. Some vegetables and fruits, such as carrots, asparagus, apples, and potatoes, have relatively thin skins or peels.

Peeling a thick-skinned vegetable such as winter squash requires the use of a chef's knife. Chef's knives are better for larger vegetables or those with very tough rinds, such as celeriac or winter squash. Remove fibrous or tough skins from broccoli or similar vegetables with a paring knife or swivel-bladed peeler to trim away the skin; often it can be pulled away after the initial cut.

Peel vegetables with relatively thin skins or peels using a swivel-bladed peeler. These peelers can be used in both directions, so that the skin or peel is removed on both the downward and upward strokes. A paring knife can be used in place of a peeler in some instances. Hold the blade's edge at a 20-degree angle to the vegetable's surface and shave the blade just under the surface to remove a thin layer.

CHOPPING

Rinse and dry herbs well, and then strip the leaves from the stems. Gather the herbs into a tight ball before slicing them to produce a very coarse chop. Use your guiding hand to hold them in place. Position the knife so that it can slice through the pile and chop the herbs coarsely.

Once the herbs are coarsely chopped, use the fingertips of your guiding hand to hold the tip of the chef's knife in contact with the cutting board. Keeping the tip of the blade against the cutting board, lower the knife firmly and rapidly, repeatedly cutting through the herbs. Continue chopping until the herbs are the desired coarseness.

FIGURE **19.2a** Keep the tip of the knife in contact with the cutting board while continuing to chop the herbs

FIGURE **19.2b** Finely chopped herbs

MINCING

Mincing is a very fine cut that is suitable for many vegetables and herbs. Onions, garlic, and shallots are often minced. Remember, a very sharp knife is the best defense against the harsh effects that cutting onions can have on your eyes. Mince onions or shallots by cutting a grid of cross cuts to create an extremely fine dice. Finely mince herbs by continuing to cut until the desired fineness is attained. Green onions and chives are minced differently. Rather than cutting repeatedly, slice them very finely.

FIGURE 19.3 Green onions and chives are minced by simply slicing them very fine

FIGURE 19.4 For chiffonade, make parallel cuts to thinly shred the leaves. For leafier vegetables, remove, stack, and roll the leaves before cutting into shreds

CHIFFONADE/ SHREDDING

The chiffonade cut is used for leafy vegetables and herbs. The result is a fine shred, often used as a garnish or bed on which to place an item. For Belgian endive, remove the leaves from the core and stack them. Make parallel cuts to produce a shred. For greens with large leaves, such as romaine, roll individual leaves into cylinders before cutting. Stack smaller leaves, such as basil, one on top of the other, then roll them into cylinders and cut. Use a chef's knife to make very fine, parallel cuts to produce fine shreds. Again, a very sharp blade will mean the difference between cleanly cutting greens and crushing their delicate texture.

STANDARD VEGETABLE CUTS

The standard cuts are outlined in the chart on page 279. The dimensions indicated are guidelines and may be modified as necessary. Determine the size of the cut by the requirements of the recipe or menu item, the nature of the vegetable being cut, the desired cooking time, and appearance.

Before chopping or cutting fruits and vegetables, trim them to remove roots, cores, stems, or seeds. They may also be trimmed by slicing away one side of a rounded vegetable. This makes vegetable cutting tasks safer, because the vegetable will not roll or slip as it is cut. To produce very regular and precise cuts, such as julienne or dice, cut a slice from each side and both ends of the vegetable to make an even rectangle or square. Be sure to save and quickly utilize all edible trim to get the maximum yield and value from the produce.

STANDARD VEGETABLE CUTS	
Fine julienne	1/16 by 1/16 by 1 to 2 in / 1.50 mm by 1.50 mm by 3 to 5 cm
Julienne/allumette	1/8 by 1/8 by 1 to 2 in / 3 mm by 3 mm by 3 to 5 cm
Batonnet	1/4 by 1/4 by 2 to 2-1/2 in / 6 mm by 6 mm by 5 to 6 cm
Fine brunoise	1/16 by 1/16 by 1/16 in / 1.50 by 1.50 by 1.50 mm
Brunoise	1/8 by 1/8 by 1/8 in / 3 by 3 by 3 mm
Small dice	1/4 by 1/4 by 1/4 in / 6 by 6 by 6 mm
Medium dice	1/2 by 1/2 by 1/2 in / 1 by 1 by 1 cm
Large dice	3/4 by 3/4 by 3/4 in / 2 by 2 by 2 cm

FIGURE **19.5a** Fine Julienne

FIGURE **19.5b** Julienne/Allumette

FIGURE **19.5c** Batonnet

FIGURE **19.5d** Fine Brunoise

(Continues)

(Continued)

FIGURE **19.5e** Brunoise

FIGURE **19.5f** Small Dice

FIGURE **19.5g** Medium Dice

FIGURE **19.5h** Large Dice

JULIENNE AND BATONNET

Julienne and batonnet are long, rectangular cuts. The difference between these cuts is the final size. Trim and square off the vegetable by cutting a slice to make four straight sides. Cut both ends to even the block off. These initial slices make it easier to produce even cuts. The trimmings can be used for stocks, soups, purées, or other preparations where the shape is not important. After squaring off the vegetable, slice the vegetable lengthwise, making parallel cuts of even thickness. Stack the cut slices, aligning the edges, and make even, parallel cuts of the same thickness for a batonnet.

FIGURE **19.6a** After squaring off the vegetable, make parallel cuts to produce slices of even thickness

FIGURE **19.6b** Stack the cut slices and make even, parallel cuts to create batonnets

FIGURE **19.6c** Line up the batonnet cuts and cut across them to produce a small dice

DICING

Dicing produces cube shapes. Different preparations require different sizes of dice. The names given to the different-sized dice are fine brunoise/brunoise, and small, medium, and large dice. To begin, trim and cut the vegetable as for julienne or batonnet. Gather the julienne or batonnet pieces and cut through them crosswise at evenly spaced intervals.

FIGURE **19.7a** Paysanne

FIGURE **19.7b** Fermière

FIGURE **19.7c** Lozenge

FIGURE **19.7d** Rondelle

FIGURE **19.7e** Tourné

ADDITIONAL VEGETABLE CUTS

These vegetable cuts are made using precise standards for a more upscale presentation. They may be cut so that the natural shape of the vegetable is visible in each slice. Tourné cuts (see page 285) may be the classic football shape shown here or modified to suit different vegetable types.

ADDITIONAL VEGETABLE CUTS	
Paysanne	1/2 by 1/2 by 1/8 in/1 cm by 1 cm × 3 mm
Fermière	Cut to desired thickness: 1/8 to 1/2 in/3 mm to 1 cm
Lozenge	Diamond shape: 1/2 by 1/2 by 1/8 in/ 1 cm by 1 cm by 3 mm
Rondelle	Cut to desired thickness: 1/8 to 1/2 in/6 mm to 1 cm
Tourné	Approximately 2 in/5 cm long with 7 faces

PAYSANNE/FERMIÈRE

Cuts produced in the paysanne (peasant) and fermière (farmer) styles are generally used in dishes intended to have a rustic appeal. When used for traditional regional specialties, they may be cut in such a way that the shape of the vegetable's curved or uneven edges is still apparent in the finished cut. However, even with cuts having this rustic appearance, it is important to cut them all to the same thickness so that they will cook evenly. Square off the vegetable first and make large batonnets, 3/4 in/2 cm thick. Make even, parallel cuts crosswise at 1/8 in/3 mm intervals to produce the paysanne cut.

For a more rustic presentation, cut the vegetable into halves, quarters, or eighths, depending on its size. The pieces should be roughly similar in dimension to a batonnet. Make even, thin crosswise cuts at roughly 1/8-in/3-mm intervals.

DIAMOND/LOZENGE CUTS

The diamond, or lozenge, cut is similar to the paysanne. Instead of cutting batonnets, trim and thinly slice the vegetable. Cut the slices on the bias into strips 1/8 in/3 mm thick of the correct width. Make an initial bias cut

FIGURE **19.8** For paysanne, cut the vegetable into large batonnet and make even, parallel cuts crosswise at 1/8-inch intervals to produce the paysanne cut

FIGURE **19.9** For diamonds, cut the slices on the bias into 1/8-inch strips of the correct width. Cut the strips on the bias to create the diamond shape

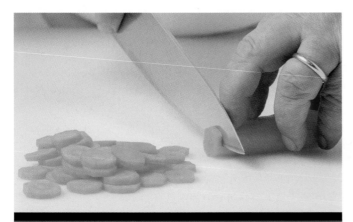

FIGURE **19.10** For rondelles, make parallel slicing cuts through the vegetable at the desired interval

FIGURE **19.11** To make diagonal, or bias, cuts, hold the blade so that it cuts through the vegetable at an angle

FIGURE **19.12** For oblique cuts, holding the knife in the same position, roll the vegetable a quarter turn and slice through it, forming a piece with two angled edges

to begin. This will leave some trim (reserve the trim for use in preparations that do not require a neat, decorative cut). Continue to make bias cuts, parallel to the first one.

ROUNDS/RONDELLES

Rounds, or rondelles, are simple to cut. Just evenly cut a cylindrical vegetable, such as a carrot or cucumber, crosswise. The basic round shape can be varied by cutting the vegetable on the bias to produce an elongated or oval disk or by slicing it in half for half moons. Score the vegetable with a channel knife to produce flower shapes. Trim and peel the vegetable if necessary. Make parallel slicing cuts through the vegetable at even intervals. Guide the vegetable as you are cutting by pushing on the end of it with your thumb.

DIAGONAL/BIAS CUTS

This cut is often used to prepare vegetables for stir-fries and other Asian-style dishes because it exposes a greater surface area and shortens cooking time. To make a diagonal cut, place the peeled or trimmed vegetable on the work surface. Hold the blade so that it cuts through the food on an angle. The wider the angle, the more elongated the cut surface will be. Continue making parallel cuts, adjusting the angle of the blade so that all the pieces are approximately the same size.

OBLIQUE OR ROLL CUTS

This cut is used primarily with long, cylindrical vegetables such as parsnips or carrots. Place the peeled vegetable on a cutting board. Make a diagonal cut to remove the tip. Hold the knife in the same position and roll the vegetable a quarter turn (approximately 90 degrees). Slice through it on the same diagonal, forming a piece with two angled edges. Be sure to decrease the angle of the diagonal as the vegetable gets larger in diameter. This will ensure uniform cuts that will cook evenly. Repeat until the entire vegetable has been cut.

DECORATIVE CUTS

Decorative cuts can add an attractive visual component to a dish. Basic tools such as a paring knife or a swivel-bladed peeler (for curled or shaved Parmesan to top carpaccio or Caesar salad, for example) or parisienne scoops or melon ballers (for balls of different sizes) can be used to create special effects. More-specialized tools include a mandoline, a Japanese "turner," an apple peeler, a ripple cutter, or a box grater for hand cutting. For large-volume operations, specialized cutting machines and tools are available. Be sure to read any instructions that come with special cutters, and use all of the safety guards that come with them.

FIGURE **19.13** Push the vegetable down the entire length of the mandoline, turning the vegetable 45 degrees on each pass

WAFFLE/GAUFRETTE

Use a mandoline to make waffle, or gaufrette, cuts. Potatoes, sweet potatoes, beets, and other large, relatively solid foods can be made into this cut. The blades of the mandoline are set so that the first pass of the vegetable doesn't actually cut away a slice but only makes grooves. Turn the potato 45 degrees and make the second pass to create waffle cut potatoes. Run the vegetable the entire length of the mandoline. Turn the vegetable 45 degrees and repeat the entire stroke. Repeat this procedure, turning the vegetable 45 degrees on each pass over the mandoline.

FLUTING

Fluting takes some practice to master, but it makes a very attractive garnish. It is customarily used on mushrooms. Hold the mushroom between the thumb and forefinger of your guiding hand. Remove the outer layer of the mushroom cap by peeling the mushroom. Start at the underside of the cap, going toward the center. Place the blade of a paring knife at a very slight angle against the mushroom cap center. Rest the thumb of your cutting hand on the mushroom and use it to brace the knife. Rotate the knife toward the base of the cap while turning the mushroom in the opposite direction. Finish the fluted mushroom by lightly pressing the tip of your paring knife into the top of the mushroom to create a star pattern. Turn the mushroom slightly and repeat the cutting steps. Continue until the entire cap is fluted. Pull away the trimmings. Trim away the stem.

CUTTING TURNED/TOURNÉ VEGETABLES

Turning vegetables (*tourner* in French) requires a series of cuts that simultaneously trim and shape the vegetable. The shape is similar to a small barrel or football. Peel the vegetable, if desired, and cut it into pieces of manageable size. Cut large round

FIGURE **19.14a** Hold the mushroom between your thumb and forefinger. Starting at the underside of the cap and working toward the center, remove the outer layer of the mushroom cap

FIGURE **19.14b** Place the blade of a paring knife at a slight angle against the center of the mushroom cap. Rotate the knife toward the base while turning the mushroom in the opposite direction

FIGURE **19.14c** Lightly press the tip of the paring knife into the top of the mushroom; turn the mushroom slightly and repeat the cut. Continue around until the cuts form a star pattern

FIGURE **19.14d** Finished fluted mushrooms

or oval vegetables, such as beets and potatoes, into quarters, sixths, or eighths (depending on the size), to form pieces slightly larger than 2 inches/5 centimeters. Cut cylindrical vegetables, such as carrots, into pieces 2 inches/5 centimeters in size. Carve the pieces into barrel or football shapes. Try to make as few cuts as possible to create the 7 sides so that the faces of the tourné remain distinct. The faces should be smooth, evenly spaced, and tapered so that both ends are narrower than the center.

FANNING

The fan cut uses one basic, easy-to-master cut to produce complicated-looking garnishes. It is used on both raw and cooked foods, such as pickles, strawberries, peach halves, avocados, zucchini, and other somewhat-pliable vegetables and fruits. Leaving the stem end intact, make a series of parallel, lengthwise slices. Spread the cut fruit or vegetable into a fan shape.

FIGURE 19.15 Leaving the stem end in tact, make a series of parallel, lengthwise slices. Spread the fruit or vegetable into the fan shape

PREPARING SPECIFIC FRUITS AND VEGETABLES

A typical foodservice kitchen's vegetable and herb mise en place often includes vegetables that grow in layers, have seeds, grow in bulbs, or are otherwise unique. These types of fruits and vegetable require special cutting techniques, which are detailed in the following text.

APPLES

Peel apples as thinly as possible to avoid trim loss. To prevent discoloration of the cut surfaces of apples, as well as pears, peaches, and bananas, toss them in water that has been acidulated by adding a little citrus juice. Choose a juice with a flavor that complements the fruit's flavor. There shouldn't be so much acid that it overwhelms the fruit. To clean and peel an apple, use the tip of a paring knife to remove the stem and blossom ends. Use a paring knife or peeler to cut away the skin. Once the peel is removed, halve the apple from top to bottom and cut into quarters. To core the quarters, work from the stem end, angling your cut to the midpoint of the core, where it is deepest. Make a second cut working from the opposite direction.

To cut very even slices, use a mandoline. Working with a whole peeled apple, make slices from one side of the apple until just before the core is reached. Turn and repeat on the opposite side. When the flesh has been removed from the two wide sides, slice the flesh from the now narrow sides of the apple.

ARTICHOKES

Artichokes are members of the thistle family. Their leaves have sharp barbs, like thorns. The edible meat of the artichoke is found at the base of each leaf, which grows from a stem, as well as at the fleshy base of the vegetable, known as the bottom. Artichokes have a purple, feathery center—the "choke"—that is inedible in mature artichokes. The choke in baby artichokes may be tender enough to eat.

To prepare whole artichokes, first cut away the stem. The amount of stem removed is determined by how the artichoke is to be presented, as well as by how tender or tough the stem is. Cutting the stem away even with the bottom of the artichoke makes a flat surface, allowing the artichoke to sit flat on the plate. If the artichoke is to be halved or quartered, some of the stem may be left intact; any part of the stem that is not woody can be eaten and adds to the value of the choke. Peel the stem with a paring knife. Cut off the top of the artichoke. Snip the barbs from each leaf with kitchen scissors. Rub the cut surfaces with lemon juice to prevent browning, or hold the trimmed artichoke in acidulated water (a mixture of lemon juice and water). The artichoke can be simmered or steamed at this point, if desired, or the center of the artichoke, the choke, may be removed prior to cooking. To remove the choke, spread the leaves of the cooked or raw artichoke open. The choke can now be scooped out using a spoon.

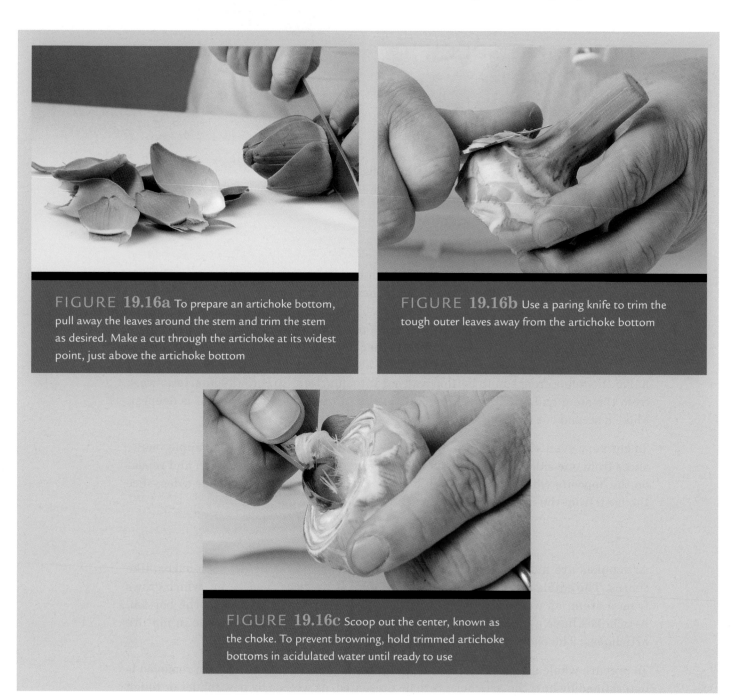

FIGURE **19.16a** To prepare an artichoke bottom, pull away the leaves around the stem and trim the stem as desired. Make a cut through the artichoke at its widest point, just above the artichoke bottom

FIGURE **19.16b** Use a paring knife to trim the tough outer leaves away from the artichoke bottom

FIGURE **19.16c** Scoop out the center, known as the choke. To prevent browning, hold trimmed artichoke bottoms in acidulated water until ready to use

ASPARAGUS

Young asparagus may need no further preparation than a simple trim to remove the very ends of the stalk, and a quick rinse. More mature asparagus may need to have the stalk trimmed a little more and partially peeled to remove the outer skin, which can be tough and stringy. As asparagus matures, the stalk becomes tough. To remove the woody portion, bend the stalk gently until it snaps. Using a special asparagus peeler or a swivel-bladed peeler, peel the remaining stalk partway up; this enhances palatability and also makes it easier to cook the asparagus evenly.

Asparagus may be tied into loose portion-sized bundles to make it easier to remove them from boiling water when they are blanched or boiled. Don't tie them too tightly or make the bundles more than a few inches in diameter, otherwise the asparagus in the middle will not cook properly.

AVOCADOS

Avocados have a rough, thick skin and a large pit. The flesh is soft enough to purée easily when properly ripened. Avocados, like potatoes, bananas, and artichokes, turn brown when they are exposed to air. To prevent browning, cut avocados as close to the time of service as possible. Citrus juices both brighten the flavor of this rich but relatively bland food and prevent the flesh from turning brown.

FIGURE **19.17a** Young asparagus may need no further preparation than a simple trim and rinse, but as asparagus matures, the stalk becomes tough. To remove the woody portion, bend the stalk gently until it snaps

FIGURE **19.17b** Using a swivel-bladed peeler, peel the remaining stalk partway up. This ensures more even cooking and enhances palatability

To remove the skin and pit from an avocado, hold it securely but gently with the fingertips of your guiding hand. Insert a knife blade into the bottom of the avocado. Turn the avocado against the knife blade to make a cut completely around it. The cut should pierce the skin and cut through the flesh up to the pit.

Twist the two halves of a sliced avocado away from each other and pull gently to separate them. Because it can be difficult to pick out the pit with your fingertips without mangling the flesh, scoop it out with a spoon, removing as little flesh as possible, or carefully chop the heel of the knife into the pit, then twist and pull it free from the flesh. To remove the pit from the knife safely, use the edge of the cutting board or the lip of a container to pry the pit free. To peel the avocado, catch the skin between the ball of your thumb and the flat side of a knife blade and pull it free from the flesh. If the flesh is under-ripe, this may not be possible; in that case, use the knife to cut the skin away.

To slice the avocado, cut it lengthwise into wedges or slices. To dice the avocado, cut crosswise through the wedges. To dice an avocado while it is still in the skin, use the tip of a knife to score the flesh into dice of the desired size. Use the edge of a kitchen spoon to slice through the flesh. As the flesh is sliced away and lifted from the avocado, it is cut into dice. Make each layer as thick or as thin as desired.

FIGURE **19.18a** To halve an avocado, insert the knife blade into the bottom of the avocado; the cut should pierce the skin and pass through the flesh right up to the pit. Turn the avocado against the knife blade to make a cut completely around it. Twist the two halves in opposite directions and pull gently to separate them

FIGURE **19.18b** Holding the avocado half in the palm of your hand, carefully chop the heel of the knife into the pit, then twist the knife to pull the pit free of the flesh. To remove the pit from the knife safely, use the edge of the cutting board to pry the pit free

FIGURE **19.18c** Scoop the flesh from the skin with a spoon or use a knife to pull the skin back from the flesh. If the flesh is under-ripe, making this technique impossible, simply use the knife to cut the skin away

CITRUS FRUITS

Citrus fruits, including oranges, lemons, limes, and grapefruit, are used to add flavor, moisture, and color to dishes. They also serve as a functional garnish with some foods—for instance, a slice of lime with Cuban-style black bean soup or a wedge of lemon with broiled fish.

Before juicing citrus fruits, allow them to come to room temperature if possible. Roll the fruit under the palm of your hand on a cutting board or other work surface before juicing to break some of the membranes. This helps to release more juice. Remember to strain out the seeds and pulp before using the juice, either by covering the fruit with cheesecloth before squeezing it or by straining it after juicing. There are numerous special tools to juice citrus fruits, including reamers, extractors, and hand-operated and electric juicers.

FIGURE **19.19** The zest includes only the brightly colored part of the skin, which contains much of the fruit's flavorful and aromatic volatile oils; it does not include the underlying white, bitter pith. To make grated zest, you can use the fine openings of a box grater, a peeler, or a zester

ZESTING CITRUS

Citrus zest is the outer portion of the fruit's peel or rind. It is used to add color, texture, and flavor to dishes. The zest includes only the skin's brightly colored part, which contains much of the fruit's flavorful and aromatic volatile oils. It does not include the underlying white pith, which has a bitter taste. You can use the fine openings on a box grater to make grated zest or a paring knife, peeler, or zester to make long strips of zest.

Zest is often blanched before it is used in a dish in order to remove any unpleasant bitter flavor. To blanch zest, cook it briefly in simmering water, then drain. Repeat as often as necessary; generally two to three blanchings are best. Add sugar to the blanching water for a sweetened zest.

MAKING CITRUS SUPRÊMES

Cutting the flesh away from all the connective membranes of the fruit makes citrus suprêmes, also called sections or segments. After cutting away the ends of the fruit, use a paring knife to remove just the peel of the orange. Be careful to cut away as little flesh as possible. To make suprêmes, use a paring knife to cut along each side of the membrane that divides the orange segments. Have a bowl ready to catch the suprêmes as you work.

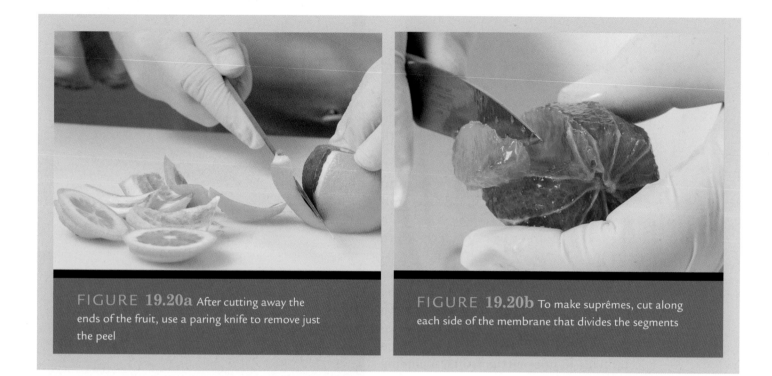

FIGURE **19.20a** After cutting away the ends of the fruit, use a paring knife to remove just the peel

FIGURE **19.20b** To make suprêmes, cut along each side of the membrane that divides the segments

FIGURE **19.21** To cut the kernels off the cob, hold the ear upright and cut downward as close to the cob as possible

CORN

Whole ears of corn can be boiled or steamed after the husk has been peeled away. The fine threads, known as silk, that cling to the corn should be pulled away. Once husked, be certain to cook the corn as soon as possible. Remove the silk, but leave much of the husk intact if you intend to grill the corn instead of boiling it. This method will give the corn a rich, smoky flavor. To cut the kernels away from the cob, hold the ear upright and cut downward as close to the cob as possible. To "milk" the corn, remove the husk and silk. Lay the ear down on a cutting surface and lightly score each row of kernels. Then, use the back of a knife, a spoon, or a butter curler to scrape out the flesh and milk.

FRESH PEPPERS AND CHILES

Peppers and chiles are used in dishes from cuisines as diverse as those of Central and South America, many Asian countries, Spain, and Hungary. As the interest in peppers and chiles has grown, many special varieties have become available, both fresh and dried. For more information about working with dried chiles, see page 303. Whenever handling very hot chiles, be sure to wear plastic gloves to protect your skin from the irritating oils they contain.

CUTTING AND SEEDING FRESH PEPPERS AND CHILES

Cut through the pepper from top to bottom. Continue to cut it into quarters, especially if the pepper is large. Use the tip of a paring knife to cut away the stem and seeds. This cut removes the least amount of usable pepper. Chiles retain a good deal of their heat in the seeds, ribs, and blossom ends. The degree of heat can be controlled by adjusting how much, if any, of these parts of the chile is added to a dish.

You can make very fine, even julienne or dice by filleting the pepper—that is, removing the seeds and ribs—before cutting it. Cut away the top and bottom of the pepper to create an even rectangle. Roll the pepper away from the paring knife as you cut the seeds and ribs away to create a long rectangle of pepper that can be cut as desired. Peel away the skin, if desired, and then cut the flesh into neat julienne or dice. For a more precise preparation, use a chef's knife to cut away a thin layer of the flesh to make a completely flat surface. This will create a more square, uniform julienne or dice. Reserve any edible scraps to use in coulis or to flavor broths, stews, or court bouillons.

PEELING FRESH PEPPERS OR CHILES

Peppers and chiles are often peeled before they are used in a dish to improve the dish's flavor or texture, or both. The thin, but relatively tough, skin can be removed using a swivel-bladed peeler or paring knife. This approach is often taken when the peppers are to be served raw, as in a salad or salsa, or in a dish that is intended to retain the pepper's sweet, fresh flavor.

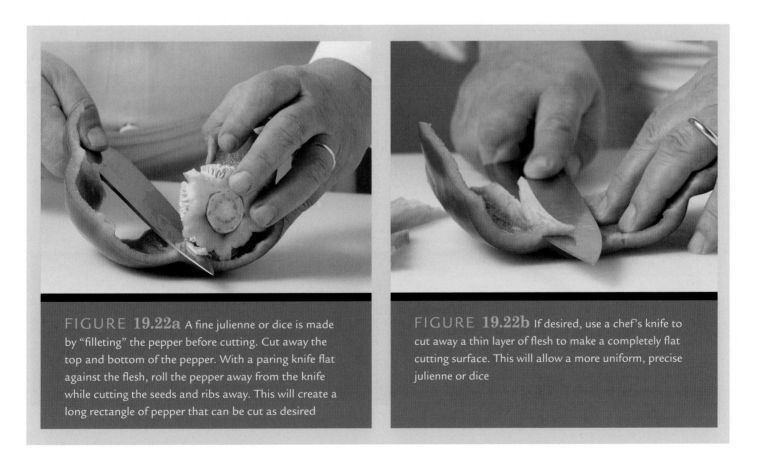

FIGURE **19.22a** A fine julienne or dice is made by "filleting" the pepper before cutting. Cut away the top and bottom of the pepper. With a paring knife flat against the flesh, roll the pepper away from the knife while cutting the seeds and ribs away. This will create a long rectangle of pepper that can be cut as desired

FIGURE **19.22b** If desired, use a chef's knife to cut away a thin layer of flesh to make a completely flat cutting surface. This will allow a more uniform, precise julienne or dice

To peel raw peppers with a swivel-bladed peeler, first section the pepper with a knife and cut along the folds to expose the skin. Then remove the core, seeds, and ribs and peel with a swivel-bladed peeler.

GARLIC

Garlic has distinctly different flavors depending upon how it is cut. It can be purchased already peeled or chopped, but many chefs feel strongly that the loss in flavor and quality is not worth the convenience for all but volume cooking situations. Once cut, garlic (like onions) starts to take on a stronger flavor. Mashed or minced garlic is called for in many preparations, so it is important to have enough prepared to last through a service period, but not so much that a significant amount has to be thrown out at the end of a shift. To prevent bacterial growth, store uncooked minced garlic covered in oil in the refrigerator and use within 24 hours.

To separate the garlic cloves, wrap an entire head of garlic in a side towel and press down on the top. The cloves will break cleanly away from the root end. The towel keeps the papery skin from flying around the work area.

To loosen the skin from each clove, place it on the cutting board, place the flat side of the knife blade on top, and hit the blade using a fist or the heel of your hand. Peel off the skin and remove the root end and any brown spots. An alternative to smashing the clove of garlic in order to remove the peel is to peel the garlic clove using a paring knife.

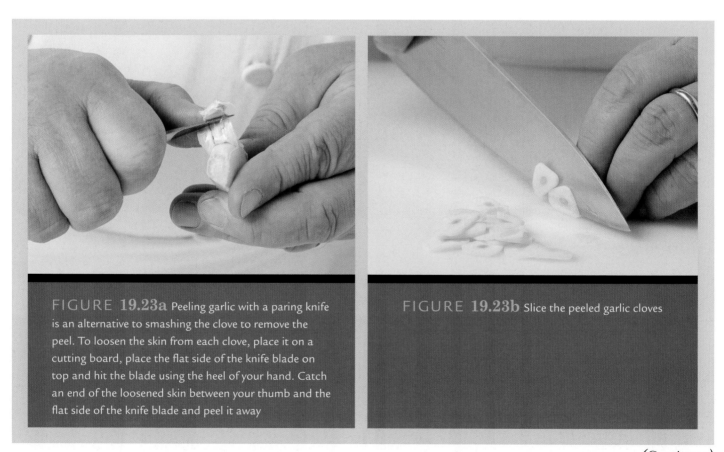

FIGURE **19.23a** Peeling garlic with a paring knife is an alternative to smashing the clove to remove the peel. To loosen the skin from each clove, place it on a cutting board, place the flat side of the knife blade on top and hit the blade using the heel of your hand. Catch an end of the loosened skin between your thumb and the flat side of the knife blade and peel it away

FIGURE **19.23b** Slice the peeled garlic cloves

(Continues)

(Continued)

FIGURE **19.23c** Cut the slices to create a rough chop

FIGURE **19.23d** Mince the cloves using a rocking motion, as though mincing herbs

At some times of the year and under certain storage conditions, the garlic may begin to sprout. Split the clove in half and remove the sprout for the best flavor.

To crush the cloves, lay the skinned cloves on the cutting board with the flat of the knife blade over them. Using a motion similar to that for cracking the skin, hit the blade firmly and forcefully with a fist or the heel of your hand. For chopped garlic, slice the peeled garlic cloves before chopping them. Cut the garlic slices to the appropriate size to create roughly chopped garlic. Mince garlic cloves like you would mince an onion. Mince or chop the cloves fairly fine, using a rocking motion, as for herbs.

To mash the garlic, hold the knife nearly flat against the cutting board and use the cutting edge to mash the garlic against the board. Repeat this step until the garlic is mashed to a paste. If desired, sprinkle the garlic with salt before mashing. The salt acts as an abrasive, speeding the mashing process and preventing the garlic from sticking to the knife blade. To mince large quantities of peeled garlic, use a food processor, if desired. Or crush and grind salt-sprinkled garlic to a paste with a mortar and pestle.

KIWI

Although the fuzzy kiwi peel is edible, it is almost always removed before serving. Cut the top and bottom off of the kiwi to create a flat surface. Carefully cut away the remaining peel from top to bottom using a sharp paring knife. Try to remove as little flesh as possible. Another method for removing the peel after trimming off the top and bottom is to use a spoon. Carefully wedge a spoon between the peel and the flesh of the fruit and rotate it around the fruit to remove the peel. The curved bowl of the spoon should remove very little of the fruit's flesh.

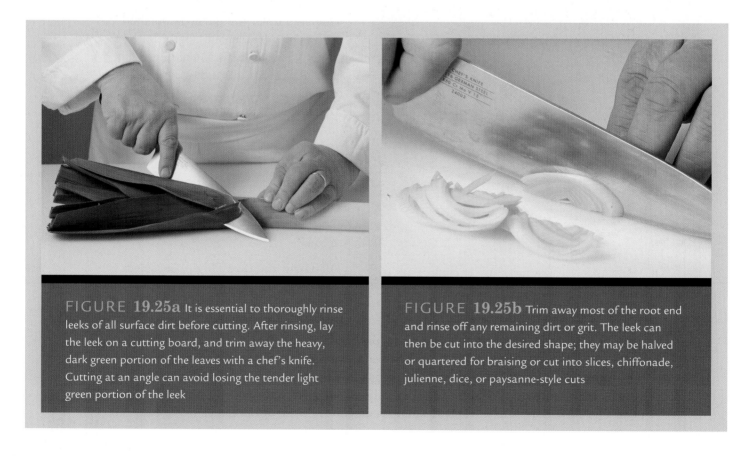

FIGURE **19.24** Carefully wedge a spoon between the peel and the flesh of the fruit and rotate it around the fruit to remove the peel

LEEKS

A leek grows in layers, trapping grit and sand between each layer. Therefore, one of the biggest concerns when working with leeks is removing every trace of dirt. Careful rinsing is essential. To clean leeks, rinse off all surface dirt, paying special attention to the roots, where dirt clings. Lay the leek on the cutting board and, using a chef's knife, trim away the heavy, dark green portion of the leaves. Cutting on an angle avoids losing the tender light green portion of the leek. The dark green portion of the leek may be reserved to make bouquet garni or for other uses. Trim away most of the root end. Cut the leek lengthwise into halves, thirds, or quarters. Then rinse the leek under running water to remove any remaining grit or sand. Cut the leek into the desired shape. Leeks may be left in halves or quarters with the stem end still intact for braising. Or they may be cut into slices, chiffonade, julienne, dice, or paysanne-style cuts.

FIGURE **19.25a** It is essential to thoroughly rinse leeks of all surface dirt before cutting. After rinsing, lay the leek on a cutting board, and trim away the heavy, dark green portion of the leaves with a chef's knife. Cutting at an angle can avoid losing the tender light green portion of the leek

FIGURE **19.25b** Trim away most of the root end and rinse off any remaining dirt or grit. The leek can then be cut into the desired shape; they may be halved or quartered for braising or cut into slices, chiffonade, julienne, dice, or paysanne-style cuts

MANGOES

A mango has a flat seed in the center of the flesh. The peel is left on to produce a special cut, known as the hedgehog cut, or the fruit may be peeled before cutting the flesh from the pit, if desired. If cut from the stem end to the pointed end of the mango, the flesh comes away from the pit more easily.

For the hedgehog cut, the mango is not peeled before the flesh is sliced from the pit. This technique can be used to prepare mangoes for salads or other uses, or it may be

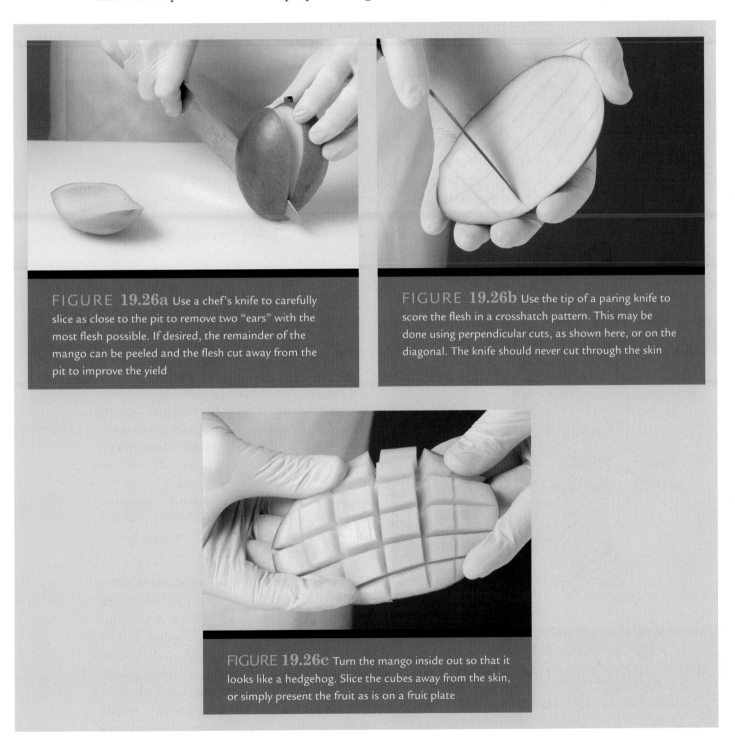

FIGURE **19.26a** Use a chef's knife to carefully slice as close to the pit to remove two "ears" with the most flesh possible. If desired, the remainder of the mango can be peeled and the flesh cut away from the pit to improve the yield

FIGURE **19.26b** Use the tip of a paring knife to score the flesh in a crosshatch pattern. This may be done using perpendicular cuts, as shown here, or on the diagonal. The knife should never cut through the skin

FIGURE **19.26c** Turn the mango inside out so that it looks like a hedgehog. Slice the cubes away from the skin, or simply present the fruit as is on a fruit plate

used for a decorative presentation on a fruit plate. Use a chef's knife to carefully slice as close to the pit as possible to remove the most flesh. If desired, the remainder of the mango can be peeled and the flesh cut away from the pit in order to improve the yield. Use the tip of a paring knife or a utility knife to score the flesh in a crosshatch pattern. This may be done on the diagonal, or using perpendicular cuts to produce cubes. The tip of the knife should not cut through the skin. Turn the mango half inside out; it will look like a hedgehog. Slice the cubes away from the skin now, or present the fruit as is on a fruit plate.

To dice the mango for puréeing or for a less decorative approach, peel it by making a series of cuts, removing as little edible fruit as possible. Cut a slice from the other side of the pit, cutting as close to the pit as possible for the best yield. Cut the remaining flesh from the two narrow sides, following the curve of the pit. Cube or slice the mango as desired.

MELONS

Melons are served in wedges, slices, cubes, or balls. To make the melon more stable as you work, cut a slice from both ends. You may remove the entire rind before halving the melon and removing the seeds to streamline production of fruit plates and salads. Or you may prefer to leave the rind on. After cutting the top and the bottom off of the melon, cut the rind away. Use a utility or chef's knife to follow the curve of the melon. Cut the melon in half and scoop out the seeds. Be careful not to gouge the flesh of the fruit. The melon can now be made into melon balls, cut into slices or cubes, or diced. Scoop melon balls out of the cleaned melon half using a parisienne scoop.

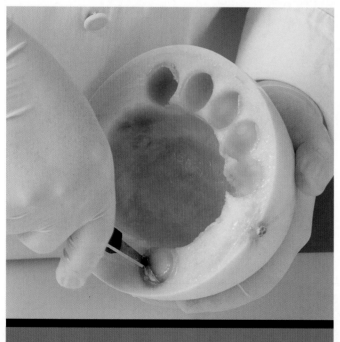

FIGURE **19.27** Remove the rind, cut the melon in half, and scoop out the seeds. Now balls can be scooped out of the melon using a parisienne scoop. Firmly press the scoop into the flesh and twist to create a round ball

MUSHROOMS

Clean mushrooms just before preparing them by rinsing quickly in cool water, only long enough to remove any dirt. Do not allow the mushrooms to soak; they absorb liquids quickly, and excess moisture causes them to deteriorate rapidly. Some people clean mushrooms by wiping them with a soft cloth or brushing them with a soft-bristled brush but this is not always practical in a professional kitchen. Let the mushrooms drain and dry well on layers of absorbent toweling before slicing or mincing.

Cook mushrooms as soon as possible after they are cut for the best flavor, color, and consistency in the finished dish. Avoid cutting more product than is needed at any given time to prevent loss of quality from discoloration and dehydration. Some mushrooms must have the stems removed. Shiitakes, for example, have very tough, woody stems; cut them away from the caps and save for stocks or to flavor sauces. The stems of other mushrooms, such as white mushrooms, morels, and cèpes, can usually be left intact, although a slice should be cut away from the stem end to trim dried or fibrous portions.

If possible, rest the mushroom on a flat side to provide more stability as you slice through the mushroom. Holding the mushroom cap with your guiding hand, make slices through the cap and stem, if it has not been trimmed off. To cut a large amount efficiently, slice the mushrooms so that the slices are layered. Then cut across the slices at the desired thickness to create julienne strips. Turn the julienne strips so that they are parallel to the edge of the work surface. Make crosswise cuts to mince the mushrooms for use in duxelles or other applications.

ONIONS

All types of onions taste best when cut as close as possible to the time to be used. The longer cut onions are stored, the more flavor and overall quality they lose. Once cut, onions also develop a strong, sulfurous odor that can spoil a dish's aroma and appeal.

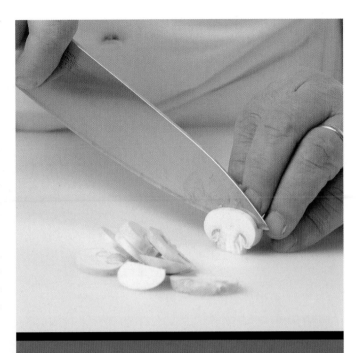

FIGURE **19.28** Holding the mushroom cap with the guiding hand, make slices through the cap and stem, if it has not been trimmed off. To create julienne strips, layer the slices and cut crosswise at the desired thickness. To then mince the mushroom, arrange the julienne strips so that they are parallel to the edge of the work surface and make crosswise cuts

When peeling an onion, remove as few layers as possible. One technique for peeling uses a paring knife to remove the outer layers of skin. Using a paring knife, cut a thin slice away from the stem and root ends of the bulb. Catch the peel between the pad of the thumb and the flat side of the knife blade and pull away the peel. Trim away any brown spots from underlying layers if necessary before cutting the vegetable to the desired size or shape. There is an alternative peeling method that is especially good when cutting and using the onion right away. Halve the onion lengthwise through the root before trimming and peeling. Trim the ends, leaving the root end intact if the onion will be diced, and pull away the skin from each half.

Leave the onion whole after peeling if you need slices or rings. To cut onion rings from a whole onion, be sure to hold the onion securely with your guiding hand. The rounded surface of the onion can slip on the cutting surface. To obtain slices, cut the onion in half, making a cut that runs from the root end to the stem end in order to cut julienne or dice. The root end, though trimmed, is still intact. This helps to hold the onion layers together as it is sliced or diced. To cut julienne from a halved onion, make a V-shaped notch cut on either side of the root end to remove it before slicing.

To dice or mince an onion half, lay it cut-side down on a cutting board. Using a chef's knife, make a series of evenly spaced, parallel, lengthwise cuts with the tip of the knife, leaving the root end intact. Cuts spaced 1/4 inch/6 millimeters apart will make

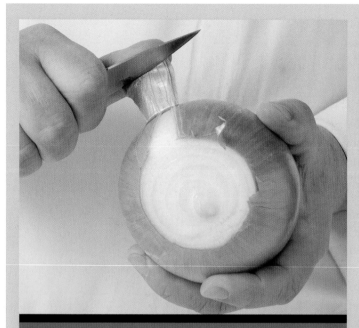

FIGURE **19.29a** Use a paring knife to cut a thin slice away from the stem and root ends of the bulb. Catch the peel between your thumb and the flat side of the knife blade and pull away the peel. If necessary, trim away any brown spots from the underlying layers, but it's best to take off as few layers as possible

FIGURE **19.29b** To mince or dice: Halve the onion with the grain and lay it cut-side down. Using a chef's knife, make two or three horizontal cuts parallel to the work surface. Work from the stem end to the root end, but do not cut all the way through

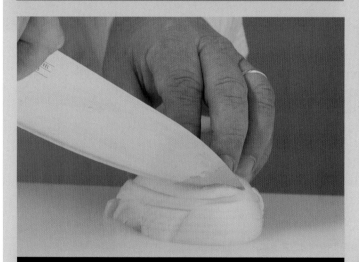

FIGURE **19.29c** Make a series of evenly spaced, parallel, lengthwise cuts with the tip of the chef's knife, still leaving the root end intact. Cuts spaced 1/4 inch/ 6 millimeter apart will create small dice; cuts spaced 1/2 inch/1 centimeter apart will produce medium or large dice

FIGURE **19.29d** To complete the mince or dice, make even, crosswise cuts through all layers of the onion. Work from the stem end to the root end, and reserve any usable trim for mirepoix

(Continues)

(Continued)

FIGURE **19.29e** To slice, first peel the onion and halve it with the grain. Place each half cut-side down, and make even, parallel cuts with a chef's knife

small dice; cuts spaced 1/2 inch/1 centimeter or 3/4 inch/2 centimeters apart will produce medium or large dice. While gently holding the vertical cuts together, make two or three horizontal cuts parallel to the work surface, from the stem end toward the root end, but do not cut all the way through. Holding the previous cuts together will produce a more uniform mince. To complete the dice, make even, crosswise cuts working from the stem end up to the root end, cutting through all layers of the onion. Reserve any usable trim for mirepoix.

Remove the root from the onion before making even cuts that follow the natural curve of the onion. Some chefs prefer to cut onions by making a series of evenly spaced cuts that follow the natural curve of the onion. These cuts are sometimes referred to as radial cuts. Radial cuts result in even julienne or batonnet, which can then be cut crosswise into dice if desired.

PEAPODS

Snow peas and sugar snap peas both have edible pods and are typically eaten raw, steamed, or stir-fried. They should be carefully selected for freshness as their quality

FIGURE **19.30** Some varieties of pea pods have a rather tough string that should be removed before cooking. Snap the stem end off, using your fingers or a paring knife, and pull the string away from the pod

FIGURE 19.31 A pineapple has thick, spiny skin, and the flesh near its skin has "eyes" that need to be removed before using the flesh in any preparations. To begin, slice away the pineapple's top and base. Use a chef's knife to cut away the skin. Make the cuts deep enough to remove the eyes but not so deep that a great deal of edible flesh is removed

FIGURE 19.32 Using a chef's knife, quarter the pomegranate. Working over a bowl of water, use your fingers to pry the seeds out of the quarters. The seeds will sink to the bottom of the bowl, while any pieces of membrane will float to the surface

and flavor deteriorate quickly. Snow peas and sugar snap peas, depending upon the variety, often have a rather tough string that runs along one seam. This string should be removed before the peas are cooked. Snap off the stem end, using either a paring knife or your fingers, and pull. The string will come away easily.

PINEAPPLES

A pineapple has a thick, spiny skin. The flesh near the skin has "eyes" that should be completely removed before using the flesh in a salad or other presentations. Slice away the pineapple top with a chef's knife, and cut a slice from the base of the pineapple. Use a chef's knife to peel the pineapple. Make the cuts deep enough to remove the eyes but not so deep that a great deal of edible flesh is removed. For even slices or to make neat dice or cubes, slice the pineapple vertically at the desired thickness until you reach the core on the first side. Turn the pineapple, and make slices from the opposite side as well as from both ends. Cut the slices into neat julienne, batonnet, or dice as desired.

POMEGRANATES

Pomegranates may be one of the toughest produce items to fabricate but it is well worth the effort. The jewel-like seeds add an acidic punch and eye-catching appeal to any dish. Cut off the crown to extract the seeds. Scoop out the white core and then score the shell to pull it apart into manageable pieces. Carefully remove the seeds from the white pith. Any white pith that adheres to the seeds should be washed off under water.

TOMATOES

Fresh and canned tomatoes are used in numerous dishes. Tomatoes can be cut into slices using a special tomato knife, which has a serrated blade, but a sharp chef's, utility, or paring knife also works well. Large quantities can be sliced on an electric slicer. Tomatoes have a skin that clings tightly to the flesh and the interior contains pockets of seeds and juice. When the tomato is peeled, seeded, and chopped, it is known as tomato concassé. The blanching technique for tomatoes is also used for peaches and nuts, such as almonds and chestnuts. The techniques for seeding and chopping or dicing can be used for both fresh and canned tomatoes. Whole or sliced tomatoes can be roasted to intensify their flavor and change their texture.

SPECIFIC CUTS FOR PEELED TOMATOES

To prepare tomatoes so that they can be cut into precise julienne, dice, lozenge, or similar cuts, the tomato flesh must be trimmed so that it has an even thickness. Halve or quarter the peeled tomato, cutting from stem to blossom end. Using the tip of a knife, cut away any seeds and membranes from the thick outer flesh of the tomato. This technique is sometimes referred to as filleting and is also used for peppers and chiles. Cut the flesh into julienne or other shapes, as desired.

Tomatoes prepared in this way may be used as garnish for hot items such as soups or sauces. They may also be used in cold preparations such as salads or in the production of hors d'oeuvres, where they can be used as a base or finely chopped for a colorful and flavorful garnish. Peeled and cut tomatoes will have a tendency to weep, so when using for cold preparations be sure to cut and assemble as close to service as possible.

WORKING WITH DRIED VEGETABLES AND FRUITS

Dried vegetables and fruits have always been used in many cuisines. Drying makes foods suitable for long-term storage and concentrates their flavors. Even today, some vegetables and fruits are too perishable to transport great distances or they have a very short season. The rest of the year, they can be found only in a preserved form. The flavor of dried chiles, mushrooms, tomatoes, and fruits such as apples, cherries, and raisins are special even though those same ingredients may be purchased fresh throughout the year.

To get the most from these ingredients, recipes may often call for them to be rehydrated or "plumped" by letting them soak in a liquid. To rehydrate dried vegetables and fruits, check first for insect infestation and remove any obvious debris or seriously blemished or moldy specimens.

Place the vegetable or fruit in a bowl or other container and add enough boiling or very hot liquid (water, wine, fruit juice, or broth) to cover. Let the vegetable or fruit steep in the hot liquid for several minutes until soft and plumped. Pour off the liquid, reserving it if desired for another use. If necessary, strain it through a coffee filter or cheesecloth to remove any debris. Other dried fruits and vegetables may be toasted or charred in a flame or on a griddle or heated pan to soften them. Some may be toasted and then rehydrated.

Toast dried chiles in the same manner as dried spices, nuts, and seeds, by tossing them in a dry skillet over moderate heat. Or pass them repeatedly through a flame until toasted and softened. Scrape the pulp and seeds from the skin, or use the whole chile, according to the recipe. Break or cut open the chile and shake out the seeds. After toasting, rehydrate the chile in a hot liquid.

RECIPES

VOL AU VENT WITH MUSHROOM RAGOUT

YIELD: 10 PORTIONS

Vol au Vents

Puff pastry sheets, 9 by 13 in/23 by 33 cm	2	2
Egg wash	as needed	as needed

Mushroom Ragout

Minced shallot	1 Tbsp	15 mL
Butter	as needed	as needed
Minced garlic	2 Tbsp	10 mL
Sliced cremini mushrooms	8 oz	227 g
Sliced oyster mushrooms	8 oz	227 g
Sliced shiitake mushrooms	8 oz	227 g
Chopped fines herbes	2 Tbsp	30 mL
Madeira	6 Tbsp	90 mL
Heavy cream	1/2 cup	120 mL
Salt	as needed	as needed
Freshly ground black pepper	as needed	as needed

METHOD

1. Preheat the oven to 350°F/177°C.
2. For the vol au vents: Cut 20 rounds from the puff pastry using a medium circular biscuit cutter. Using a biscuit cutter that is 1/4 in/6 mm smaller than the original cutter, cut out an inner circle from 10 of rounds and reserve the rings of dough. Be sure to cut straight down so that the vol au vents don't bake up lopsided.
3. Brush the rounds of dough lightly with egg wash. Place the round rings on top of the dough rounds, making sure to line up the edges of the circles. Lightly brush more egg wash on top of the dough rings.
4. Bake the vol au vents until golden brown, about 20 minutes. Remove the vol au vents from the oven and cool to room temperature. If necessary, remove some of the puff from the center of the vol au vent to make space for the mushroom ragout.

(Continues)

5. For the mushroom ragout: Sweat the shallots in the butter over medium-high heat, about 2 minutes. Add the garlic and sweat until light golden brown, stirring constantly, about 1 minute.
6. Add the mushrooms to the pan and do not touch. Let the mushrooms brown in the pan before stirring and then sauté until browned uniformly. Stir every 1 to 2 minutes.
7. When all of the mushrooms have completely browned, deglaze the pan with Madeira and allow the Madeira to reduce slightly. Add the cream and season with salt and pepper.
8. Remove the mixture from the heat. Fill the vol au vents with the mushrooms and serve hot.

SICILIAN-STYLE BABY ARUGULA

YIELD: 10 PORTIONS

Olive oil	3 Tbsp	45 mL
Small-dice pancetta	4 oz	113 g
Anchovy fillets, mashed to a paste	4	4
Minced onions	8 oz	227 g
Minced garlic	1/4 cup	60 mL
Golden raisins	6 oz	170 g
Slivered almonds	6 oz	170 g
Baby arugula, cleaned	4 lb	1.81 kg
Salt	as needed	as needed
Freshly ground black pepper	as needed	as needed

METHOD

1. Heat olive oil in a large sauté pan over medium heat. Add the pancetta and sauté until the fat renders and the pancetta is translucent, 2 to 3 minutes. Raise the heat to high and add the anchovy, onion, and garlic. Sauté until the garlic is aromatic and the anchovy has dissolved into the oil, about 1 minute more. Add the raisins and almonds and sauté until the almonds are toasted and the raisins are puffy, 2 to 3 minutes. Add the arugula and sauté until deep green, tender, and softened, 3 to 4 minutes more.
2. Drain the mixture, if necessary, and season generously with salt and pepper. Serve immediately.

SAFFRON CAULIFLOWER WITH ONIONS

YIELD: 10 PORTIONS

Olive oil	3 Tbsp	45 mL
Pearl onions, peeled	1 lb 8 oz	680 g
Minced garlic	3/4 oz	21 g
Dry white wine	3/4 cup	180 mL
Lemon juice	6 Tbsp	90 mL
Cauliflower florets	1 lb 8 oz	680 g
Water	2 1/4 cups	540 mL
Saffron threads	1 1/2 tsp	7.5 mL
Coriander seeds	1 1/2 tsp	7.5 mL
Bay leaves	3	3
Kosher salt	1 1/2 tsp	7.5 mL

METHOD

1. Heat the oil in a medium sauté pan over medium heat. Add the onions and garlic and cook, stirring occasionally, over medium heat until a deep golden color appears on the onions, about 12 minutes.
2. Deglaze the pan with the wine and lemon juice.
3. Add the cauliflower, water, saffron, coriander, bay leaves, and salt. Cook until the cauliflower is tender, about 15 minutes. Serve immediately.

ASPARAGUS WITH HOLLANDAISE

YIELD: 10 PORTIONS

Hollandaise

Minced shallots	1/2 oz	14 g
Cracked black pepper	3/4 tsp	3.75 mL
White wine	3 Tbsp	45 mL
Cider vinegar	6 Tbsp	90 mL
Cold water	3/4 cup	180 mL
Large egg yolks	6	6
Clarified butter, at 130°F/54°C	1 lb	454 g
Lemon juice	2 1/4 tsp	11.25 mL
Kosher salt	1 tsp	5 mL
White pepper	1/4 tsp	1.25 mL
Tabasco sauce	1/4 tsp	1.25 mL

Asparagus

Water	2 gal	7.68 L
Kosher salt	2 oz	57 g
Asparagus, ends trimmed and peeled if necessary	2 lb 8 oz	1.13 kg

METHOD

1. For the hollandaise: Place the shallots, cracked black pepper, white wine, and cider vinegar in a small sauce pan over medium heat. Allow to simmer until almost dry, about 5 minutes. It should begin to get glossy.

2. Pour the cold water into the pan immediately to stop the reduction. Strain the cool mixture into the bowl with the egg yolks and whisk together.

3. Place the bowl over a sauce pan of simmering water. The water should never touch the bottom of the bowl. Whisk the mixture until it is light and fluffy and when the whisk is removed from mixture, ribbons fall off the whisk and back to the bowl. Whisk quickly during the cooking process. Remove from the heat about once a minute and continue whisking for about 10 seconds to allow the temperature to stabilize, then place back on

(Continues)

pot and continue whisking. The ribbons should remain visible for a couple seconds before fading back. Remove from the heat and continue whisking to prevent the mixture from overcooking from carryover heat.

4. Begin slowly drizzling the clarified butter into the yolk mixture while whisking constantly. The stream should be about the thickness of a pencil. If the butter is not incorporating completely, stop and whisk until it has disappeared and then resume.

5. Once butter is completely incorporated, whisk for an additional 10 seconds and adjust seasoning.

6. Pass through a strainer to remove clumps and serve immediately or place in a metal container in a 150°F/66°C water bath.

7. For the asparagus: Bring the water and salt to a boil in a stockpot over high heat.

8. Trim the asparagus to where the stalk breaks if you hold the head and base and bend slightly.

9. Add asparagus to the water and boil until cooked through, about 5 minutes.

10. Remove from the water and serve with sauce immediately.

JALAPEÑO COLESLAW

Crème fraîche	6 oz	170 g
Mayonnaise	6 oz	170 g
Cider vinegar	1/4 cup	60 mL
Dry mustard	1 Tbsp	15 mL
Granulated sugar	1 1/2 oz	43 g
Celery seed	1 1/2 tsp	7.5 mL
Tabasco sauce	1 1/2 tsp	7.5 mL
Salt	as needed	as needed
Freshly ground black pepper	as needed	as needed
Green cabbage, cored, sliced 1/16 inch/1.50 mm thick	1 lb 8 oz	680 g
Small-dice pineapple	1 1/2 cups	360 mL
Grated carrots	6 oz	170 g
Minced red onion	1/4 cup	60 mL
Minced jalapeños	1/4 cup	60 mL

METHOD

1. Mix the crème fraîche, mayonnaise, vinegar, mustard, sugar, celery seed, and Tabasco together in a large mixing bowl until smooth. Season the mixture with salt and pepper.
2. Add the cabbage, pineapple, carrots, onion, and jalapeños, and toss until evenly coated.
3. Refrigerate and serve cold.

ONION FOCCACIA

Biga

Bread flour	6 1/2 oz	184 g
Water	3 1/2 oz	100 g
Instant yeast	pinch	pinch

Dough

Bread flour	1 lb 4 oz	567 g
Instant yeast	3/4 oz	21 g
Salt	1/2 oz	14 g
Water	15 1/4 oz	432 g
Olive oil, plus as needed	1 1/2 oz	43 g
Malt syrup	1/4 oz	7 g
Yellow onions, sliced thin	2	2
Grated Parmesan	6 oz	170 g
Thyme leaves, finely chopped	1 Tbsp	15 mL
Kosher salt	4 tsp	20 mL

METHOD

1. For the biga: Mix the flour, water, and yeast in the bowl of an electric mixer fitted with a dough hook on medium speed mix until completely combined and homogenous. Store at 75°F/24°C for 18 hours.
2. For the dough: Mix the flour, yeast, and salt with the biga on low speed. Slowly add the water, olive oil, and malt syrup. Once incorporated, mix on low speed for 4 minutes and then on medium low speed for 2 more minutes.
3. Turn out the dough into an oiled bowl, cover with plastic wrap, and allow to rise for 45 minutes.
4. Turn out the dough onto a floured work surface and fold the dough together to punch it down. Place the dough back into the bowl and allow to rest, covered, for 10 minutes.
5. Divide the dough into 1 lb/454 g loaves and coat the bottoms with semolina flour.
6. Shape into balls and allow to rest for 10 more minutes.
7. Shape the balls into rectangles 12 by 6 in/30 by 15 cm using your fingertips, then stipple the dough with olive oil.
8. Allow the dough to rest for a final 30 minutes.
9. Brush the dough with more olive oil and evenly sprinkle the onions, Parmesan, and salt over the dough. Bake at 465°F/241°C until golden brown and baked through, about 18 minutes.

GLAZED CARROTS AND PARSNIPS WITH THYME

YIELD: 10 PORTIONS

Butter	3 oz	85 g
Carrots, peeled and cut into obliques	1 lb 8 oz	680 g
Parsnips, peeled and cut into obliques	1 lb 8 oz	680 g
Sugar	1 1/2 oz	43 g
Chicken stock	1 1/2 cups	360 mL
Salt	1 tsp	5 mL
Freshly ground white pepper	1/4 tsp	1.25 mL
Chopped thyme	1 Tbsp	15 mL

METHOD

1. Melt the butter in a large sauté pan and add the carrots. Cover and sweat over medium-low heat for 3 to 4 minutes and the parsnips. Cover and sweat over medium-low heat for 2 to 3 minutes.
2. Add the sugar and stock. Bring to a simmer over medium heat. Cover and cook over low heat until almost tender, about 5 minutes
3. Remove the lid and add salt, pepper, and thyme.
4. Continue to simmer until liquid reduced to a glaze and the vegetables are tender, 2 to 3 minutes.
5. Adjust seasoning and serve.

BRAISED RED CABBAGE

YIELD: 10 PORTIONS

Cinnamon stick	1	1
Juniper berries	8	8
Bay leaf	2	2
Minced bacon	8 oz	227 g
Granny Smith apples (about 7 ounces), thinly sliced	2	2
Onion, sliced 1/8-inch thick	8 oz	227 g
Shredded red cabbage	2 lb	907 g
Red wine	1 cup	240 mL
Red wine vinegar	1 cup	240 mL
Sugar	4 oz	113 g
Red currant jelly	3 oz	85 g
Salt	1 tsp	5 mL
Freshly ground black pepper	1/2 Tbsp	2.5 mL

METHOD

1. Tie the cinnamon, juniper berries, and bay leaves into a sachet.
2. Render the bacon in a sauce pot over medium-low heat, stirring occasionally, until just crisped, about 10 minutes.
3. Add the apple slices, cabbage, and onion to the rendered fat and sweat over medium heat until softened, about 5 minutes.
4. Add the remaining ingredients and sachet. Bring the mixture to a simmer, cover, and place in a 350°F/177° oven.
5. Cook for 45 minutes, stirring every 10 minutes, or until the cabbage is tender.
6. Adjust seasoning and serve hot.

BAKED TOMATOES WITH GOAT CHEESE

YIELD: 10 PORTIONS

Ingredient	US	Metric
Pine nuts	1/4 cup	60 mL
Panko	1/4 cup	60 mL
Plum tomatoes	10	10
Crumbled goat cheese	7 oz	198 g
Diced roasted red peppers	3 oz	85 g
Grilled zucchini, small dice	3 oz	85 g
Cranberries, plumped and chopped	2 Tbsp	30 mL
Basil, chopped	2 Tbsp	30 mL
Chervil, chopped	2 Tbsp	30 mL
Lemon zest	1/2 tsp	2.5 mL
Kosher salt	2 tsp	10 mL
Freshly ground black pepper	1/2 tsp	2.5 mL

METHOD

1. Preheat oven to 350°F/177°C.
2. Lightly toast the pine nuts in the oven. Allow to cool slightly then crush the nuts and combine with Panko. Reserve.
3. Remove the cores from the tomatoes and cut in half lengthwise. Scoop out the seeds and reserve the tomato halves.
4. Combine the goat cheese, red peppers, zucchini, cranberries, basil, chervil, lemon zest, salt, and pepper in a large bowl.
5. Divide the filling among the tomatoes and pack the filling tightly. Press the tomatoes, filling side down, into the pine nut/Panko mixture.
6. Bake until the tomatoes are hot and the topping has slightly browned, 8 to 10 minutes.

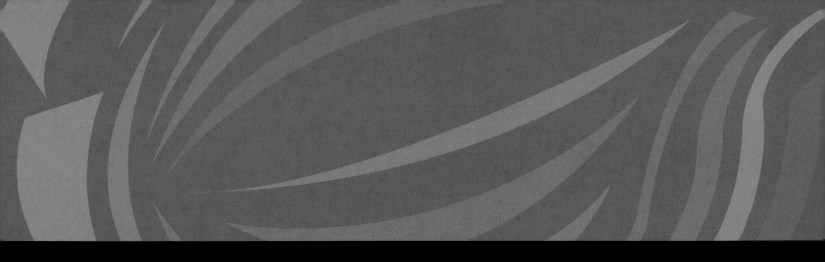

FRESH HARISSA

YIELD: 2 CUPS

Fresno peppers	1 lb	454 g
Habañero peppers, or as needed	1/2	1/2
Sundried tomatoes in oil	4 oz	113 g
Garlic cloves, crushed with salt	3	3
Ground turmeric	1 Tbsp	15 mL
Ground coriander	1/2 tsp	2.5 mL
Ground cumin	1/2 tsp	2.5 mL
Ground caraway	1/2 tsp	2.5 mL
Kosher salt	1/2 tsp	2.5 mL
Lemon juice, or as needed	1/2 tsp	2.5 mL
Olive oil, or as needed	1/4 cup	60 mL
Water, or as needed	1/4 cup	60 mL

METHOD

1. Remove the seeds and stems from the fresh chiles.
2. Combine all ingredients in a blender and blend until smooth.
3. Adjust the consistency with lemon juice, olive oil, and water, if necessary.

ONION SOUP GRATINÉE

YIELD: 10 PORTIONS

Soup

Bay leaf	1/2	1/2
Thyme sprig	1/2	1/2
Black peppercorns	8	8
Thinly sliced onions	2 lb 8 oz	1.13 kg
Clarified butter	2 Tbsp	30 mL
Calvados	1/4 cup	60 mL
White beef stock	9 cups	2.16 L
Kosher salt	2 Tbsp	30 mL
Freshly ground black pepper	1/2 tsp	2.5 mL

Croutons

Baguette	1/2	1/2
Grated Gruyère	6 oz	170 g
Salt	1/2 tsp	2.50 mL
Freshly ground black pepper	1/8 tsp	0.6 mL

METHOD

1. For the soup: Tie the bay leaf, thyme, and peppercorns into a sachet.
2. In a large sauce pot or rondeau, caramelize the onions in the butter over medium-high heat, stirring occasionally, until browned, 40 to 45 minutes. Do not add any salt at this time to prevent the extraction of moisture and to allow for optimum caramelization.
3. Deglaze the pan with the Calvados and reduce over moderately high heat until it reaches a syrupy consistency.
4. Add the stock and the sachet and simmer until the onions are tender and the soup is properly flavored, about 30 to 35 minutes. The soup is ready to finish now, or it may be rapidly cooled and refrigerated for later service.
5. To finish the soup for service, return it to a boil and season with salt and pepper.
6. Top each crouton generously with grated Gruyère, season with salt and pepper, and brown under a salamander or broiler until lightly browned, 3 to 5 minutes.
7. Serve the soup in heated bowls or cups garnished with a crouton.

ITALIAN SAUSAGE WITH ONION AND PEPPER SAUTÉ ON ITALIAN ROLL

YIELD: 10 PORTIONS

Sun-dried Tomato Pesto

Chopped basil	3 Tbsp	45 mL
Sun-dried tomatoes in oil	3 oz	85 g
Garlic cloves, peeled and crushed	3	3
Grated Parmesan	1 oz	28 g
Pine nuts, toasted	1 oz	28 g
Olive oil	3/4 cup	180 mL
Kosher salt	1 tsp	5 mL
Freshly ground black pepper	1/2 tsp	2.5 mL

Sandwich

Olive oil	2/3 cup	160 mL
Onions, thinly sliced	1 lb 8 oz	680 g
Garlic cloves, minced	8	8
Dried oregano	1 tsp	5 mL
Dried basil	1 tsp	5 mL
Dried thyme	1 tsp	5 mL
Yellow mustard seed	2 Tbsp	30 mL
Red peppers, sliced 1/4 in/6 mm thick	2	2
Green peppers, sliced 1/4 in/6 mm thick	2	2
Jalapeños, minced	2	2
Sweet Italian sausage links	10	10
Dijon mustard	3 Tbsp	45 mL
Italian rolls, split	10	10
Aged provolone, thinly sliced	2 lb	907 g
Kosher salt	4 tsp	20 mL
Freshly ground black pepper	1/2 tsp	2.5 mL

(Continues)

METHOD

1. For the pesto: Combine the basil, tomatoes, garlic, Parmesan, and pine nuts in a food processor and pulse the ingredients until they are evenly chopped.
2. With processor running, add the olive oil and purée into an even-textured paste that will hold its shape. Adjust seasoning with salt and pepper.
3. For the sandwich: Preheat the oven to 400°F/204°C and turn on the grill.
4. Heat the olive oil in a large sauté pan over medium heat. Sweat the onions, garlic, dried herbs, and mustard seed in the olive oil, stirring often, until the onions are translucent, about 5 minutes. There should be no color on the onions and take care not to burn the spices.
5. Add all of the peppers and cook over low heat until the peppers are tender but not soft, 5 to 7 minutes. Remove the pan from the heat and reserve until needed.
6. Place the sausages on the grill. Cook, rotating often until they reach an internal temperature of 165°F/74°C, 7 to 10 minutes.
7. In the meantime, spread a thin layer of pesto and Dijon mustard on each side of each roll. Divide the cheese among the rolls and place them in the oven. Bake until the cheese is melted and bubbly. Remove from the oven.
8. Divide the pepper-onion mixture evenly among the bottom halves of the rolls. Place a sausage on top and serve hot.

ZUCCHINI PANCAKES WITH TZATZIKI SAUCE

YIELD: 8 PORTIONS

Tzatziki Sauce

Plain yogurt	1/2 cup	120 mL
Sour cream	1/2 cup	120 mL
Grated cucumber, squeezed dry	1/2 cup	120 mL
Minced garlic	1 tsp	5 mL
Extra-virgin olive oil	1 Tbsp	15 mL
Chopped mint *or* dill	1 Tbsp	15 mL
Lemon juice	1/2 tsp	2.5 mL
Lemon zest	1 tsp	5 mL
Salt	as needed	as needed
Fresh ground black pepper	as needed	as needed

Zucchini Pancakes

Coarsely grated zucchini	12 oz	340 g
Salt	as needed	as needed
Chopped scallions	1 cup	240 mL
Large eggs, lightly beaten	4	4
All-purpose flour	3 oz	85 g
Chopped dill	1/2 oz	14 g
Chopped flat leaf parsley	1/2 oz	14 g
Chopped tarragon	1 Tbsp	15 mL
Freshly ground black pepper	as needed	as needed
Crumbled feta cheese	3 oz	85 g
Chopped toasted pine nuts	2 1/2 oz	71 g
Olive oil for pan frying, or as needed	2 cups	480 mL

(Continues)

METHOD

1. For the tzatziki sauce: Combine the yogurt, sour cream, cucumber, and garlic in a food processor and purée until smooth. Transfer to a bowl and fold in the olive oil, mint *or* dill, lemon juice, and zest. Stir until combined and season to taste with salt and pepper. Keep refrigerated until ready to serve.

2. Place the grated zucchini in colander. Sprinkle with salt and let stand for 30 minutes. Squeeze the zucchini to remove as much liquid as possible. Dry the zucchini by pressing it between several layers of paper towels.

3. In a large bowl, combine the zucchini, scallions, eggs, flour, dill, parsley, tarragon, salt, and pepper until evenly blended. Fold in the feta cheese. (The pancake mixture can be prepared to this point up to 3 hours ahead. Cover tightly and refrigerate. Stir to blend before continuing.) Fold the pine nuts into the zucchini mixture.

4. Preheat the oven to 300°F/149°C to keep the pancakes warm as you work. Place a baking sheet in the oven.

5. Add enough oil to a large skillet to come to a depth of about 1/8 in/3 mm, and heat the oil over medium-high heat until the surface of the oil shimmers. Working in batches, drop heaping tablespoons of the zucchini mixture into the hot oil, leaving enough room for the pancakes to spread as they cook. Fry until the pancakes are golden brown and cooked through, about 3 minutes per side. Transfer each batch of pancakes to the baking sheet in the oven to keep warm. Serve immediately with the tzatziki sauce.

PESTO

YIELD: 2 CUPS

Basil leaves, lightly packed	2 cups	480 mL
Grated Parmesan	4 oz	113 g
Pine nuts, toasted	4 oz	113 g
Minced garlic cloves	2 Tbsp	30 mL
Extra-virgin olive oil	1 cup	240 mL
Salt	as needed	as needed
Freshly ground black pepper	as needed	as needed

METHOD

1. Place the basil in a food processor and pulse until the basil is evenly chopped. Add the parmesan, pine nuts, and garlic and purée into a paste, scraping down the sides of the food processor bowl as you go.
2. While the food processor is running, gradually add the oil until a thick, heavy paste forms. It should have a distinctly course texture, but should not appear oily. Season the mixture with salt and pepper.
3. The pesto is ready to use now. Store it covered in the refrigerator for up to 2 weeks or in the freezer for up to 2 months.

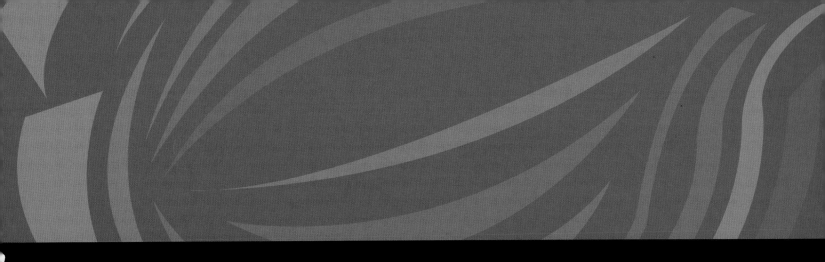

PORT POACHED PEARS WITH ROQUEFORT AND WALNUTS

YIELD: 10 PORTIONS

Port Poaching Liquid

Port	1 quart	960 mL
Sugar	1 lb 4 oz	567 g
Cinnamon stick	1/2	1/2
Vanilla bean, split	1	1
Orange zest	3/4 oz	21 g

Poached Pears

Forelle pears	10	10
Port Poaching Liquid, or as needed	1 quart	960 mL
Roquefort cheese	10 oz	284 g
Lightly toasted, chopped walnuts	5 oz	142 g
Mandarin oranges or clementines	6	6
Cornstarch	1/2 oz	14 g
Water	1/4 cup	60 mL
Butter	1 Tbsp	15 mL

METHOD

1. For the poaching liquid: Combine all ingredients and bring to a simmer, stirring to dissolve the sugar.
2. For the pears: Peel the pears, leaving the stems on. Using a melon baller, core the pears from the bottom, making an opening 1/2 in/1 cm in diameter. Using a clean scouring pad, sand the outside of the pears to smooth the sides and remove any lines or ridges from peeling.
3. Put the pears in a pot and cover with the poaching liquid. Poach until tender, about 30 to 40 minutes. Let cool to room temperature and then refrigerate the pears in the liquid overnight.
4. Gently mix together the Roquefort and walnuts.
5. Remove the pears from the liquid and reserve 2 cups/480 mL of the poaching liquid. Cut the pears in half, keeping the half with the stem with its sister half. Stuff cavity with 3/4 oz/21 g of the filling.

(Continues)

6. Cut the oranges into suprême segments and reserve.
7. Strain the reserved poaching liquid and reduce it by one third to about 10-1/2 fl oz. Make a cornstarch slurry from the cornstarch and water and add it to the simmering liquid. Stir to combine and return to a boil. When the liquid is thick enough to coat the back of a spoon, whisk in the butter and hold warm.
8. Place the stuffed pears in a 375°F/191°C oven on a parchment-lined sheet tray until the Roquefort softens but does not brown. Remove the pears from the oven and allow to cool for 10 minutes.
9. Serve 2 pear halves in a bowl with 2 Tbsp/30 mL of the sauce and orange suprêmes.

RED SNAPPER WITH GRAPEFRUIT SALSA

YIELD: 10 PORTIONS

Grapefruit Salsa

Chopped cilantro	2 Tbsp	30 mL
Minced red onion	1/3 cup	80 mL
Minced Scotch bonnet peppers	2 tsp	10 mL
Chopped parsley	1 1/2 tsp	7.5 mL
Kosher salt	1/2 tsp	2.5 mL
Freshly ground black pepper	1/8 tsp	6 mL
Ruby red grapefruit, cut into suprêmes	4	4
Oranges, cut into suprêmes	2	2

Snapper

Red snapper fillets	10	10
Kosher salt	1 Tbsp	15 mL
Freshly ground black pepper	1 tsp	5 mL
Olive oil	1/4 cup	60 mL

METHOD

1. For the salsa: Combine the cilantro, onion, peppers, parsley, salt, and pepper.
2. When ready to serve, carefully add the grapefruit and oranges as to not break the suprêmes.
3. For the snapper: Season the fillets with salt and black pepper.
4. Heat the olive oil over medium-high heat in a large sauté pan. Sauté the fillets, in batches if necessary, until browned on the first side, 2 to 3 minutes. Flip the fillets and sauté until cooked through, 2 to 3 minutes. Serve with the salsa.

Chef's Note: The fish can also be grilled but be sure to brush the grill with oil to prevent sticking. Place the fillets on the grill presentation side down.

SUMMER PUDDING

YIELD: 10 PORTIONS

Brioche Dough

Bread flour	1 lb	454 g
Instant yeast	1 Tbsp	15 mL
Butter, soft, divided	15.1/2 oz	439 g
Eggs	3	3
Whole milk	6 Tbsp	90 mL
Sugar	3 1/2 Tbsp	52.5 mL
Salt	1 Tbsp	15 mL
Eggs, mixed with 1 Tbsp/15 mL milk	2	2

Filling

Strawberries	12 oz	340 g
Berry Schnapps	3/4 cup	180 mL
Lemon juice	2 Tbsp	30 mL
Sugar	8 oz	227 g
Raspberries, halved	11 oz	312 g
Blueberries	11 oz	312 g
Blackberries, quartered	11 oz	312 g

METHOD

1. For the brioche dough: Combine the flour and yeast. Add 4 oz/113 g butter, eggs, milk, sugar, and salt and mix on low speed for 4 minutes.

2. Gradually add 9 1/2 oz/269 g butter with the mixer running on medium speed, scraping down the sides of the bowl as necessary. After the butter has been fully incorporated (you will still see clumps but it is integrated with the dough), mix on medium speed for 15 minutes, or until the dough pulls away from the bowl. A gluten window should form and dough will wrap around kneading arm.

3. Place the dough on a sheet pan that has been lined with parchment paper and greased. Cover tightly with plastic wrap and refrigerate overnight.

4. Brush two cylindrical molds 6 3/4 in/16.8 cm diameter by 8 in/20 cm tall with the remaining 2 oz/57 g of butter.

5. Divide the dough into two 1 lb/454 g pieces. Round each into a ball and place one in each of the prepared molds.

6. Allow the dough to proof for 1 hour, until it springs back lightly to the touch; there should be an indentation left in the dough, but it should not collapse. Brush lightly with egg wash.

7. Bake in a 325°F/163°C deck oven until the brioche is dark golden brown on top and golden brown in the center cracks, about 45 minutes. Toward the end, if brioche is a deep brown it may be necessary to remove the brioche from the molds and dry it out slightly in the oven. Cool to room temperature.

8. Unmold the brioche if necessary, and slice crosswise into rounds 3/8 in/9 mm. Using a 2-1/2 in/6.25 cm cutter, cut 30 disks out of the brioche slices.

9. For the filling: Cut the strawberries into medium dice; the pieces should be about the same size.

10. Combine schnapps, lemon juice, and sugar in a large pot and bring to a boil. Reduce heat to a low simmer, add the strawberries, and poach until they just release their juices. Add the remaining fruit and poach until tender. Remove from the heat.

11. Place 1 disk on the bottom of each of ten 4 fl oz/120 mL soufflé cups. Place 1 oz/28 g fruit on each disk and top with a disk. Repeat until all disks are used.

12. Cover the puddings with parchment and place a sheet tray on top. Weight down. Refrigerate overnight.

13. Carefully unmold and serve.

SUMMER MELON SALAD WITH PROSCIUTTO

YIELD: 10 PORTIONS

Cantaloupe, scooped into balls or cut into slices	1 lb	454 g
Honeydew, scooped into balls or cut into slices	1 lb	454 g
Thinly sliced prosciutto	10 oz	284 g
Aged balsamic vinegar	2 Tbsp	30 mL
Cracked black peppercorns	as needed	as needed
Lemon juice	2 Tbsp	30 mL
Olive oil	1/4 cup	60 mL
Mesclun mix	5 cups	1.2 L

METHOD

1. Arrange the melons and prosciutto on chilled plates.
2. Drizzle the melon and prosciutto with the vinegar and garnish with the cracked pepper.
3. Whisk together the lemon juice and olive oil. Toss together with the mesclun greens. Divide the salad among the plates and serve immediately.

AVOCADO AND BLACK BEAN CROSTINI

YIELD: 10 PORTIONS

Baguette, sliced 1/4 inch thick (about 20 slices)	1/2	1/2
Small-dice Vidalia onions	3 oz	85 g
Small-dice plum tomatoes	3 oz	85 g
Cooked black beans	3/4 cup	180 mL
Chopped cilantro	2 Tbsp	30 mL
White wine vinegar	1 tsp	5 mL
Salt	as needed	as needed
Freshly ground black pepper	as needed	as needed
Avocadoes, cut into small dice	2	2
Lime juice	2 Tbsp	30 mL
Garlic clove, minced	1	1
Dark chili powder	1/4 tsp	1.25 mL
Ground cumin	1/8 tsp	0.6 mL
Crumbled Cotija cheese	4 oz	113 g

METHOD

1. Preheat the oven to 400°F/204°C.
2. Toast the baguette slices in the oven until golden brown, about 5 to 7 minutes.
3. Cook the onions, tomatoes, black beans, and vinegar over medium heat until just softened, about 5 minutes. Season with salt and pepper. Remove the pan from the heat and allow to cool to room temperature.
4. Combine the avocado with lime juice, garlic, chili powder, and cumin. Season with salt and pepper.
5. To assemble, on each crostini place a heaping tablespoon of the black bean mixture, followed by another heaping tablespoon of the avocado mixture. When all are done, garnish with the crumbled Cotija cheese.

SPICY GARLIC STIR-FRIED GREEN BEANS

YIELD: 10 PORTIONS

Green beans	2 lb	907 g
Tamari	2 Tbsp	30 mL
Hoisin	2 Tbsp	30 mL
Rice wine vinegar	1/4 cup	60 mL
Sambal oelek, or as needed	2 tsp	10 mL
Peanut oil	4 tsp	20 mL
Garlic cloves, thinly sliced	12	12
Dark sesame oil	2 tsp	10 mL

METHOD

1. Trim the stem ends from the beans, rinse well with cold running water, and drain. Cut the beans into 2 in/5 cm pieces. Place in a steamer basket in a pan with an inch of water. Cover and steam until tender, about 5 minutes. Remove and reserve briefly, if necessary.
2. While the beans are cooking, combine the tamari, hoisin, vinegar, and sambal in a small bowl and reserve.
3. Heat a wok over high heat. Add the peanut oil and heat until it shimmers. Add the garlic and cook until golden, stirring continuously, 5 to 10 seconds. Add the green beans and toss with the garlic. Cook until lightly browned, about 2 minutes, tossing constantly. Add the sauce and toss until covered. Place the green beans on a plate and drizzle with sesame oil.

SAUTÉED BRUSSELS SPROUTS WITH PANCETTA

YIELD: 10 PORTIONS

Brussels sprouts	2 quarts	1.92 L
Olive oil	3 Tbsp	45 mL
Small-dice pancetta	3 1/4 oz	92 g
Chopped onion	3/4 cup	180 mL
Butter	4 tsp	20 mL
Water	2 1/2 Tbsp	37.5 mL
Salt	1 1/2 tsp	7.5 mL
Freshly ground black pepper	3/4 tsp	3.75 mL

METHOD

1. Slice each Brussels sprout in half and remove the core. Gently pull the layers of leaves apart.
2. Heat a large sauté pan and add the olive oil and pancetta. Render the fat from the pancetta, until it is lightly crispy. Remove the pancetta and reserve.
3. Add the onions and cook until translucent, about 5 minutes.
4. Add the butter and swirl to melt. Add the sprouts and water.
5. Cook over medium heat, tossing to coat, until leaves are tender and bright green, about 6 to 8 minutes. Adjust seasoning, fold in remaining pancetta, and serve immediately.

VARIATION

Sautéed Brussels Sprouts with Beurre Noisette: Omit the pancetta, decrease the amount of olive oil to 2 Tbsp/30 mL, and increase the amount of butter to 2 oz/57 g. Cook the entire amount of butter separately. As the sprouts are finishing cooking, heat a small sauté pan over medium heat. Just before the sprouts are done, add the whole butter to the pan; if it sizzles, remove the pan from the heat and swirl until the sizzling stops. Place the pan back on the burner and gently cook the butter until it has a nutty smell and is a medium dark brown color. Toss the cooked Brussels sprout with the brown butter and serve.

GLOSSARY

Al Dente—Literally, "to the tooth"; refers to an item, such as pasta or vegetables, cooked until it is tender but still firm, not soft.

Allium Genus—This is the genus that contains onions and garlic. It is also related to the lily family.

Ancho—A dried poblano pepper.

Anthocyanins—The color compounds that look purple in produce. These compounds are believed to supply antioxidants that aid in cardiac and brain function as well as aid in cancer protection.

Antioxidants—Substances that may protect your cells against the effects of free radicals.

Artichoke Heart—The meaty lower part of the base of an artichoke.

Bell Peppers—Block-shaped, sometimes tapered peppers that are either green or red in color. The green pepper is tart, whereas the red pepper has a sweet flavor.

Berries—The name for any of a number of small edible fruits. Botanically a berry is a fruit that has seeds surrounded by pulp and comes from a single ovary. True berries in the food industry include lingonberry, huckleberry, and currants.

Beta-Carotene—A color pigment responsible for the orange color of the carrot for which it is named, and many other fruits and vegetables (for example, sweet potatoes and orange cantaloupe melon).

Betalain—A class of red and yellow indole-derived pigments that causes the red color in beets and in chard.

Bolting—The term that describes what happens if lettuce is not harvested in time and the stalk continues to grow through the head and that may flower.

Bouquet Garni—A classic method of flavoring stocks and sauces by bundling herbs together with twine or in a cheesecloth sack so they can be easily removed once the cooking process has ended. Typically this consists of parsley, bay leaf, and thyme.

Bract—The scale or petal of an artichoke plant.

Brassica—A genus of plants in the mustard family including cabbages, broccoli, and cauliflower.

Butterhead Lettuces—Consists of two main types, Boston and Bibb and are characterized by soft, tender, silky leaves and small stalks.

Caesar Salad—Comprises romaine lettuce and croutons dressed with parmesan cheese, lemon juice, olive oil, egg, anchovies, Worcestershire sauce, and black pepper originally prepared tableside.

Cajun Trinity—A term used in Cajun and Southern cooking to describe a group of aromatic seasoning vegetables such as onion, bell pepper, and celery. These three items are the base seasoning mixture for most recipes such as gumbos, jambalayas, étouffées, sauces, chilis, and stews.

Cap—The top round portion of a mushroom that contains most of the meat.

Capsaicin—The active component of chili peppers that can produce a strong burning sensation in the mouth.

Capsicum—A genus of plants from the nightshade family; this includes all peppers and chiles.

Cara Cara Orange—A sweet navel eating orange with reddish flesh that is less acidic than typical navel orange.

Caramelization—The process of browning sugar in the presence of heat. The temperature range in which sugar begins to caramelize is approximately 320° to 360°F/160° to 182°C.

Chipotle—A dried jalapeño pepper sold dried or canned packed in Adobo sauce that exhibits a smoky flavor with mild heat.

Clingstone—The pit or stone is more tightly adhered to the flesh of the fruit. (stone fruit)

Commercially Grown Mushroom—These are mushrooms that have been grown in captivity under the watchful eye of a gardener, as opposed to wild mushrooms.

Crudités—An appetizer consisting of a variety of raw vegetables, usually cut into strips or bite-size pieces, and served with a dip.

Deep-Fry—To cook food by immersion in hot fat; deep-fried foods are often coated with breadcrumbs or batter before being cooked.

Dry Onions—The round or flat bulbs of the Allium cepa category. These are the mature bulb of the onion with tight layer of flesh and a dry, papery skin that can be white, red, or yellow. This includes yellow or Spanish, white boiling, shallots, and red onions.

Fines Herbes—A mixture of several minced herbs used as seasoning in may classic dishes. The most classic combination of flavors would include tarragon, chervil, chives, and parsley.

Florets—Individual flower stems of the heads of vegetables such as broccoli and cauliflower.

Freestone—The seed or stone easily separates itself from the flesh. (stone fruit)

Gazpacho—A soup made with chopped tomatoes, onions, cucumbers, peppers, and herbs that is served cold.

Gill Veils—A veil is the thin covering underneath the mushroom cap over the gills, which are plate-like structures arranged on the underside of a mushroom's cap.

Gremolata—Classic spicy garnish consisting of parsley, garlic, lemon, and orange zest that is best known as an accompaniment to Veal Osso Buco.

Grill—A cooking technique in which foods are cooked by a radiant heat source placed below the food. Also, the piece of equipment on which grilling is done. Grills may be fueled by gas, electricity, charcoal, or wood.

Head Forming—This type will either form into a dense, firm, rounded bolting head or a dense, squat barrel shape. These include Green Cabbage, Red Cabbage, Savoy Cabbage, and Napa.

Hearts of Palm—The edible inside portion of the stem of the cabbage palm tree. They are slender, ivory-colored, and have a delicate flavor reminiscent of artichoke.

Heirloom Tomato—Open-pollinated tomato varieties that were introduced before 1940, or tomato varieties more than 50 years in circulation.

Herbs—The fragrant leafy parts of certain plants having non-woody stems and prized for the aroma and flavor they impart to the food we cook.

Hoppin' John—The Southern United States' version of the rice and beans dish traditional throughout the Caribbean. It consists of black-eyed peas and rice, with chopped onion and sliced bacon, seasoned with a bit of salt.

Hydroponics—A method of growing plants using mineral nutrient solutions, without soil.

Legumes—The seed of the vegetable is enclosed in a pod; some pods are tender and edible and others require the seed to be shelled from their tough inedible pod casing.

Lily Family—A category of vegetables that consists of leeks, asparagus, and garlic.

Micro Green—A tiny form of edible greens produced from the seeds of vegetables, herbs, or other plants. They range in size from 1 to 2 in/3 to 5 cm long, including the stem and leaves and the flavor is very concentrated.

Muskmelons—These can have netted veins covering their rind, such as cantaloupe or smooth waxy rinds like honeydew. They may or may not have a netted rind, may or may not be ribbed, and most are orange fleshed, but others are green to white.

New Potato—A freshly dug potato that hasn't been put into storage; these are characterized by a thin, more tender skin and finer texture to the flesh.

Non-head Forming—See stalk forming.

Persillade—A mix of finely minced parsley and garlic used to garnish broiled meat.

Pesto—A rich thick paste made from pine nuts, parmesan cheese, garlic, olive oil, and basil that is used as a flavoring paste and to dress pasta.

Rellenos—Literally meaning "stuffed pepper" in Spanish this is usually a poblano pepper stuffed with meat and cheese and deep-fried.

Rhizome—An underground stem that produces roots and supports above-ground stems.

Root—The actual root portion of a plant that stores the plant's nutrition in a swollen bulb.

Sachet d'Epices—A combination of parsley stems, thyme, bay leaf, peppercorns, and optional garlic wrapped in cheesecloth and used to flavor soups, sauce, and stocks.

Stalk Forming—Or non-head forming, stalk forming cabbaged grow on stalks of varying thickness. Some, but not all, of the stalks are edible.

Sweet Onions—This type is generally more oblate than round in shape. They have a higher sugar and water content than yellow onions and a lower ratio of those irritating sulfur compounds. They have a full sweetness and lighter flavor profile.

Thistle—A family of spiny plants that includes the artichoke.

Tropical Fruit—These have an inability to survive a frost, or any temperature below 50°F/10°C.

Tuber—The plant whose stem grows underground and swells as that plant's means to store nutrition.

Wild Mushrooms—These are mushrooms that have been harvested from the wild. They usually have stronger flavor characteristics than commercially grown mushrooms but are much more expensive.

READINGS AND RESOURCES

The Professional Chef 8th Edition
The Culinary Institute of America, Wiley
and Sons Inc, 2006

*The Compleat Squash: A Passionate Grower's
Guide to Pumpkins, Squashes, and Gourds*
Amy Goldman, Artisan, 2004

The Heirloom Tomato: From Garden to Table
Amy Goldman, Artisan, 2008

Melons for the Passionate Grower
Amy Goldman, Artisan, 2002

*Field Guide to Produce: How to Identify,
Select, and Prepare Virtually Every Fruit
and Vegetable at the Market*
Aliza Green, Quirk Books, 2004

The Great Chile Book
Mark Miller and John Harrisson, Ten Speed
Press, 1991

The Food Lover's Companion
Sharon Tyler Herbst, Barron's Educational
Series, 2007

*The Buying Guide for Fresh Fruits, Vegetables,
Herbs, and Nuts*
Hugh Oakley, Blue Goose, 1986

*The Encyclopedia of Herbs, Spices
and Flavorings*
Elisabeth Lambert Ortiz, Dorling
Kindersley Inc. 1992

*Uncommon Fruits and Vegetables: A Common
Sense Guide*
Elizabeth Schneider, Harper Collins, 1990

Vegetables, From Amaranth to Zucchini
Elizabeth Schneider, William Morrow
Cookbooks, 2001

Websites:

U.S. Department of Agriculture
http://www.usda.gov

Foodreference.com
http://www.foodreference.com

The Cook's Thesaurus
http://www.foodsubs.com

The Gourmet Sleuth
http://www.gourmetsleuth.com

Produce Pete
http://www.producepetes.com

The Produce Hunter
http://www.producehunter.com

Sensitech–Cold Chain Visibility
http://www.sensitech.com

**Glynwood Center–Guide to Serving Local
Food on Your Menu**
http://www.glynwood.org

The World's Healthiest Foods
http://www.whfoods.com

INDEX

PHOTO CREDITS

KEITH FERRIS

BEN FINK

We would like to extend a special thanks to Montgomery Place Orchard, Talliafero Farms, and Wigsten Farm for generously opening their doors and allowing us to photograph their gorgeous produce. These are just some of the beautiful farms that neighbor The Culinary Institute of America; be sure to visit the farms or greenmarkets in your neck of the woods.

CIA CONVERSION CHARTS

TEMPERATURE, WEIGHT AND VOLUME CONVERSIONS

TEMPERATURE CONVERSIONS

32°F = 0°C	205°F = 96°C	380°F = 193°C
35°F = 2°C	210°F = 99°C	385°F = 196°C
40°F = 4°C	**212°F = 100°C**	390°F = 199°C
45°F = 7°C	215°F = 102°C	395°F = 202°C
50°F = 10°C	220°F = 104°C	**400°F = 204°C**
55°F = 13°C	**225°F = 107°C**	405°F = 207°C
60°F = 16°C	230°F = 110°C	410°F = 210°C
65°F = 18°C	235°F = 113°C	415°F = 213°C
70°F = 21°C	240°F = 116°C	420°F = 216°C
75°F = 24°C	245°F = 118°C	**425°F = 218°C**
[room temp]	**250°F = 121°C**	430°F = 221°C
80°F = 27°C	255°F = 124°C	435°F = 224°C
85°F = 29°C	260°F = 127°C	440°F = 227°C
90°F = 32°C	265°F = 129°C	445°F = 229°C
95°F = 35°C	270°F = 132°C	**450°F = 232°C**
100°F = 38°C	**275°F = 135°C**	455°F = 235°C
105°F = 41°C	280°F = 138°C	460°F = 238°C
110°F = 43°C	285°F = 141°C	465°F = 241°C
115°F = 46°C	290°F = 144°C	470°F = 243°C
120°F = 49°C	295°F = 146°C	**475°F = 246°C**
125°F = 52°C	**300°F = 149°C**	480°F = 249°C
130°F = 54°C	305°F = 152°C	485°F = 252°C
135°F = 57°C	310°F = 154°C	490°F = 254°C
140°F = 60°C	315°F = 157°C	495°F = 257°C
145°F = 63°C	320°F = 160°C	**500°F = 260°C**
150°F = 66°C	**325°F = 163°C**	505°F = 263°C
155°F = 68°C	330°F = 166°C	510°F = 266°C
160°F = 71°C	335°F = 168°C	515°F = 268°C
165°F = 74°C	340°F = 171°C	520°F = 271°C
170°F = 77°C	345°F = 174°C	**525°F = 274°C**
175°F = 79°C	**350°F = 177°C**	530°F = 277°C
180°F = 82°C	355°F = 179°C	535°F = 279°C
185°F = 85°C	360°F = 182°C	540°F = 282°C
190°F = 88°C	365°F = 185°C	545°F = 285°C
195°F = 91°C	370°F = 188°C	550°F = 288°C
200°F = 93°C	**375°F = 191°C**	

WEIGHT CONVERSIONS

For weights less than 1/4 oz: use tsp/tbsp for U.S. measure with gram or mL equivalent
(see specific conversion tables).

Formula to convert ounces to grams: number of oz $\times$ 28.35 = number of grams (round up for .50 and above)

1/4 ounce = 7 grams
1/2 ounce = 14 grams
1 ounce = 28.35 grams
4 ounces = 113 grams
8 ounces (1/2 pound) = 227 grams
16 ounces (1 pound) = 454 grams
32 ounces (2 pounds) = 907 grams
40 ounces (2 1/2 pounds) = 1.134 kilograms

VOLUME CONVERSIONS

Formula to convert fluid ounces to milliliters: number of fluid ounces $\times$ 30 = number of milliliters

1/2 fl oz = 15 mL	20 fl oz = 600 mL
1 fl oz = 30 mL	24 fl oz = 720 mL
1 1/2 fl oz = 45 mL	30 fl oz = 900 mL
1 3/4 fl oz = 53 mL	**32 fl oz = 960 mL [1 qt]**
2 fl oz = 60 mL	40 fl oz = 1.20 L
2 1/2 fl oz = 75 mL	44 fl oz = 1.32 L
3 fl oz = 90 mL	**48 fl oz = 1.44 L [1 1/2 qt]**
3 1/2 fl oz = 105 mL	64 fl oz = 1.92 L [2 qt]
4 fl oz = 120 mL	**72 fl oz = 2.16 L [2 1/2 qt]**
5 fl oz = 150 mL	80 fl oz = 2.4 L
6 fl oz = 180 mL	96 fl oz = 2.88 L [3 qt]
7 fl oz = 210 mL	128 fl oz = 3.84 L [1 gal]
8 fl oz = 240 mL [1 cup]	1 1/8 gal = 4.32 L
9 fl oz = 270 mL	1 1/4 gal = 4.8 L
10 fl oz = 300 mL	1 1/2 gal = 5.76 L
11 fl oz = 330 mL	**2 gal = 7.68 L [256 fl oz]**
12 fl oz = 360 mL	3 gal = 11.52 L
13 fl oz = 390 mL	4 gal = 15.36 L
14 fl oz = 420 mL	5 gal = 19.20 L
15 fl oz = 450 mL	10 gal = 38.40 L
16 fl oz = 480 mL [1 pt]	20 gal = 76.80 L
17 fl oz = 510 mL	25 gal = 96 L
18 fl oz = 540 mL	50 gal = 192 L
19 fl oz = 570 mL	

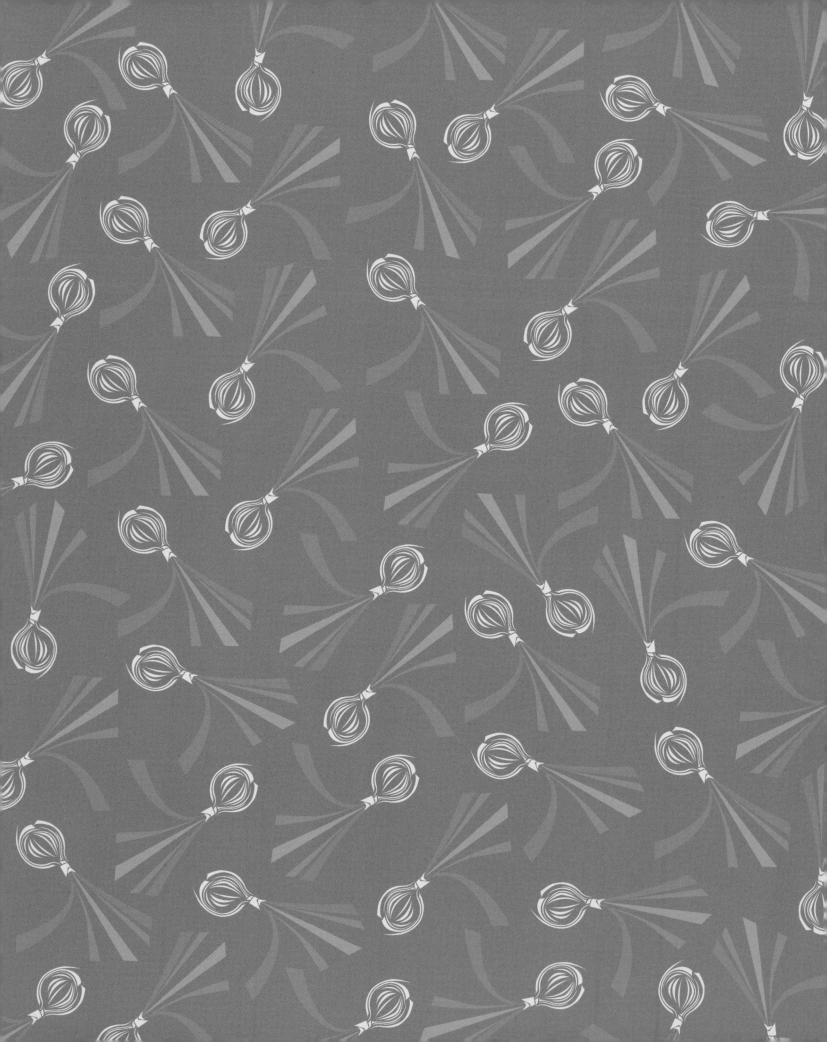